Chinese Social Media

T0270870

This book brings together scholars from a variety of disciplines to address critical perspectives on Chinese language social media, internationalizing the state of social media studies beyond the Anglophone paradigm. The collection focuses on the intersections between Chinese language social media and disability, celebrity, sexuality, interpersonal communication, charity, diaspora, public health, political activism and non-governmental organisations (NGOs). The book is not only rich in its theoretical perspectives but also in its methodologies. Contributors use both qualitative and quantitative methods to study Chinese social media and its social–cultural–political implications, such as case studies, in-depth interviews, participatory observations, discourse analysis, content analysis and data mining.

Mike Kent is head of department and a senior lecturer in the Internet Studies Department at Curtin University, Australia.

Katie Ellis is a senior research fellow in the Internet Studies Department and convenor of the Critical Disability Studies Research Network at Curtin University, Australia.

Jian Xu is a research fellow at the School of Communications and Creative Arts at Deakin University, Australia.

Routledge Research in Digital Media and Culture in Asia
Edited by Dal Yong Jin
Simon Fraser University

1 Chinese Social Media
   Social, Cultural, and Political Implications
   Edited by Mike Kent, Katie Ellis and Jian Xu

Chinese Social Media

Social, Cultural, and
Political Implications

Edited by Mike Kent, Katie Ellis
and Jian Xu

Routledge
Taylor & Francis Group

LONDON AND NEW YORK

First published 2018 by Routledge

2 Park Square, Milton Park, Abingdon, Oxfordshire OX14 4RN

52 vanderbilt Avenue, New York, NY 10017

Routledge is an imprint of the Taylor & Francis Group,
an informa business

First issued in paperback 2019

Library of Congress Cataloging-in-Publication Data
CIP data has been applied for.

ISBN: 978-1-138-06477-5 (hbk)
ISBN: 978-0-367-88941-8 (pbk)

Typeset in Sabon
by codeMantra

To our colleagues at Curtin University in the Digital China Lab, and the China Writing Centre.

Contents

List of Figures and Tables

Figures

Tables

Acknowledgements

We would like to thank the authors both for their contributions to this collection and also for acting as anonymous readers of this book. Everyone offered both insightful and encouraging feedback at every stage – it has been a pleasure working with you all. Of course, this book is a reflection of the authors' efforts and we are grateful to each of them. We also want to acknowledge the work of Ceri Clocherty who helped to shape their manuscripts. A number of people have read or heard pieces of this book and generously gave of their time to discuss ideas with us: Gerard Goggin, Michael Keane, John Hartley, Henry Li, Lucy Montgomery, Susan Leong, Liz Byrski, Haiqing Yu, Karen Fisher, Wanning Sun, Elaine Jeffreys, Guobin Yang and Matthew Allen.

Mike would like to thank his colleagues in the School of Media Culture and Creative Arts for their support and advice throughout this project. He would also like to acknowledge the significant contribution to this collection from all the authors. He would also like to thank the staff at Epic Expresso where much of his editing work was done. Finally, Mike would like to thank Katie and Jian for their tireless work in bringing this book together.

Katie would like to thank her colleagues at Curtin University in the Digital China Lab, the China Writing Centre and those who attended the Culture+8 seminar for their mentoring and valuable critiques. To Mike and Jian it was a privilege working with you both on this project. And Chris, Stella and Connor, your love and support make this possible.

Jian would like to thank his colleagues in the School of Communication and Creative Arts, Deakin University and Professors Wanning Sun, Haiqing Yu, Gerard Goggin, Elaine Jeffreys, Michael Keane and Guobin Yang for their generous support and insightful comments. Jian is particularly grateful to Mike and Katie for their trust, support and guidance throughout this project.

Foreword

Michael Keane

Outside of the Chinese mainland people are familiar with an image of the world's factory', the point of origin of countless products found in global markets. Within China itself many millions of people are employed in sweatshops or in component assembly plants. In many of these ventures the intellectual property is owned by multinationals, for example, a case in point being the production of the iPhone chassis and other components in Southern China. Scholars and policy makers within China have lamented that the nation has lacked the innovative culture to produce breakthrough products such as the iPhone, hybrid cars or movies that win universal acclaim. However, this situation is changing – and digital technology is driving the change. Over the past two decades China has leapfrogged technologies largely thanks to the knowledge gained from foreign direct investment in China, from contract manufacturing projects in southern China to today's start-up incubators and so-called 'accelerators' in first tier cities like Beijing and Shanghai. The race to patent innovations has accelerated with domestic internet technology and communications companies like Alibaba and Huawei investing heavily in research and development, as well as luring overseas talent to their 'campuses.'

The backdrop is the unprecedented roll out of information services and broadband. In March 2015, the government announced a blueprint called Internet Plus (*hulianwang jia*). At the turn of the millennium as China's manufacturing industries were propelling its economy to commanding heights the objectives of this blueprint would have sounded like science fiction. China now plans to integrate mobile internet, cloud computing, big data and the internet of things with modern manufacturing. All this is possible because of a combination of enabling policy and investment from above, the dynamism of grassroots user communities, and the power of China's internet communication companies with their assets of big data. At the end of 2016, the number of registered internet users in China totalled 770 million. More significantly perhaps, mobile phone usage had reached 1.3 billion (roughly the same as the population) and more than 50 percent of these users were using the mobile internet. In a population heavily skewed towards one-child families 'connectivism' has become the new collectivism.

In 2013, two years before Internet Plus was rolled out the State Council had issued a blueprint to promote 'information consumption.' If China's economy were to transition from a low-cost export model to a consumption-based model the fix would include the roll out of digital services. China was once seen as a market where internet users expected digital products to be free, from software to music, movies, and e-books. Now users are increasingly prepared to pay for online video subscriptions, digital music and other digital services. The rise of the BAT, the so-called 'three kingdoms' – Baidu, Alibaba and Tencent – have provided the foundations for the growth of the mobile economy. With the digital transformation of the economy Chinese language apps have boomed, led by Tencent's WeChat service ecosystem that allows people to send messages by text, voice and video as well as make payments, play games, order a taxi, and book tickets for hotels. Smart cities plans are now also part of the policy landscape. The sharing economy is evidenced in the way that people are collaborating online, not just in sharing memes but also in looking for new ways of financing ventures.

The Chinese government has realised the potential of the digital era, launching an ambitious campaign called 'mass entrepreneurship, mass innovation' (*dazhong chuangye, wanzhong chuangxin*) based on the ubiquity of low-cost digital technologies. The technological frontier includes next generation information networks, core electronics, high-end software and new information services. Particularly in coastal cities such as Beijing and Shanghai the emerging technologies of mobile internet, cloud computing and big data are driving the 'upgrade' of cultural and creative industries. More significantly, the 13th Five Year Plan has prioritised technological innovation, following a vision originally laid out by President Hu Jintao and Premier Wen Jiabao in 2006, at the beginning of the 11th Five Year Plan.

Much territory is currently unexplored in respect to the Chinese government's deployment of digital technologies. To date academic researchers have largely focused on political control of traditional media channels, censorship and online activism on the internet. There are good reasons for such critical perspectives, not the least being a strong tradition of critique in the Western academy. Another perspective is to view the media and communication industries in China as fundamentally capitalist. Certainly, China's new internet champions are fond of talking up the liberating power of being able to consume online services. However, the internet has many manifestations that need to be investigated, including its potential to impact on the workforce, to benefit elderly and marginalised communities, to provide assistive technologies for people who are disabled, to promote social innovation and social entrepreneurship, and to activate grassroots volunteerism. From social media to digital affordances, this collection of essays is therefore timely, signalling a new pathway for research. The collection introduces the work of several new scholars from mainland China, highlighting important social developments that are often overlooked by Western scholars.

Much discussion focuses on how the whole of Chinese society can 'upgrade,' particularly in regard to the millions of people with low levels of education living outside the large urban centres. The aging of China's population, a consequence of the One Child Policy established in 1978 by Deng Xiaoping, is having a direct impact on the numbers of people registered in work. Such a decline is to be expected over time but combined with increasing minimum wages and growing average incomes, the nation is moving inexorably closer to what economists call the 'Lewis Turning Point.' This occurs when the economy can no longer create wealth by adding cheap labour. Can new technologies solve the problems facing China or will they add to the challenges facing China as more of its low-cost production moves to cheaper locations? Knowledge is crucial and social media provides a platform to extend social capital and hence create a new society, one in which ordinary people are able to have a voice. Meanwhile China is borrowing ideas – and technology – from the rest of the world and innovation is occurring in unlikely places. Apps are the new currency, from those that enable people to find taxis to apps to allow people to purchase online, to those that allow people to watch content and engage with traditional Chinese culture, to those that provide medical and food safety information to people. This is only the tip of the iceberg. China is setting its course for a digital revolution and this excellent collection of essays from a range of disciplinary perspectives illustrates this phenomenon.

Michael Keane, Professor of Chinese Media and Cultural
Studies and leader of the Digital China Lab,
Curtin University, Australia

1   Chinese Social Media Today

Mike Kent, Katie Ellis and Jian Xu

The idea for this collection came about in early 2015 when Kent and Ellis were in the process of bringing together another edited collection, *Disability and social media: Global perspectives* (Ellis & Kent, 2017). They noted that while there were many excellent submissions from around the world for the collection, China, and more specifically Chinese social media, was a notable exception. At that time the rapidly expanding Chinese social media sphere had already been embraced by China's many internet users – China has both the world's largest population (1.38 billion) and the world's largest internet user base (710 million) – and social media was an established and active site of participation, particularly on sites unique to China. Of particular note was that while for other language groups the global dominance of US-centric social media such as Facebook, Twitter and Google has encroached on, and in many cases supplanted, any native language-specific social media platform, this has not been the case in China. This is to an extent due to the Chinese government's policy of blocking many popular Western social media sites, in the space of these networks a dramatic rise of unique domestic social networking sites such as WeChat (Weixin), Sina Weibo, QQ and RenRen, has taken place resulting in the development of a uniquely Chinese language social media ecology and a vibrant and unique Chinese social media market outside the Western world.

Indeed, it has been interesting to observe the rise of social media in China – both its level of adoption and how it is used. Social media first evolved following the launch of access to the internet in China in 1994 with online forums and communities and then migrated to instant messaging, with platforms such as QQ launching in 1999. In 2009 the internet company Sina launched the Twitter-esque Sina Weibo which now has 261 million active users (Weibo, 2016). RenRen – also referred to as China's Facebook – was launched in 2011. More recently, platforms such as Tencent's WeChat – China's answer to WhatsApp – have begun to play a leading role (Statista.com, 2016), with 650 million monthly active user accounts (CNNIC, 2016). These social media platforms have their own unique patterns of use and features that set them apart from their western counterparts and make Chinese language social media a dynamic and changing environment. Further, they all represent a significant shift on what has gone before – we have seen the Chinese media model move from a government-centric control base towards a more popular enabled social interaction and communication structure, enabling users to share a wide range of media and information quickly to a large number of people. It has disrupted traditional media hierarchies, with users both generating and distributing (sharing) content in a way that challenges the traditional understanding of mass media. As a result, China has a large and growing modern social media landscape, surpassing many of the more globally popular social media platforms dominated by English language. More than 700 million people in the country actively engage with mobile internet, blogs, social networking sites, microblogs and other online communities (CNNIC, 2016).

For a book on social media to not include at least one chapter that addressed Chinese language social media from a western perspective therefore seemed to undermine its premise. Seeking to fill this notable gap, we reached out to our professional and academic networks in social media, media studies and disability studies; however, we found that we were initially unable to find any research for this much needed chapter in the English literature despite the emergent spread of Chinese-based networks to western based audiences (as is explored in Chapter 13 in more detail). Indeed, much of the previous research on the internet in China focused on issues around government control and involvement in the internet, censorship and international relations (see deLisle, Goldstien, & Yang 2016; Yang, 2015) – albeit arguably an unavoidable part of the internet environment in China – rather than a consideration of social media as a popular tool.

We eventually teamed up with some excellent emerging Chinese media scholars who worked with us to research and then develop a chapter for that collection looking at the role of social media in enabling disability-focused non-governmental organisations (NGOs) in China (see Xu, Kent, Ellis, & Zhang, 2017). However, it was felt that more research was required to more fully address this gap in the literature. Alongside one of our co-authors on that chapter, Jian Xu, as a co-editor, we set about to develop this edited collection to consider and explore contemporary Chinese language social media and its social, cultural and political implications – with the focus firmly on a Chinese rather than western-facing perspective. We sought to provide a collection of writing based on people's lived experience of Chinese language social media in mainland China and beyond.

It is often argued that social media is merely a continued extension of the development of the internet and how it is used. While to an extent this is true, the rise of social media in both its level of adoption, and how it is used represents a significant shift on what has gone before. Social media presents people with low barriers to entry with easy access provided through web interfaces and Apps, large active user bases and the ability to share a wide range of media and information quickly to a large number of people through easily enabled social interaction and communication. The book brings together scholars from a diversity of backgrounds and areas of expertise – both established academics in this field as well as upcoming new researchers in this area – to address critical perspectives on Chinese language social media and explore its social, cultural and political implications.

Outline

The book is divided into five parts. Part 1 is concerned with Chinese social media and the public. Chapter 2, Microphilanthropy and New Grassroots associations: Social Media and the Rights Discourse in China by Haiqing Yu, is the first of four in this section and links social media and citizen activism through microphilanthropy in China. Drawing on the case study of Deng Fei's Free Lunch initiative (*Mianfei wucan*) for schoolchildren, the chapter notes how these movements are "built on small amounts in donation, small pieces of information, small words of kindness and small acts of courage, all mediated and transmitted via social media". Chapter 3 in this section by Dianlin Huang looks at another case study, this time the NGO Love Save Pneumoconiosis (LSP) (*Da'ai qingchen*). Through this study, the chapter explores how "Chinese grassroots non-governmental organisations (NGOs) have taken a non-profit public approach to social media by tactfully utilising these new alternative outlets to promote their specific activism goals" and how NGOs are using social media in collective actions for resource mobilisations and self-legitimacy construction.

Chapter 4 by Tianyang Zhou and Lianrui Jia then looks at the role of social media in the portrayal of 'celebrities' An Wei and Wu Yebin, a rural gay couple from Hebei province in northern China who found fame through photo galleries on Ifeng.com. Using Bourdieu's concept of symbolic capital, the chapter explores "the idiosyncratic characteristics of Chinese non-for-profit organisations, the non-oppositional, family-centric orientation of the gay rights movements in China, and traditional family values in assessing the role that social media has played in social changes". Chapter 5 then continues this focus on social media celebrity. Zixue Tai, Xiaolong Liu and Jiang Liang turn our attention to the social media platform Weibo – and in particular the top 50 Weibo microbloggers known as the 'Big Vs' – and how they make use of this social media space.

Part 2 of this collection focuses on Chinese social media and (re)presentation. It opens with Chapter 6 by Yang Wang that explores how the bottom up civil discourse from social media challenges the top down approach by more traditional state-controlled media.

It does so through a framing analysis of the *People's Daily* and *South Metropolitan Daily* newspapers and Sina Weibo during the cadmium rice contamination scandal in Guangzhou province in 2013. In Chapter 7 Xiaoli Tian looks at how students from mainland China studying in Hong Kong both utilise and present themselves differently on Facebook and RenRen and how they negotiate maintaining face (*mianzi*) across these social media platforms. Chapter 8 continues the exploration of RenRen, this time in mainland China where David Holmes and Naziat Choudhury explore how this network can act to facilitate bridging social capital to help connect the social gaps created by a rapidly urbanising population, exploring this through the lens of social ties and *guanxi* practice, the fostering of strong commercial and interpersonal networks and relationships.

Part 3 of the book looks at Chinese social media and disability. Chapter 9 from Mike Kent, Katie Ellis, He Zhang and Joy Zhang explores the case study of the WeChat Voice Donor Project – a joint project from the social media company Tencent and the United Nations. This study looks at the interplay between social media, Chinese companies' enactment of corporate social responsibility and the development of accessible audiobooks against the backdrop of the position of people who are blind or who have vision impairments in China. In Chapter 10 Yao Ding and G. Anthony Giannoumis then turn directly to the accessibility of social media in China for people with disabilities through a policy analysis and interviews of information and communications technology (ICT) design staff working on one of the major social media platforms. Then in Chapter 11, Weiqin Chen, Way Kiat Bong and Nan Li bring elements of these two earlier chapters together as they explore the accessibility of the WeChat platform for people with disabilities through a heuristic evaluation of WeChat against the World Wide Web Consortium's *Web content accessibility guidelines 2.0*. Here they find that Tencent may have focused more on usability rather than accessibility for the platform and offer a set of recommendations for improvements.

Part 4 then turns to Chinese social media in greater China and overseas. It starts with Joshua Cader's investigation of the PTT bulletin board system in Taiwan in Chapter 12. He discusses how one of the earliest social media platforms is still used and relevant in Taiwan today and considers its role in forging a Taiwanese identity through language. Chapter 13 presents Gianluigi Negro's exploration of the big three Chinese internet and social media companies Baidu, Alibaba and Tencent, known collectively as BAT, and their expansion beyond mainland China as part of the government's "going out" strategy (*Zouchuqu zhanlue*). Chapter 14 concludes this section with an exploration of the adoption of QQ and WeChat by the Chinese diaspora in Australia. Jiajie Lu uses interviews with members of this diaspora to explore reasons behind the adoption of these networks and the role of Chinese government censorship in this process.

The final section of the book turns to critiques of Chinese social media. In Chapter 15 Wilfred Wang Yang looks at looks at how Weibo is used to enable a distinct geographic sense of place and locality (*difang*) for people in the city of Guangzhou, and in doing so argues against the notion that China's internet is conceptualised as "placeless" or geographically indifferent. In the final chapter in the volume, Chapter 16, Jonathan Benny and Jian Xu look at the relative decline of the Weibo social media platform and the rise of WeChat. Their phasic study explores the role of both government control and censorship through Weibo – as well as the market factors in the dynamic ecology of the Chinese social media environment that are driving this change – and they point to potential further developments in the future.

As the first book in English that specifically addresses research and writing about Chinese language social media, we hope that it will facilitate a much-needed dialogue between English language, western-based scholars and their Chinese language counterparts around their respective, and increasingly overlapping and integrated, digital and social media environments. The chapters in this book represent an exciting first step in addressing this area in this context. We hope that there will be many to follow.

References

CNNIC. (2016). Statistical report on internet development in China. 2016. China Internet Network Information Centre. Retrieved November 20, 2016 from www.cnnic.cn/hlwfzyj/hlwxzbg/hlwtjbg/201608/P020160803367337470363.pdf.

deLisle, J., Goldstien, A., & Yang, G. (2016). *The internet, social media and a changing China*. Philadelphia: University of Pennsylvania Press.

Ellis, K., & Kent, M. (Eds.). (2017). *Disability and social media: Global perspectives*. New York: Routledge.

Statista.com. (2016). *Number of monthly active WeChat users from 2nd quarter 2010 to 3rd quarter 2016 (in millions)*. Retrieved from www.statista.com/statistics/255778/number-of-active-wechat-messenger-accounts/.

Weibo. (2016). *Weibo reports first quarter 2016 financial results* [Press release]. Retrieved from http://ir.weibo.com/phoenix.zhtml?c=253076&p=irol-newsArticle&ID=2167667.

Xu, J., Kent, M., Ellis, K., & Zhang, H. (2017). One plus one: Online community radio for the blind in China and social media. In K. Ellis & M. Kent (Eds.), *Disability and social media: Global perspectives*. New York: Routledge.

Yang, G. (2015). *China's contested internet*. Copenhagen: Nias Press.

Part I

Chinese Social Media and the Public

2 Social Media and the Experience Economy in China's Microphilanthropy

Haiqing Yu

Introduction

Since 2011, the idea of citizen-led philanthropy has been emerging in China (Yu, 2015a). This is represented by media-savvy, socially engaged and globally connected individuals who, aided by social media, wedge into the 'grey' areas of social welfare, charity and philanthropy, including environmental protection, education, food security, labour rights, animal rights and health. They call on fellow citizens to pay attention to particular issues, rally support for a particular cause, and mobilise donors and volunteers to help those in need. Such citizen-initiated and -led philanthropic action is, in the first instance, unofficial, unplanned, uncoordinated, spontaneous and grassroots. It often derives from an individual's wish or drive to help those in need, and it builds upon individual social networks to rally support and resources. It is built on small amounts in donation, small pieces of information, small words of kindness and small acts of courage, all mediated and transmitted via social media such as Weibo (the Chinese term for microblogging), Weixin (the Chinese term for micromessaging and China's most popular social application) or WeChat (the English version of Weixin) and QQ (China's oldest and still most popular instant messaging tool). The two 'micro' (*wei*) social media platforms, Weibo and Weixin, are central to the emergence and development of this microphilanthropy. Microphilanthropy thus can be defined as altruistic, social media-enabled, citizen-driven, unofficial, sustained and often small-to-large scale civic activism. This definition excludes ad hoc and once-off efforts initiated by individuals that ask for donations to cover private expenses, such as medical costs of a sick child; unlike charity, philanthropy emphasises 'enabling' rather than simply 'giving'. These digitally connected, mediated and sustained, and loosely connected civic associations are core to our understanding of citizen activism in Web 2.0 China.

This chapter makes explicit links between a particular genre of digital media (social media), a specific form of citizen activism (microphilanthropy) and the implication of such activism on the 'experience economy' – the desire to experience stimulation and motivation rather than to purchase – of the social movement in China. It examines the role of social media in the rise of microphilanthropy and grassroots associations in China, with a focus on journalist/activist Deng Fei's Free Lunch 免费午餐 (for school kids) initiative. In particular, it discusses the new type of philanthropy that Free Lunch represents in contemporary China, its philosophy and experience. Many themes and topics can be distilled from such a discussion of the rise of social media-enabled microphilanthropy in China, such as the state–civil society relationship in the framework of "contested symbiosis" (Zhang, 2015) or "contingent symbiosis" (Spires, 2011); operational and organisational or survival strategies of civic associations with different sizes and missions (Hildebrandt, 2011; Spires, 2007); situational opportunities for civic associations; leadership skills, qualities and embeddedness within the political system (Hildebrandt, 2013; Tai, 2012); and the role of media (traditional, digital and mobile) in constructing active citizenship and civil society (such as a green public sphere) in China (Sima, 2011;Yang, 2003; Yang & Calhoun, 2007).

The Free Lunch campaign is one compelling example of younger civic associations that have taken social media to solve their resource strategy problems, to "scale up impact without having to raise large amounts of funds or hire a lot of people" and to "outsource work by breaking it down into tiny components and parceling it out among large populations of volunteers/clients accessed through internet-based social networking technologies" (Hsu, 2011, p. 126). It calls for a critical reflection of the nature, operation, and composition of microphilanthropy, its interaction and relationship with governmental and non-governmental agencies, and its impact on the Chinese moral landscape and democratic future. This chapter will discuss these issues, with particular attention to the relationship between activism and personalised experience, in order to bring to light the political economy of philanthropy-themed civic activism. This research takes a qualitative analysis based on informal interviews with Deng Fei (twice, in Beijing and Hangzhou, respectively) and his team (five persons in Hangzhou) from June to July 2015. Questions were asked towards understanding the ideology that drove Deng and his team to devote their careers to provide care and support to rural children, their families, villages and environment. Secondary sources gathered through subscription to Deng's public account on Weixin/WeChat are also used in the following analysis, which starts with the discussion of the role of social media in shaping microphilanthropy in China.

Philanthropy: Traditional Mores and Its Modern Social Media Presence

The Chinese understanding of charity and philanthropy has evolved with the transformation in their techno-socio-political culture. It also reflects and shapes a changing and multifaceted moral landscape which is framed by Chinese tradition, socialist experience, post-socialist neoliberal discourse and globalisation; the rise of online-based micro-philanthropy is situated in this complex web of history, tradition and techno-socialist modernity. In particular, it goes hand in hand with the rise of social media in China, particularly Weibo (since 2009) and Weixin (since 2011), known as 'double micro' (*liang wei* 两微).

Doing public good has traditionally been regarded as the job of a 'benevolent government' or that of social, intellectual and political elites to fulfil their obligation to the state or their community/clan. For example, Chinese Confucian tradition encouraged a relational structure of philanthropy and benevolence directed towards known individuals or groups out of a sense of duty or indebtedness (Tucker, 1998). These Confucian and Buddhist traditions of doing good to others prompted people to carry out socially responsible projects to help the needy – it was morally uplifting to individual donors, socio-economically beneficial to the merchant philanthropists who were eager to secure their legitimate place in the moral economy of charitable activities and hence politically advantageous to keep up family and clan reputation (Smith, 2009). Nowadays, this tradition has seen private businesses and individuals being called upon to donate to or engage in social projects as a form of patriotism and social responsibility. Thus, it can be argued that the modern seemingly altruistic charity and philanthropic initiatives are deeply rooted in a narrowly defined Confucian moral structure, which is essentially a patron–client structure. It reflects a deeply politicised and personalised relationship on the one hand, and hinges upon a clearly acknowledged social hierarchy on the other hand, with state officials and monied entrepreneurs at the top and the needy supplicants at the bottom. This 'philanthropy on demand' is organised and participated by big corporate and government agencies. There is a low need for transparency, as 'quid pro quo donations' are tied to specific rewards such as media exposure, meetings with the mayor and tax breaks. Neither is there any question about the impact of such charitable actions.

Independent charity activities were not existent in the Mao era – there were very few even in the 1990s, mainly in the care for children with intellectual disabilities, orphans or the elderly. In a book written in the 1990s, Vivienne Shue (1998) comments, "Statism, social hierarchy, Chinese family value remain as prominent features today of Chinese philanthropic thought and practice as they were in the past" (p. 351). She identifies four major categories of charitable activities in China – state-initiated and -managed nationwide charity causes, projects and associations (e.g. the Project Hope 希望工程 that brings education to China's rural poor); local government initiated and managed charity drives and community-chest-like provincial and municipal foundations raising donations; merchant–entrepreneur and corporates giving upward (to state) and downward (to special petitioners and clients); and independent charity activists. The latter category is relatively small, and the very few truly independent philanthropists rarely regard their work as social and political activism; instead, they are often driven by a very deep and personal desire to redeem themselves from personal 'failures' such as failed marriages (Jeffreys, 2010); this can be called 'philanthropy for redemption'. For example, women who lead in self-help initiatives after having suffered domestic or sexual violence themselves are representative of this type of personalised philanthropy. Their participation in philanthropic and charitable activities is regarded as a way to redeem themselves of the stigma that they carry as 'impure' women (having been violated, divorced or discarded), so that they can be like the lotus, emerging as pure as possible from muddy waters.

However, the state-centred and elite-driven 'philanthropy on demand' or the narrowly defined 'philanthropy for redemption' as outlined above stand in stark contrast with the idea of 'engaged philanthropy' which is citizen-led and relies heavily on social media for communication, co-ordination, mobilisation and publicity. This idea of microphilanthropy and civil society emerged in the late 1990s during disaster relief efforts and mushroomed following the 7.9-magnitude Wenchuan earthquake in Sichuan province in May 2008 (e.g. Shieh & Deng, 2011; Teets, 2009; Xu, 2014). The earthquake took at least 68,000 lives and prompted tens of thousands of volunteers and millions of Chinese citizens to donate their money and time to support the relief efforts through loosely formed citizen associations (Shieh & Deng, 2011). Such actions were not all called upon by the government or prompted by any potential reward for their generosity – they were just individual actions that trickled into a large onrush of kindness. Loosely organised, grassroots and connective civic associations were born from this disaster relief effort, and have continued to grow in subsequent natural disaster relief efforts (such as the 2010 Yushu earthquake and the 2012 Ya'an earthquake). Some of them have grown from loosely organised citizen actions groups into non-governmental organisations (NGOs) with a mission, leadership, operational structure, and even official status through registration; some have grown from smaller organisations into influential NGOs such as Jet Li's One Foundation 壹基金 (Song, 2015).

The development of microphilanthropy as an 'engaged' social engineering project participated in by millions of individuals has been particularly interesting in relation to the development of social media as an enabling tool. While in 2008 it was the 'old' social media such as QQ (including Qzone and QQ groups), BBS forums and SNS (e.g. Xiaonei and Kaixin) that functioned as the nexus of communication, mobilisation and facilitation in civic actions, since 2009 it has been the 'new' social media like Weibo (especially Sina Weibo and Sohu Weibo) that has taken the spotlight in facilitating its growth. In particular, the year 2011 marked a milestone in the development of grassroots philanthropic activism in China. Several Weibo-facilitated grassroots philanthropy campaigns stole the headlines of Chinese mainstream media and became the hot topics in various online spaces (Yu, 2015a). They included "Random snapshots to rescue child beggars" initiated by Yu Jianrong and Deng Fei et al., "Love save pneumoconiosis" founded by Wang Keqin (see Chapter 3 by Huang in this volume) and the Free Lunch campaign initiated by Deng Fei and 500 journalists, the focus of this chapter.

Case Study: Free Lunch

Free Lunch was initiated by Deng Fei, a renowned investigative journalist with the Hong Kong-based *Phoenix Weekly*, in collaboration with some 500 fellow journalists from his QQ group *Lanyi* (Blue Shirt). It started from a conversation between Deng and a volunteer teacher from a rural school in Guizhou province, which led Deng to a field trip to the school. This in turn led to the idea of providing free lunches for schoolchildren from poor and deprived areas. It then took off online with Deng's posts on Sina Weibo in early 2011 to his 1.4 million followers – poor left-behind children had to endure starvation at school without lunch... how could they help? Within hours, he was overwhelmed by responses from his followers who wished to donate and participate in the programme. Through his connection with mainstream media via his Lanyi QQ group, the initiative also got extensive media coverage beyond cyberspace. More publicity and support poured in as Deng's fellow journalists, microbloggers and their followers spread the word and mobilised their own followers to participate in his programme. In less than 2 months, Deng and his collaborators raised more than 10 million yuan and provided free lunches for over 3,000 kids in four of the poorest provinces; in the following 4 years until 2015, Free Lunch received more than 150 million yuan in donations and provided free lunches to more than 110,000 kids from over 400 schools in 23 provinces (Deng, 2014). It also prompted the Chinese government into action. Six months after the Free Lunch programme kicked off in Guizhou, on 26 October 2011, Premier Wen Jiabao declared a Rural Nutrition Improvement Plan, modelled on the programme, with a pledge of 16 billion yuan per year to provide free lunches to 2.6 million students in 699 pilot areas – the state and the society working together to provide a duty of care to China's poorest children. Just as Deng Fei writes in his book *Free Lunch: Softness Changes China* (2014), "This is a citizen philanthropy movement that involves everybody from students, workers, farmers and intellectuals to business leaders, celebrities, government officials and state leaders. It is a landmark event in China's structural transformation in the e-era" (p. 1).

Deng Fei's Free Lunch has been officially registered as a sub-project of the China Social Welfare Foundation in order to 'legally' receive and manage donations, although the programme is managed at the local level by Deng's team with its headquarters in Hangzhou. Apart from Free Lunch, Deng and his team run a series of programmes under the banner United Philanthropy for Rural Children in China, which cover healthcare, environmental protection, cultural heritage conservation, water conservation, philanthropy training programmes for youths and protection of girls (against sexual abuse) and of orphans (including kids who do not live with their parents) in rural China. They also run an e-agricultural programme, Hope Farm, which is a social enterprise jointly launched by Deng and his 170 alumni from the China Europe International Business School in 2013. It aims to help reduce poverty in poor rural areas by selling agricultural products via social media (e.g. Weixin) and e-commerce platforms (e.g. Taobao.com).

Deng and his team rely heavily on the internet and mobile communication through social media platforms such as Weibo, Weixin and QQ, as well as e-commerce platforms such as Taobao, for all activities from brainstorming, crowdsourcing and fundraising to volunteer recruitment, social participation, project implementation and fund auditing. Digital media and communication networks help Deng and his team achieve a large-scale flow of information at a minimum cost, realise organisational management and societal collaboration across a wide range of geographical and professional boundaries, and enable a snowballing effect in galvanising support and publicity for Free Lunch through enacting a personalised experience economy, an idea which will be discussed in the next section.

Deng Fei has transformed himself from an observer and commentator (as a journalist) to a doer and social experimentalist (as a philanthropist and social entrepreneur). The 'double micro' digital platforms have enabled him and his team to experiment with innovative and pragmatic initiatives that aim at solving concrete social problems. In his words, "complaints and criticism cannot solve problems that China faces; instead individual citizens can work together to solve these problems, because we have the platforms for expression and association" (Interview, June 2015, Beijing). This enthusiasm about digital communication is shared across the board by academics and practitioners in the philanthropy movement in China, as declared in an open letter from Anping Foundation of Philanthropic Communication (2015) – "Never before are we empowered with a platform and channel to record, express and communicate; to become doers and to care, record and promote the progress and transformations in China".

Deng Fei and his enthusiastic team have adopted a 'discourse oblivious' approach to doing good for others – that is, they focus on solving concrete and real problems without making any grand narrative or claim. They talk highly of resource integration and network integration in order to achieve high efficiency while getting as many people as possible to be involved in their projects and through skilful use social media to garner social capital from pre-existing social networks and hyperlinked online networks. Indeed, social media is central to the success of Free Lunch as an example of China's growing microphilanthropy, not only in terms of organisation, mobilisation and communication but also in terms of the democratic model of operation and management. It sets the model and precedence of complete transparency, public supervision and open audition via social media (Weibo and Weixin). In doing so, they adopt a cooperative approach with the Party and government at all levels, who then give their support to civic associations like Deng's for doing work in the interests of the government and within the limits of political boundaries. They also enlist largesse by getting private entrepreneurs and the business sector involved. This offers not only philanthropic recognition and status for China's wealthy elite but also possible economic and political opportunities (Graham-Harrison, 2015; Hildebrandt, 2013, 2015).

Deng Fei reported having encountered no censorship thus far, as he and his team are doers (*xingdong zhe*) rather than activists (*hudong zhe*). He encourages his team to think big but act small, to engage in solving concrete problems rather than ideological debates – "this [the latter] is the job of academics and ideologues" (Interview, July 2015, Hangzhou). This pragmatic approach has guided China throughout its open and reform era under Deng Xiaoping's leadership and has been internalised by Generation X (such as Deng Fei and his collaborators) and the millennium generation (Deng Fei's team) in the post-Deng era. This pragmatism is key to our understanding of the personalised experience economy that Free Lunch and its breed of microphilanthropy enact and represent.

Social Media and Experience Economy

Experience economy is a business and marketing concept to describe a new movement for sales and profit, after the agriculture, manufacturing and services economies (Pine & Gilmore, 1999). People are attracted to certain products and services, tangible or intangible, because their physical, intellectual or emotional needs can be fulfilled. This concept is also used to describe experience-stimulating activities in the public sector, such as culture events, festivals and architecture. For many people volunteering in the third sector is an experience, and many events, including charity and philanthropy-related events, rely on volunteers' free work to fulfil their missions with limited budgets. In fact, civic organisations like Free Lunch have utilised this experience economy to garner support from concerned individuals in creating a sustained philanthropy.

As discussed earlier, Deng Fei and his team are doers, not dreamers – they are guided by pragmatism rather than ideology and do not regard themselves as, nor claim to be, 'activists'. Rather, they *enact* what they believe to be their duty and responsibility towards fellow citizens. To use Deng Fei's words, it is not enough to find and analyse problems or ask other people's (including the government's) help to solve the problems, but citizens should also be self-empowered to take the course of action into their own hands with available technologies, apps and tools (Interview, June 2015, Beijing). Indeed, *enacti*vism and experience economy are the two sides of the same coin. Both result from the emerging post-material values among China's middle class – after settling into their newly found wealth and fortunes, China's wealthy elite, middle class and their children have attached greater importance to social recognition, quality of life, and political and social rights (Cheng, 2010). At the same time, a growing number of idealistic and resourceful youths (the so-called post-1990s, '90 *hou*') volunteer in social services and philanthropy as 'technology of self' in order to transform themselves into moral, entrepreneurial, responsible and functional subjects; this also blends with 'technology of power' that taps into the state's neoliberal aspirations to refashion its citizens into responsible and self-reliant subjects in an increasingly competitive world (Fleischer, 2011). Individual accounts regarding their volunteering experience in projects led by Deng Fei testify to Deng's skilful use of the experience economy framework in campaigning Free Lunch as a brand for microphilanthropy and to his ability to attract volunteers, through digital, mobile, social and experiential means and platforms as well as word of mouth. They also testify to the personalised politics of enactivism by individual volunteers, claiming it to be experience-based, personal and transformative.

A common thread of the individual accounts is 'experience', that is, a personalised experience that cannot be replicated. Each project is different, each situation is unique, and participating in philanthropy is therefore a deeply personal and transformative experience. In Deng Fei's (2015) words, "you are helping yourself while helping others", that is, altruistic and self-interested motivations are mixed with doing good for others. Another common thread is 'trust', a total trust by Deng Fei – known as 'Brother Fei' – in individual volunteers to initiate an idea, design and implement a project and fundraise. Such trust enables individuals to immerse in the experience economy as a technology of self, when one gains intellectual and emotional maturity through volunteering in civic associations and activities (Liu, 2015). Such experience economy in turn brings about the technology of power that both the Chinese state and middle class wish to harness to refashion young Chinese citizens and citizenship. The experience economy, as utilised by Deng Fei and his team, hence creates value for all parties concerned in doing good for others.

At the individual and personal level, the experience economy is realised through personalised engagement in individual projects. Quite often, this personalised politics is built on friendship through one's circles of friends, that is, friends are used as a basic information infrastructure in carrying out grassroots philanthropic efforts. Friends can be more easily trusted and connected in collective actions than strangers in the Chinese context.

Word-of-mouth mobilisation in one's friends groups on Weixin and Weibo can often get a large number of followers and large amounts of donation – Deng Fei and his team are keenly aware of and able to skilfully utilise these personalised connective politics; he knows how to diffuse emotional power from individuals to the collective and turn people's emotion and admiration into actions. These personal and personalised collective actions are often taken by individuals who join in loosely coordinated activities centred on personal emotional identifications, aspirations or simply obligation to one's group or circle of friends. In other words, individuals are mobilised around personal lifestyle values as well as friendship to engage in collective causes. Online platforms and social media are core to individuals committed to "DIY politics" that can be amplified beyond personal networks (Bennett, 2012). Indeed, Free Lunch has been called the "best university" by student volunteers because it enables young people to act out their individual beliefs, ideals and potentials (Du, 2015). The personal dimension and morally uplifting effect of enactivism has been marketed by Deng Fei and his team (including thousands of volunteers throughout the country) as central to the experience politics of the Free Lunch brand, as they write numerous personal accounts about their involvement in various programmes on Weibo, Weixin, various blogs, online forums and personal networks. Despite being censored in China, Facebook has also been added to Deng Fei's arsenal of social media marketing in order to attract international followers and supporters. Such witness accounts of enactivism have further galvanised an increasing number of people to extend a helping hand without engaging in any form of 'activism' (a politically loaded term and hence sensitive in the Chinese context) or stepping out of their personal space through what Guobin Yang calls "transboundary interactions" (Yang, 2006, p. 5). As Deng Fei (2015) summarises,

> What is interesting is that our volunteers and donors often write their actions in their Weibo, which were seen by his or her friends and followers in social media, and often forwarded and commented on their microblogs. Theirs attracted more followers. In this way, they also help communicate and publicise Free Lunch, as doers and communicators, like a kind of fissionable power.

It can therefore be argued that these small-scale, localised, issue-focused and sometimes private and unplanned forms of microphilanthropy can have a greater net effect on Chinese society than more 'organised' events due to their unofficial and grassroots nature (which gives them social legitimacy); the sheer number of participants (including thousands of volunteers across the country); the complete transparency in fundraising, operation and auditing process (in contrast to government organised non-governmental organisations, or GONGOs); and, at the individual level, the transformative experience for all involved – donors, doers, givers, volunteers and receivers.

Conclusion

The role of the internet in facilitating online activism and social movement in China has been central to academic discussions in recent years (e.g. Chen, 2015; Chen & Reece, 2015; Yang, 2009). This development of digital communication technologies parallels the rise of urban, consumerist and individualised lifestyles and politics (Damm, 2007). The boundaries between private and public domains, and between personal problems and collective demands, are increasingly porous and easily crossed, often at one's fingertips with the help of mobile communication. The revival of civic associations also parallels this development of the internet and mobile internet as civil society actors are often early adopters of new technologies. As a technological tool, a strategic resource and opportunity and spatial haven, social media has produced a web of civic associations, given birth to fledgling citizen groups, and enabled new, small and resource-poor organisations to achieve social change and construct alternative identities (Sullivan & Xie, 2009; Yang, 2003; Yuan, 2015). Deng Fei's Free Lunch is one of the new breed of citizen associations and microphilanthropy initiatives that are born of, mature and expand via social media.

Previous research has shown that despite the increasingly sophisticated state control and censorship effort, digital media and communication networks provide individuals with an alternative space to exercise citizenship, not through overt resistance, but through a skilful play of humour, music, videos, games, symbols, words and memes – such digital remix creates new forms of expression and association that are intrinsically subversive of and yet at the same time confirm to political and cultural tradition and establishment (e.g. Meng, 2011; Yang & Jiang, 2015; Yu, 2015b). Through their informal, sporadic, spontaneous, personal networks, netizens can connect and network across different cyber communities. Communities that are formed online can become actors in the real world, especially when they concern themselves with areas in which the government has been more tolerant of citizen involvement, such as poverty alleviation, public health and environmental protection.

Digital media and communication networks have enabled Deng Fei, his team and volunteers to achieve economies of scale and scope at a minimum cost. They have done so without challenging the state ideology and authority. Rather, Deng Fei and his Free Lunch initiative have been incorporated into a GONGO (China Social Welfare Foundation) and received positive publicity through various awards, public and media events, and media reports for their efforts in providing services to poor rural children and their families. All these are achieved not just through effective use of social media but also through a pragmatic experience economy, which is both personal and collective.

The personal dimension of experience economy calls for a reflection on social movement in the era of digital communication. The concepts of "personalized politics" or "DIY politics" (Bennett, 2012) and "connective actions" (Bennett & Segerberg, 2012) are useful in describing personalised engagement in digitally networked actions and political associations. As this chapter has argued, self-reliant individuals are mobilised through personal networks to engage in loosely coordinated activities centred on personalised identifications and experience. The engaged philanthropy has an intrinsically personalised emotional fabric that binds individuals together in the experience economy of doing good for others. Hence, what starts as personal and personalised experience in volunteering for Free Lunch and other microphilanthropy initiatives can turn into a collective tide and drive to transform Chinese society.

The explosion of grassroots civil associations in the past decade in China indexes the emergence of volunteerism, rights consciousness and alternative politics on self-governance, with well connected, knowledgeable and entrepreneurial individuals as the lead sheep to guide the herd to new fields. Social media and apps provide the timely platforms and tools to carry out individual "altruistic action[s] in an egoistic society" (Yang, 2009, p. 180). Microphilanthropy, though capable of being co-opted by vested interests and agendas, represents the "utopian impulse" and "a yearning for justice, trust, and solidarity" among the Chinese commons (p. 184).

References

Anping. (2015). 历史从未像今天，赋权我们以记录、表达、传播 [*History has never empowered us to record, express, and communicate as today*]. Retrieved from http://mp.weixin.qq.com/s?__biz=MjM5MjAyNDY1Ng==&mid=40048738 0&idx=2&sn=5c1cf580b28cfeaf43878b6bc5f20b76&scene=5&srcid= 1110QMk6B1GGSclu90rIxC5v#rd.

Bennett, W. L. (2012). The personalization of politics: Political identity, social media, and changing patterns of participation. *The ANNALS (AAPSS), 644,* 20–39.

Bennett, W. L., & Segerberg, A. (2012). The logic of connective action: Digital media and the personalization of contentious politics. *Information, Communication & Society, 15*(5), 739–768.

Chen, W. (Ed.). (2015). *The internet, social networks and civic engagement in Chinese societies.* London, UK & New York: Routledge.

Chen, W., & Reece, S. D. (Eds.). (2015). *Networked China: Global dynamic of digital media and civic engagement: New agendas in communication.* London, UK & New York: Routledge.

Cheng, L. (Ed.). (2010). *China's emerging middle class: Beyond economic transformation.* Washington, DC: Brookings Institution Press.

Damm, J. (2007). The internet and the fragmentation of Chinese society. *Critical Asian Studies*, 39(2), 273–294.

Deng, F. (2014). 免费午餐：柔软改变中国 [*Free Lunch: Softness changes China*]. Beijing: Huawen Press.

Deng, F. (2015). 公益项目的运营模式创新与可持续发展 [*Operational innovation and sustained development of philanthropic programs*]. Retrieved from http://mp.weixin.qq.com/s?__biz=MjM5NjEwMTQ4OA==&mid=400849186&idx=1&sn=6e1382d89988221580431f412d4e1032&scene=5&srcid=1117ajlkSQ9C72KpmOtDpVDI#rd.

Du, X. (2015). 免费午餐是我最好的大学 [*Free Lunch is my best university*]. Retrieved from http://mp.weixin.qq.com/s?__biz=MjM5NjEwMTQ4OA==&mid=400663650&idx=1&sn=c3f6a25780b0d43c88b90da34487f2e3&scene=5&srcid=1118d8SSpOLtN8teijoFrVIr#rd.

Fleischer, F. (2011). Technology of self, technology of power: Volunteering as encounter in Guangzhou, China. *Ethnos*, 76(3), 300–325.

Graham-Harrison, E. (2015). *Why China's super-rich are now eager to invest in philanthropy*. The Guardian. 15 November. Retrieved from www.theguardian.com/world/2015/nov/15/china-super-rich-philanthropy-corruption.

Hildebrandt, T. (2011). The political economy of social organization registration in China. China Quarterly, 208, 970-989.

Hildebrandt, T. (2013). *Social organizations and the authoritarian state in China*. New York: Cambridge University Press.

Hildebrandt, T. (2015). From NGO to enterprise: The political economy of activist adaptation in China. In R. Hasmath & J. Y. J. Hsu (Eds.), *NGO governance and management in China* (pp. 121–136). London, UK & New York: Routledge.

Hsu, C. L. (2011). Even further beyond civil society: The rise of internet-oriented Chinese NGOs (response to Kin-Man Chan and Li Zhang). *Journal of Civil Society*, 7(1), 123–127.

Jeffreys, E. (2010). Accidental celebrities: China's chastity heroines and charity. In L. Edwards & E. Jeffreys (Eds.), *Celebrity in China* (pp. 67–84). Hong Kong: Hong Kong University Press.

Liu, J. (2015). 乡村学校"会飞的宿舍"诞生记 [*The birth of 'Flying Dorms' for rural schools*]. Retrieved from http://zhenhua.163.com/15/0628/18/AT7GGIDE000465FI.html.

Meng, B. (2011). From steamed bun to grass mud gorse: E'gao as alternative political discourse on the Chinese internet. *Global Media and Communication*, 7(1), 33–51.

Pine, B. J. II, & Gilmore, J. H. (1999). *The experience economy: Work is theater and every business a stage*. Boston, MA: Harvard Business School Press.

Shieh, S., & Deng, G. (2011). An emerging civil society: The impact of the 2008 Sichuan earthquake on grassroots associations in China. *The China Journal*, 65, 181–194.

Shue, V. (1998). State power and the philanthropic impulse in China today. In W. F. Ilchman et al. (Eds.), *Philanthropy in the world's traditions* (pp. 332–354). Bloomington & Indianapolis: Indiana University Press.

Sima, Y. (2011). Grassroots environmental activism and the internet: Constructing a green public sphere in China. *Asian Studies Review*, 35(4), 477–497.

Smith, J. H. (2009). *The art of doing good: Charity in late Ming China*. Berkeley: University of California Press.

Song, Z. (2015). 坚固的东西都在消失 [*Anything hard is disappearing*]. Retrieved from http://mp.weixin.qq.com/s?__biz=MzA3NzI0MjUzMw==&mid=4000 71700&idx=1&sn=28d76e621bd8e28fd5596cb7d3982c51#rd.

Spires, A. J. (2011). Contingent symbiosis and civil society in an authoritarian state: Understanding the survival of China's grassroots NGOs. *American Journal of Sociology*, 117(1), 1-45.

Spires, A. J. (2007). *China's un-official civil society: The development of grassroots NGOs in an authoritarian state*. (PhD dissertation). Yale University, CT, USA.

Sullivan, J., & Xie, L. (2009). Environmental activism, social networks and the internet. *The China Quarterly*, 198, 422–432.

Tai, J. W.-C. (2012). *Embedded civil society: NGO leadership and organizational effectiveness in authoritarian China*. (PhD dissertation). The George Washington University, DC, USA.

Teets, J. C. (2009). Post-earthquake relief and reconstruction efforts: The emergence of civil society in China? *The China Quarterly*, 198, 330–347.

Tucker, M. E. (1998). A view of philanthropy in Japan: Confucian ethics and education. In W. F. Ilchman et al. (Eds.), *Philanthropy in the world's traditions* (pp. 169–196). Bloomington & Indianapolis: Indiana University Press.

Xu, B. (2014). Consensus crisis and civil society: The Sichuan earthquake response and state-society relations. *The China Journal*, 71, 91–108.

Yang, G. (2003). The co-evolution of the internet and civil society in China. *Asian Survey*, XLIII(3), 405–22.

Yang, G. (2006). Activists beyond virtual borders: Internet-mediated networks and informational politics in China. *First Monday*, 7, 1–22.

Yang, G. (2009). *The power of the internet in China: Citizen activism online*. New York: Columbia University Press.

Yang, G., & Calhoun, C. (2007). Media, civil society, and the rise of a green public sphere in China. *China Information*, 21, 211–236.

Yang, G., & Jiang, M. (2015). The networked practice of online political satire in China: Between ritual and resistance. *The International Communication Gazette*, 77(3), 215–231.

Yu, H. (2015a). Micro-media, micro-philanthropy, and micro-citizenship in China. In Q. Luo (Ed.), *Global media worlds and China* (pp. 79–92). Beijing: Communication University of China Press.

Yu, H. (2015b). After the "steamed bun": E'gao and its postsocialist politics. *Chinese Literature Today*, 5(1), 55–64.

Yuan, E. (2015). The new political of mediated activism in China: A critical review. In W. Chen & S. D. Reese (Eds.), *Networked China: Global dynamic of digital media and civic engagement: New agendas in communication* (pp. 214–230). London, UK & New York: Routledge.

Zhang, J. Y. (2015). Contested symbiosis: State-NGO relations in China. *Open Democracy/ISA RC-47: Open Movements*. Retrieved from https://opendemocracy.net/joy-y-zhang/contested-symbiosis-statengo-relations-in-china.

3 Social Media and Activism of Grassroots NGOs in China

A Case Study of Love Save Pneumoconiosis (LSP)

Dianlin Huang

Introduction

How the interaction between social organisations and state power is mediated by new media and information technologies, in particular social media, has been an important issue attracting attention from authors working in varying areas of social sciences, including media studies. While many studies concerning this issue are focused on cases in well-developed democratic societies or contexts of progressive political change (e.g., Ghannam, 2011; Joseph, 2012), China, with a relatively stable authoritarian state–society configuration, provides an ideal site for examining dynamic contentious relationship between organised social actors, the authoritarian party–state and booming social media that offers new forms of mediation.

In recent years, Chinese social media has undergone fast development as a result of policies that have largely excluded non-Chinese services from the Chinese market and thereby constructed "a flourishing home-grown, state-approved ecosystem" for locally-originated social media platforms (Crampton, 2011). These social media platforms have quickly become important resources employed by different actor–speakers, including the party–state, the market, social organisations and individual citizens, to serve their differing and often conflicting purposes. Different from the party–state's propaganda-driven (Wang, 2012) or market actor's commercial uses (Yu, Asur, & Huberman, 2015) of social media, burgeoning Chinese grassroots non-governmental organisations (NGOs) have taken a non-profit public approach to social media by tactfully utilising these new alternative outlets to promote their specific activism goals. With social media, grassroots Chinese NGOs are now able to offset the previous shortage of media resources available for advocacy organisations in the party–state-dominated mass media sphere. They are now able to establish direct communication networks with, and moderately mobilise the general public and key stakeholders in, their respective issue areas, and also justify their own legitimacy by carefully managing discursive strategies.

In order to determine the role of social media in China, authors have tried to either evaluate the Chinese party–state's role in shaping the political–economic ecology of social media (Lagerkvist, 2011, 2012) or prescribe business rules, models or marketing strategies for making a success in the lucrative Chinese social media market (Chiu, Ip, & Silverman, 2012). Comparatively, not too much has been said about the role social media plays in facilitating activism for grassroots social organisations and mediating their relationship with the party–state and the public. In particular, how exactly social media has been used by NGOs in collective actions for the purposes of resource mobilisation and self-legitimacy construction in the Chinese context? This chapter aims to examine this issue by conducting an in-depth case study of Love Save Pneumoconiosis (LSP) (大爱清尘 *Da Ai Qing Chen*), a Beijing-based grassroots non-governmental charitable organisation dedicated to help rural migrant workers suffering from pneumoconiosis, an occupational lung disease induced by excessive workplace exposure to and inhalation of certain airborne dusts due to poor labour conditions. The chapter will begin by briefly contextualising Chinese NGOs and social media developments through a critical discussion of relevant literature that theorise the relationship between NGOs, media and the party–state. This will be followed by a case study on the tactical use of social media and other forms of communication resources by LSP activists – including organisational communication, self-legitimising strategies and promotion of a narrative rationale – to illustrate both the complex social media practice of Chinese social organisations and their limitations.

Contextualising NGOs and Social Media in China

Due to their non-state nature, Chinese NGOs have to face questions of the legitimacy of their existence in Chinese society, and carefully maintain their actions within the boundary of the party–state's political bottom line pre-emptively, and avoiding any actions that potentially undermine the one-party regime. Besides self-limiting measures, they also actively develop defensive discursive strategies by making use of all accessible resources, including media, to legitimise their existence and construct a relatively friendly political environment for their work. In terms of the issue of how NGOs interact with the authoritarian party–state, scholars have taken either a liberal civil society perspective (e.g., Saich, 2000; Yang, 2005) or a corporatist insight (Hsu & Hasmath, 2014) to theorise the existence of non-state entities such as NGOs in Chinese society. More recent studies have identified a teleological tendency in the two contrasting approaches (Hildebrandt, 2013) – overcoming the state–society dichotomy and disaggregating "both 'state' and 'society' to take into account the diverse interests and goals within them" (Lu, 2009, p. 9). Methodologically, it has been argued that ethnographic explications of NGOs' micro operations on a daily basis are necessary to illustrate exactly how NGO activists react, adapt and act on the basis of available resources (Hsu & Hasmath, 2015).

In this process, media, especially newly popularised social media represented by varying forms of social networking services (SNS), are some of the vital resources that NGOs must effectively deploy so as to discursively legitimise their existence. Strategies include constructing a positive self-image, activating public resonance and support, resetting the party–state-dominated media agenda, negotiating policy boundaries and thereby advancing their organisational goals. In other words, they need to utilise both technological forms and content resources provided by social media to create and expand discursive opportunities, an important aspect of larger political opportunity structures for collective actions engendered by changes in a political system (McAdam, 1982; McAdam, McCarthy, & Zald, 1996). While political opportunity structure includes "all of the institutional and cultural access points that actors can seize upon to attempt to bring their claims into the political forum", discursive opportunity structure refers to "the framework of ideas and meaning-making institutions in a particular society" (Ferree, Gamson, Gerhards, & Rucht, 2002, p. 62), including political and socio–cultural components.

Among others, media and relevant institutional structures are one of the focal parts of the discursive opportunity framework. Concurring with the whole neo-authoritarian developmentalist package (Karmel, 1995) prescribed by the party–state to defuse extensive crisis in the aftermath of decades of an inefficient centrally-planned economy and totalitarian politics, Chinese media institutions have changed prodigiously in the last 3 decades from a rigidly controlled hierarchical propaganda system to a moderately marketised and semi-pluralistic cultural sphere where new economic and cultural roles of the media sector have been allowed to emerge and prosper (Winfield & Peng, 2005). However, the core of the media system as the party–state's mouthpiece (*houshe* 喉舌) (Guo, 1997) – or what Lee, He and Huang (2008) call the "Chinese Party Publicity Inc". – remains institutionally and ideologically intact. This unchanged nature of a party–state ideological organ is the fundamental determinant of traditional media organisations' relatively vigilant attitudes towards NGOs, especially those with foreign or dissident political backgrounds. In comparison, although politically circumscribed by an increasingly sophisticated regulation system, the booming Chinese internet industry and internet-enabled social media – represented earlier by sites such as Bulletin Board System (BBS) and blogging, and more recently by SNS such as Sina's Weibo (微博 microblogging) and Tencent's WeChat (微信 mobile messaging app) – have provided more openness for socially engaged communication and thus alternative information platforms for social activism in China.

Chinese social organisations epitomised by environmental NGOs (ENGOs) have long relied on internet-based new media to offset insufficient support from traditional mass media. As early as 1999, Chinese ENGOs had already started to make innovative use of the internet to organise online public participation in environmental protection (Liu, 2011). Since the late 1990s, Chinese ENGOs have been one of the most active areas where internet-based new media are extensively utilised by environmental activists who have purportedly constructed a "green public sphere" of critical contention (e.g., Sima, 2011; Yang & Calhoun, 2007). More recently, realising the extensive potential for social media in communicating social initiatives, professor Jing Wang from the Massachusetts Institute of Technology, in cooperation with some other institutions, launched project NGO 2.0 in 2009 to introduce "Web 2.0 thinking and social media tools to the grassroots NGOs in the underdeveloped regions of China" (Wang, 2010), marking the rise of both academic interests and practical actions in social media-based civic engagement in China.

However, given the fact that both the information system, including social media and organisational social activism upheld by NGOs, are subject to limited political opportunity structures in a long-entrenched authoritarian party–state–society configuration, it can be expected that Chinese grassroots NGOs' use of internet and social media is also tactically limited. The general political structure in which NGOs and the media system operate has not become inclusive enough to tolerate radical discourses and actions. This results in a depoliticising or specific policy-oriented strategy widely embraced in civic engagement. Mirroring China's particular political system and reality of activism, most Chinese social organisations choose to make use of what Kingdon (1984) calls a "policy window" to promote specific goals (Goldstone, 1998) rather than appeal to systematic change. For example, in their study on Chinese ENGOs' use of websites in relationship building and policy agenda setting, Yang and Taylor (2010) suggest websites were only used to disseminate environment related information, rather than to overtly mobilise the public to take organised actions to challenge government policies, an action which can easily be regarded as attacking the regime *per se*. A similar media strategy is also recognised in a more recent study which shows how a strategy of "minimal politics" of subtly politicising the issue in question without fundamentally confronting the political system has been adopted in NGO's social media-facilitated discursive contention, concluding that "resistance is possible in repressive contexts, without necessarily leading to democratization" (Gleiss, 2015).

The above discussion of social background and scholarly enquiries shows both the growing importance and limitations of the use of social media by Chinese grassroots NGOs. However, most current literature tends to take either a political–economic oriented approach or a discursive–centric framework to understand the relationship between social media and NGOs. This overlooks the issue of how the fast development of social media has, to a certain degree, changed the communicative opportunities for advocacy organisations, and how media forms *per se*, in particular how specific technological and functional features of social media, have offered new possibilities for both political–economic and discursive nego-tiations and thereby affected Chinese NGOs' legitimisation and campaign strategies. It is necessary to adopt an integrated approach by contextual-ising grassroots NGOs' social media-based discursive contention in their actual organisational management and activism practice while keeping sensitive to broader socio–political structures.

Following this framework, this chapter will use LSP as a typical ex-ample of a Chinese grassroots NGO to examine how, while also utilising varying forms of printed and broadcasting communication at national and regional levels, social media has been more extensively used by LSP activists in both routine and event-driven communications to consolidate its legitimacy and promote organisational goals. All data were drawn from in-depth interviews with LSP media team members in Beijing con-ducted in November 2015, field observations of charity events in Beijing and Xi'an in July 2015, as well as online and offline documents from LSP's Weibo and WeChat accounts or provided by LSP media staff. The chapter will conclude with evaluative remarks on the potentials and lim-itations of social media in activism of Chinese grassroots NGOs.

Case Study: LSP's Social Media Presence

Background

LSP was founded by Wang Keqin, an influential veteran investigative journalist who had a strained relationship with the government because of his decade-long critical exposure of official misconducts such as un-masking the vaccine scandal and official corruption in Shanxi province (Branigan, 2010). He is the soul figure of the organisation and his repu-tation as a widely respected journalist plays an important constructive role in the establishment and operation of LSP ("Wang Keqin", n.d.). According to its official website (www.daaiqingchen.org), LSP was es-tablished in July 2011 in affiliation with China Social Assistance Foun-dation, a national public fundraising foundation directly regulated by the Ministry of Civil Affairs. It should be noted that this affiliation is procedurally required for NGO establishment, and does not affect LSP's relative autonomy in its daily operation.

As a domestic-originated charity NGO, LSP is dedicated to providing aid to rural migrant workers suffering from pneumoconiosis, an occu-pational lung disease caused by dust breathed in and deposited deep in the lungs after excessive exposure to a dusty work environment without enough preventive measures. The main social background of the organisation's founding was the serious problem of the prevalence of pneumoconiosis in China, particularly among mining workers. Most victims are underprivileged rural-originated migrant workers, who have been discriminatorily defined as outcast from urban citizenship, including from basic labour rights enjoyed by their urban counterparts, by the *hukou* (户口) or the household registration system, which defines differentiated categories of welfare treatment of citizens based on the dual classification of rural and urban populations (Chan & Zhang, 1999). Official records on the numbers of migrant workers infected with pneumoconiosis in China are rare; yet a recent government report admits that there are at least 720,000 cases (Li, 2015). However, according to Wang Keqin, the actual number of victims is much higher than the official one, something which has severely underestimated the intensity of the crisis (Wang's lecture at Xi'an International Studies University, personal communication, July 18, 2015). Despite LSP being an example of a charity organisation in the reform period in place since the 1990s (Hsu, 2008), its non-official background and strong stance on migrant issues differentiates it from other state-backed charities.

The salience of LSP's representativeness as a domestic-originated charitable NGO with a clear target group of pneumoconiosis victims among underclass rural migrant workers strongly presents its validity as the subject of this case study. Another justification is the fact that the trajectory of LSP's founding and development largely overlaps with key periods of Chinese social media. The time when LSP was founded was also a golden period of Chinese social media, embodied by the rise and rapid popularisation of Sina Weibo, the dominant Twitter-like microblogging service in mainland China. Weibo was launched in 2009 when most forerunning smaller domestic microblogging services were shut down and foreign SNS sites blocked because of Han-Uygur ethnic turmoil in Xinjiang. The politically-induced market vacuum gave Weibo the chance to quickly gain a monopoly in the Chinese social media market, leading to explosive growth of users and comprehensive impacts on social life by 2010, a year regarded by many as the "Year One of the Weibo Era" in China (Xie & Xu, 2011). Because of its features of faster and decentralised information diffusion among citizens, Weibo significantly empowers individuals and organisations by granting them alternative communication spaces, thus revealing potential positive effects on collective actions by fostering issue networks among social activists (Huang & Sun, 2014). The period from 2010–2012, before the government's crackdown, saw the sprouting of a large number of Weibo accounts, especially those held by the so-called 'Big Vs' or prominent verified bloggers including popular critics, activists and writers who used Weibo to foster public debates about comprehensive issues ranging from environmental protection to official corruption (Hatton, 2015). At the same time, Weibo also launched its own social media-based 'microphilanthropy' service (http://gongyi.weibo.com) whereby charitable organisations can promote their projects and receive donations.

In addition to Weibo, another new development in the Chinese social media market has been the emergence of Tencent's multi-platform mobile instant messaging app WeChat (微信 *Weixin*) in early 2011. Similarly, the government's ban on foreign counterparts created a favourable market condition for WeChat to quickly hold sway over the industry. In September 2015 Tecent reported that WeChat had 650 million monthly active users (Tencent, 2015) with a penetration rate of 93 percent in major Chinese cities (Wang, 2015), making it one of the largest and most popular messaging apps worldwide and the most dominant in the Chinese market. The platform-focused strategy makes it not just a mobile instant messaging service, but a complex hybrid of Facebook, WhatsApp and Paypal, featuring interpersonal or group chat, profile pages, individual or organisation-registered public accounts and also an increasing number of cutting edge localised commercial or public online-to-offline services (Chan, 2015). Compared with Weibo's overt publicness, WeChat only provides limited personal network-based public communication in the forms of either a personal profile page (朋友圈 *pengyouquan*, literally 'friend circle') or public accounts whereby individual or organisational users can diffuse public posts to their subscribers. In comparison, WeChat is much more intimate, more personal network-based, while Weibo is more like a public platform where individuals and organisations showcase their ideas. Thus, people mainly use Weibo to search for news and other public information, while WeChat is largely used for interpersonal or group communication. In the case of grassroots NGOs, both Weibo and WeChat have been quickly grasped to serve their respective organisational goals. As we will see in the specific case of LSP, one of the earliest NGO adopters of both services, functional differences between Weibo and WeChat have led to different usages of the two social media services in advocacy practice, with WeChat mainly used for internal management and Weibo for public education and mobilisation.

Wang opened his personal Weibo account (http://weibo.com/p/1005051700757973) in early 2010. Shortly after its establishment in June 2011, LSP also set up its verified official Weibo account (http://weibo.com/daaiqingchen) with the first message publicised being a repost of Wang's microblog titled "millions of migrant workers under death threat of pneumoconiosis". Two years later on 3 April 2013, LSP's WeChat public account (daaiqingchen010) sent out its first post. Both LSP's Weibo and WeChat accounts include some common features and functions, such as donation channels, feature stories of victims, knowledge about pneumoconiosis and so forth. In the following section of this chapter, detailed modes and tactics of utilising the two social media platforms as a complement to traditional media forms will be empirically analysed, particularly with regards to ISP's legitimisation strategies and organisational goal fulfilment.

Organisational Communication

LSP's organisational communication has been shaped by social media. In a public speech, Wang Keqin attributed the organisation's success should, to a large degree, be attributed to the rise of social media in China, in particular the popularity of Sina Weibo. He personally finds Weibo, and later WeChat, important alternative public communication spaces where he can express his opinions and diffuse information that are usually avoided by party–state controlled mass media. Indeed, he started to use Weibo to publish information and stories about China's pneumoconiosis crisis and victims' sufferings long before the founding of LSP. This use of social media platforms to disseminate knowledge and raise public consciousness of pneumoconiosis has been an integral part of LSP's public communication strategies since its establishment; as Wang said, "LSP is a non-official charitable organisation that could not have been so successful if there is no Weibo" (Wang's lecture at Xi'an International Studies University, personal communication, July 18, 2015).

The very organisational structure of LSP's media section (Figure 3.1) has also clearly demonstrated a tendency of increasing emphasis on social media with Weibo as its core component, supplemented by WeChat and other traditional mass media.

As one media staff member at the Beijing headquarters said,

> ...though we still need to keep contact and good cooperation with the central and regional mass media organisations, what all of us at the media team here do every day is mainly focused on managing our official social media accounts, planning social-media-based campaigns, and coordinating our growing nation-wide regional social media teams to promote our national or regional projects. (Interviews with LSP media staff, personal communication, November 25, 2015)

These national and regional media campaigns are regularly launched by the LSP headquarters and provincial teams to facilitate key social events; besides the verified official Weibo account of its Beijing headquarters, all provincial LSP volunteer organisations also have their own Weibo accounts. LSP volunteers are just required to use a common profile logo on Weibo to display a unified public image of the organisation and its advocacy. These LSP-owned accounts also connect with other Weibo

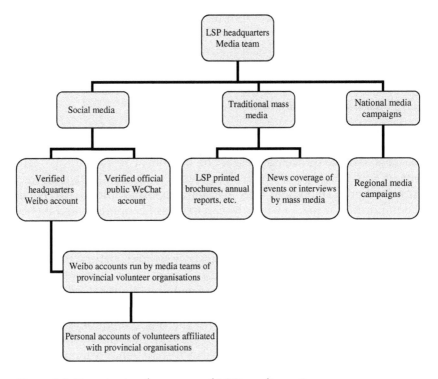

Figure 3.1 Organisational structure of LSP's media section.

accounts of relevant public organisations and important public figures who actively support LSP's initiatives.

There are two main reasons cited for why social media is such a popular medium for NGOs such as LSP. As LSP staff pointed out, there is clearly a shift from mass media to social media in today's NGO activism because "most of our appeal objects have moved from television and newspapers to various mobile devices, to Weibo and WeChat" (Interviews with LSP media staff, personal communication, November 25, 2015). In addition, according to Wang Keqin, one of the main reasons why LSP activists prefer to rely on social media is because it is difficult for an NGO headed by a critical former journalist who was purged from his position many times by the government to get frequent and enough opportunities to have its voice propagated in party–state-monopolised mass media (Wang's lecture at Xi'an International Studies University, personal communication, July 18, 2015). Both Wang Keqin and his media team members acknowledged social media has opened more information space for Chinese grassroots social organisations to more directly and effectively engage with and mobilise the general public (Interviews with LSP media staff, personal communication, November 25,

2015). This decentralised communication mode of social media empowers NGOs to directly have lateral interaction with the public, bypassing state-monopolised mass media, which, out of political concerns, usually hold cautious attitudes towards non-state organisations.

It can therefore be argued that social media has dramatically expanded Chinese grassroots NGOs' public visibility and their ability for public mobilisation in almost all aspects of their work, from fundraising to initiating moderate public actions. As a typical example of a social media-based NGO in the Chinese context, LSP has developed an integrated approach to advocacy communication using four main avenues – through key figures (Wang Keqin and his celebrity friends), event or offline face-to-face campaigns and relevant event-driven public communication and fundraising, via routine online dissemination of public education and scientific information and humanised stories of individual victims as well as using additional media campaigns to offer a 'united' front when promoting particular issues. These are discussed in more detail below.

LSP promotes advocacy communication though the use of a prominent online 'people presence', and social media is considered to be a constitutive part of its organisational management system. For example, LSP's national Weibo network links actors at different levels, including prominent key figures (Keqin Wang and other famous public figures closely connected with the organisation), the Beijing headquarters, provincial branches, individual volunteers and peripheral actors (such as medical experts who offer scientific support or entrepreneurs who give generous donations). The interviews with LSP staff also show how their WeChat-based groups are widely used in the organisation's internal management of volunteers and coordination between regional leaders.

LSP's fundraising has also been increasingly social media-facilitated as online fund donations have become an integral function of its social media channels. For example, its WeChat account includes a function for small donations in its user interface whereby users can directly give their donation through WeChat's embedded Tenpay service. At the same time, its Weibo account directly links with a public interest shop (https://daaiqc.taobao.com) at Alibaba's popular online shopping platform Taobao where users can choose from different donation options supported by Alibaba's Alipay.

LSP's public education and mobilisation are also heavily dependent on social media platforms. WeChat groups moderated by core members of regional organisations are widely used to recruit, network and mobilise LSP volunteers to participate in important events such as organised investigations into living conditions of rural pneumoconiosis victims, public lectures and information briefings, projects of helping families with pneumoconiosis victims and so on (Interviews with LSP media staff, personal communication, November 25, 2015). Both its Weibo and WeChat accounts publish a large number of feature stories about the miserable circumstances of pneumoconiosis workers as well as information about the basic facts of pneumoconiosis in China, including the severity and contributing factors of the crisis and how to resolve it. By doing so, LSP acts on behalf of the victimised rural migrant workers, calling for public support, corporate and government accountability, as well as policy and legislative change for labour rights protection. A common strategy in this respect is to publish serial posts tracking the life history of a specific representative pneumoconiosis victim. In particular, life and death stories about successful or failed LSP-funded medical treatments of pneumoconiosis patients are regularly presented on LSP's social media channels to appeal to the general public's emotional resonance.

LSP has also launched a series of additional national social media campaigns aiming to maintain a relatively high public visibility for the pneumoconiosis issue in the Chinese public sphere and brand a coherent and unified organisational public image. For example, since November 2015 the hashtag slogan 'the green orange is taking action' (青橙在行动 *qingcheng zai xingdong*) has started to be widely used by LSP activists to mark all their Weibo posts related to LSP activities, with the attempt to make LSP and pneumoconiosis trending topics on Chinese social media. As an important part of this campaign, an anthropopathic imagery of a green orange was designed and used by LSP activists as their profile pictures to construct a standardised visual identity of the campaign and LSP's enterprise in general.

Self-Legitimising Strategies

In spite of the prominent role of social media in its activism, LSP still seeks to cooperate with state-owned mass media agencies. The reason is because, compared with dispersive information flows of social media extensively connecting LSP with the general public, party–state-owned media organisations generates more political authority in the current media system embedded in a moderately pluralistic society-in-state configuration (Mertha, 2010). In the current system, they act as a pathway coordinating LSP and party–state organs at different levels and thus endow LSP with more legitimacy and political opportunities to negotiate policy boundaries or effectively alter actions of party–state officials to support LSP agendas. In this regard, LSP has tried to adopt a hybrid approach to media activism, making both social media and state-owned mass media its communicative channels to network with the public and the party–state respectively. By doing so, it has used social media to create its own alternative networks of connecting and engaging with citizens, but also made "organized 'grassroots' efforts directed to creating or influencing media practices and strategies, whether as a primary objective, or as a by-product of other campaigns" (Carroll & Hackett,

2006, p. 84). Though the two forms of media operate in different modes, LSP has largely successfully made them complementary to each other. For example, LSP has established cooperative relationships with county-level governments in regions with high pneumoconiosis prevalence such as provinces of Shaanxi, Hubei and Guizhou; major charity events organised by LSP in these areas were supported by local governments and covered by local and even national media (Interviews with LSP media staff, personal communication, November 25, 2015).

One of the major strategies LSP activists use to converge representations of its charity activism in social media and state-owned mass media is to invite famous public figures, especially celebrities, to be its 'promotion ambassadors'. As a recent phenomenon that has attracted both media publicity and public controversy, the rapid rise of celebrity philanthropy in China has been a prominent trend in NGO activism (Jeffreys, 2015). Celebrities are usually able to easily attract interests from the general public, media professionals and local government officials who eagerly need the fame of celebrities to promote the publicity of the place under his or her jurisdiction. LSP activists also resort to this strategy to attract both media and public favour and have tactically used connections with celebrities to raise the public visibility of the pneumoconiosis issue and LSP itself.

One approach is to directly invite celebrity figures to join LSP's charity actions. For example, in a campaign of donating breathing machines to pneumoconiosis victims launched by LSP in 2011, many famous Chinese actors and singers such as Chen Kun were declared to have joined the project and offered their donations ("Daaiqingchen", 2011). More recently, in July 2015 Chinese actress Yuan Li was invited by Wang Keqin to join a tour in rural areas of Shaanxi province to visit families with pneumoconiosis patients; she has since been a very active member of LSP's charity actions. Her participation has successfully attracted a lot of public attention to the pneumoconiosis issue and the plight of victims – her daily activities and thoughts are broadcast live online via her own verified Weibo account and almost every piece of information she posts or reposts on Weibo receives hundreds and even thousands of comments from Weibo users. In the context of creating 'positive energy' (正能量 *zheng neng liang*) hailed by the government, the case of Yuan Li's involvement in charity also presents a good story for local and national official mass media. Her activities in provinces of Shaanxi and Hubei were covered by xinhuanet.com, the official website of Xinhua News Agency, China's national news agency (Sun, 2015) and the story was then soon republished by people.cn, the official website of the *People's Daily*, the mouthpiece of the ruling Chinese Communist Party ("Yuan Li", 2015).

This type of coverage serves as a sign of the party–state's authorisation of the legitimacy of LSP's charity advocacy, further ensuring local governments' cooperation with LSP in pneumoconiosis prevention, financial and medical aids to victims and their families, and supervision of corporate accountability. Increasingly LSP has established a mode of cooperation with local mass media organisations, especially city or county level TV stations, in advocating LSP initiatives by producing and broadcasting public service advertising, news, documentaries and talk shows (Interviews with LSP media staff, personal communication, November 25, 2015). Further, by deploying these integrated media strategies, LSP has demonstrated a balanced approach to discursive contestation about the pneumoconiosis issue and depicted itself as both a speaker for those silenced suffering migrant workers via social media discourses and also a problem solver for the government's sake through authorised coverage on its charity actions by state-owned official media. It has carefully managed to construct its own social and political legitimacy through combined forms of old and new media.

Promotion of a Narrative Rationale

The idea of using social media to promote a narrative rationale can be seen in the example of three online videos repeatedly reposted on LSP's official Weibo account. In these, as in most of its Weibo posts, LSP activists have carefully used critical discursive tactics of humanisation narratives and a common responsibility frame to mildly disclose facts about the social roots of the pneumoconiosis crisis and the sufferings of workers. The videos represent three episodes of LSP activism – monological presentation of basic facts about the pneumoconiosis crisis, dialogical story telling of the unbearable sufferings of individual pneumoconiosis victims and paradigmatic displays of LSP activist actions aiming to change the dreadful status quo. The first video is a speech highlighting the severity and policy roots of the pneumoconiosis crisis in China delivered by Wang Keqin at a Social Responsibility Person of the Year award ceremony hosted by the influential liberal newspaper *Southern Weekly* (Xisen27, 2014). The second is a dialogue between Wang Keqin and Hong Kong based Phoenix TV hostess Zeng Zimo disclosing the suffering of pneumoconiosis families (Phoenix TV, 2012) and the third is a Philips-sponsored short documentary featuring Wang Keqin investigating conditions of rural pneumoconiosis peasants ("Feilipu", 2015).

Indeed, many posts tell either heartbreaking stories of rural migrant workers and their families suffering from unbearable inhuman conditions, or encouraging stories of individual or organisational actors spurred by LSP's advocacy taking compassionate actions to help relieve their wretched circumstances. Through these micro narratives of humanised stories of individual lives, LSP effectively utilises a 'common destiny community' or shared responsibility framework which defines pneumoconiosis victims and their families as 'our suffering brothers and sisters' and therefore moralises the issue as a problem that no one can ignore.

LSP thus has deconstructed the hierarchised social order as a result of a developmentalist ideology and concurring policies in the reform era, an order which severely devalues and thereby excludes underprivileged rural migrants from rightful and equal citizenship rights (Anagnost, 2004). It is in this realm of bio-politics where the human body of sick migrant workers becomes a site of discursive contention where LSP, by displaying the bodily suffering of pneumoconiosis workers, tactfully challenges both the hegemonic dehumanised discourse of migrant workers as a silenced and devalued 'other' and also the dominant ideology of China's development mode that underscores economic growth at expense of human dignity and basic rights. It thus subtly criticises the status quo of differentiated citizenship treatments and labour rights conditions in China, and indirectly politicises the pneumoconiosis crisis as a consequence of policy defects and governance failure. This motive of defending morality and justice and working for a better and more just society constitutes the underpinning of LSP's social legitimacy as a domestic grassroots NGO winning public resonance and support. This has been largely achieved through social media – many negative materials including astounding scenes of rural families being destroyed by pneumoconiosis could have not been presented to the general public without social media. Social media has therefore fundamentally expanded the scope and depth of discursive practice for grassroots NGOs such as LSP and thus provided a public communication space for social organisations to continuously engage with the general public.

However, while LSP promotes this idea of narrative, as discussed above it also carefully takes a self-limiting approach to its discursive contention when politicising the pneumoconiosis issue and negotiating policy boundaries, by limiting its activities within the scope of charity endeavours and thus depoliticising its work. Despite the fact that it touches labour rights protection, one of the most sensitive social issues in today's China, and therefore runs the risk of being blamed for politically stirring up social grievances, LSP has carefully kept away from radical discursive and practical actions by defining its primary target as 'saving lives and relieving sufferings'. Interviews with core staff members indicate that LSP has adopted a clear-cut self-limiting policy concerning the main scope of its public discourse and actions. Discursively, all posts published in LSP-held Weibo and WeChat accounts are not allowed to directly criticise the government and officials. In practice, LSP has discreetly avoided getting involved in individual appeals or organisational actions related to the highly politically sensitive *Weiquan* (维权) or Rights Defense Movement that covers a very broad range of rights protection activism, from scattered personal resistance to large-scale protests or 'mass incidents' (群体事件 *qunti shijian*) (Hung, 2010, pp. 333–338) (Interviews with LSP media staff, personal communication, November 25, 2015).

LSP thereby excludes itself from the confrontational realm of political struggles and limits its activism within the scope of party–state sanctioned political boundaries. As analysed above, LSP has actively sought to cooperate with official media and regional government officials to legitimise its work by defining it as saving lives and spreading 'positive energy', rather than just exposing the seamier side of society or acting as a subversive force, a basic fact signalled by the organisation's name highlighting 'love' and 'save'. This balanced strategy ensures the legitimacy of LSP's existence in Chinese society, and proves effective in fulfilling the organisation's goals of both alleviating individual migrant's sufferings and also promoting policy change and legislation towards a resolution of the pneumoconiosis crisis in China. Their hard work has paid off – after years of efforts by LSP and other organisations, in January 2016 the National Health and Family Planning Commission and several other major departments of the central government jointly issued a policy document *Opinions on strengthening the prevention and treatment of pneumoconiosis of migrant workers*, marking pneumoconiosis for the first time being recognised as an important issue in central government agenda ("Guanyu", 2016).

Conclusion

To sum up, the above analysis shows that social media use has been a core part of LSP's organisational genes, pervading almost all major facets of its operation. In this regard, LSP is a typical social media-based non-state charitable organisation which epitomises the shift in media power that social media has brought to the activism of grassroots NGOs, and the more general development of civil society and a subtle reconfiguration of the state–society relationship in China. Indeed, the LSP case study shows that the use of social media has definitely engendered new possibilities for grassroots NGOs to directly engage and mobilise the general public and major stakeholders in discursive contention and activism towards social improvement and policy change. With such technological features as instantaneity, interactivity and decentralised network structures, social media platforms thus comprise the major alternative commutation space which, to a certain degree, empowers Chinese grassroots NGOs to far more extensively reach and mobilise new social groups who would have never easily become targets of NGO advocacy without social media. In other words, social media helps lessen dependence on state-monopolised communication networks, diversifies media and public opinions about specific social or policy issues, raises autonomy and boosts networked communicative ability of non-state actors. Therefore, it can be concluded that social media affords grassroots NGOs more leverage to directly engage actor–speakers from both the party–state and civil society to maximise its advocated interests.

However, the case study of LSP's media practice also shows a continued self-limiting tendency in grassroots NGOs activism, especially in terms of managing the relationship with the party–state; the coming of the social media era has not changed that tendency too much. As mentioned earlier, both social media and the social organisations who use them are not immune to the general political economic conditions engendered by the intact authoritarian political order and concurring state–society relationship. Therefore, it would be misleading to overestimate the emancipatory potential of social media in activism of grassroots advocacy organisations or overlook the complex relationship between social media and traditional forms of mass communication. As we have seen in the LSP case, two compromises were made by the organisation to legitimise its work. On the one hand, both social media and government-controlled state media were used in a complementary manner to optimise communicative effectiveness and also politically legitimise itself by getting more visibility in state media or related party–state authorised discursive arena. On the other hand, LSP's discursive contention on social media has adopted hybridised narrative strategies which depoliticise the advocated issue in general but tactfully politicise it at partial levels in order to push the policy boundary without necessarily leading to radical results. With this self-limiting principle, LSP has carefully managed its social media content within political limits and thus has safely located itself in the corporatist space of state–society interaction. This strategy works to ensure self-legitimacy and discursive space of policy negotiation.

Given LSP's representativeness as a grassroots NGO in China, it is reasonable to infer these communicative strategies of legitimisation are not uncommon among Chinese non-profit advocacy organisations. These strategies, with their advantages and also limitations, are a result of complex interactions of specific political, technological, market and social conditions in today's China. Since its inception, the Chinese internet sphere has been continuously shaped by the intricate and dynamic configurations of party–state power, market and technological forces, and social agency of actor–speakers promoting public interests. When each of these elements changes, the power relations among them and the general landscape of internet-based communication subsequently evolve, and there is no exception for Chinese social media. The future of the relationship between social media and activism of Chinese grassroots NGOs therefore relies on continued development of these key momentums.

References

Anagnost, A. (2004). The corporeal politics of quality (Suzhi). *Public Culture*, 16(2), 189–208.

Branigan, T. (2010). Wang Keqin and China's revolution in investigative journalism. Retrieved from www.theguardian.com/world/2010/may/23/wang-keqin-china-investigative-journalism.

Carroll, W. K., & Hackett, R. A. (2006). Democratic media activism through the lens of social movement theory. *Media, Culture & Society, 28*(1), 83–104. doi:10.1177/0163443706059289.

Chan, C. (2015). *When one app rules them all: The case of WeChat and mobile in China*. Retrieved from http://a16z.com/2015/08/06/wechat-china-mobile-first/.

Chan, K. W., & Zhang, L. (1999). The Hukou system and rural–urban migration in China: Processes and changes. *The China Quarterly, 160*, 818–855. doi:10.1017/S0305741000001351.

Chiu, C., Ip, C., & Silverman, A. (2012). Understanding social media in China. *McKinsey Quarterly*. Retrieved from www.mckinsey.com/insights/marketing_sales/understanding_social_media_in_china.

Crampton, T. (2011). *Social media in China: The same, but different*. Retrieved from www.chinabusinessreview.com/social-media-in-china-the-same-but- different/.

Daaiqingchen tubu mujuan huodong juxing huhuan guanai chenfei bingren [*LSP hiking event launched for fund-raising, calling for care and love for pneumoconiosis victims*]. (2011, November 14). Retrieved 2015, August 15, from http://news.sina.com.cn/c/2011–11–14/104123462303.shtml.

Feilipu baiwei rensheng zhi xingzou zai ai de lushang [*Walking on the road of love*] [video file]. (2015, November 17). Retrieved 2015, November 18, from http://v.qq.com/page/g/5/d/g0173av1n5d.html?ptag=4_4.2.5.10120_wxf.

Ferree, M. M., Gamson, W. A., Gerhards, J., & Rucht, D. (2002). *Shaping abortion discourse: Democracy and the public sphere in Germany and the United States*. Cambridge, UK: Cambridge University Press.

Ghannam, J. (2011). *Social media in the Arab world: Leading up to the uprisings in 2011*. Washington, DC, USA: Center for International Media Assistance. Retrieved from http://www.cima.ned.org/wp-content/uploads/2015/02/CIMA-Arab_Social_Media-Report-10-25-11.pdf.

Gleiss, M. S. (2015). Speaking up for the suffering (br)other: Weibo activism, discursive struggles, and minimal politics in China. *Media, Culture & Society, 37*(4), 513–529. doi:10.1177/0163443714566897.

Goldstone, J. (1998). Social movements or revolution? On the evolution and outcome of collective action. In M. Giugni, D. McAdam, & C. Tilly (Eds.), *From contention to democracy* (pp. 125–148). Lanham, MD: Rowman and Littlefield.

Guanyu yinfa jiaqiang nongmin'gong chenfeibing fangzhi gongzuo de yijian de tognzhi [*Circular on Printing and Distributing the Opinions on Strengthening the Prevention and Control of Pneumoconiosis among Migrant Workers*] (2016, January 26). Retrieved 2016, May 2, from http://ghpf.acftu.org/art/2016/1/26/art_1123_161519.html.

Guo, C. (1997). *Houshe Lun [On mouthpiece]*. Beijing: Xinhua Chubanshe.

Hatton, C. (2015). *Is Weibo on the way out?* Retrieved from www.bbc.com/news/blogs-china-blog-31598865.

Hildebrandt, T. (2013). *Social organizations and the authoritarian state in China*. Cambridge, UK: Cambridge University Press.

Hsu, C. L. (2008). 'Rehabilitating charity' in China: The case of Project Hope and the rise of non-profit organizations. *Journal of Civil Society, 4*(2), 81–96. doi:10.1080/17448680802335144.

Hsu, J. Y. J., & Hasmath, R. (2014). The local corporatist state and NGO relations in China. *Journal of Contemporary China*, 23(87), 516–534. doi:10.10 80/10670564.2013.843929.

Hsu, J. Y. J., & Hasmath, R. (2015). Governing and managing NGOs in China: An introduction. In R. Hasmath & J. Y. J. Hsu (Eds.), *NGO governance and management in China* (pp. 1–8). London, UK & New York: Routledge.

Huang, R., & Sun, X. (2014). Weibo network, information diffusion and implications for collective action in China. *Information, Communication & Society*, 17(1), 86–104. doi:10.1080/1369118X.2013.853817.

Hung, C.-f. (2010). The politics of China's Wei-Quan movement in the internet age. *International Journal of China Studies*, 1(2), 331–349.

Jeffreys, E. (2015). Celebrity philanthropy in mainland China. *Asian Studies Review*, 39(4), 571–588. doi:10.1080/10357823.2015.1081871.

Joseph, S. (2012). Social media, political change, and human rights. *Boston College International and Comparative Law Review*, 35(1), 145–188. Retrieved from http://lawdigitalcommons.bc.edu/iclr/vol35/iss1/3.

Karmel, S. M. (1995). *The neo-authoritarian contradiction: Trials of developmentalist dictatorships and the retreat of the state in mainland China.* (Unpublished PhD Dissertation). Princeton University.

Kingdon, J. W. (1984). *Agendas, alternatives, and public policies.* Boston, MA: Little Brown.

Lagerkvist, J. (2011). New media entrepreneurs in China: Allies of the party-state or civil society. *Columbia Journal of International Affairs*, 65(1), 169–182.

Lagerkvist, J. (2012). Principal-agent dilemma in China's social media sector? The party–state and industry real-name registration waltz. *International Journal of Communication.* Retrieved from http://ijoc.org/index.php/ijoc/article/view/1643.

Lee, C.-C., He, Z., & Huang, Y. (2008). 'Chinese Party Publicity Inc.' conglomerated: the case of the Shenzhen Press Group. In K. Sen & T. Lee (Eds.), *Political regimes and the media in Asia* (pp. 11–30). London, UK: Routledge.

Li, J. (2015, July 10). Zhongguo chenfeibing baogao renshu chaoguo 72 wan ren 62% zai meitan hangye [*Report says number of pneumoconiosis victims in China reached 720,000, with 62% from coal industry*]. Xinhua. Retrieved 2015, August 15, from http://www.chinanews.com/gn/2015/07–10/7397027.shtml.

Liu, J. (2011). Picturing a green virtual public space for social change: a study of internet activism and web-based environmental collective actions in China. *Chinese Journal of Communication*, 4(2), 137–166. doi:10.1080/17544750.2011.565674.

Lu, Y. (2009). *Non-governmental organizations in China: The rise of dependent autonomy.* London, UK: Routledge.

McAdam, D. (1982). *Political process and the development of black insurgency, 1930–1970.* Chicago, IL: University of Chicago Press.

McAdam, D., McCarthy, J. D., & Zald, M. N. (1996). *Comparative perspectives on social movements: Political opportunities, mobilizing structures, and cultural framings.* Cambridge, UK: Cambridge University Press.

Mertha, A. (2010). Society in the state: China's nondemocratic political pluralization. In P. Gries & S. Rosen (Eds.), *Chinese politics: State, society and the market* (pp. 69–84). London, UK: Routledge.

Phoenix TV. (2012, December 27). *Zhongguo chenfeibing bingsilv hengao duoshu huanzhe zhineng dengsi [The case fatality rate of pneumoconiosis in China is high with most victims only waiting to die]* [video file]. Retrieved 2015, November 18, from http://v.ifeng.com/news/society/201212/9cb4a75d-c7e1-4564-90f8-6ca646244280.shtml.

Saich, T. (2000). Negotiating the state: The development of social organizations in China. *The China Quarterly, 161,* 124–141. doi:10.1017/S0305741000003969.

Sima, Y. (2011). Grassroots environmental activism and the internet: Constructing a green public sphere in China. *Asian Studies Review, 35*(4), 477–497. doi:10.1080/10357823.2011.628007.

Sun, L. (2015, July 16). Yuan Li Wang Keqin shoupin chengwei yunxixian chenfeibing fangzhi gongzuo guwen [*Yuan Li and Wang Keqin appointed consultants of pneumoconiosis prevention in Yunxi county*]. Xinhua. Retrieved 2015, August 1, from http://news.xinhuanet.com/gongyi/2015-07/16/c_128025902.htm?from=singlemessage.

Tencent. (2015). *Tencent announces 2015 third quarter results.* Retrieved from www.tencent.com/en-us/content/ir/news/2015/attachments/20151110.pdf.

Wang, J. (2010). *NGO2.0: When social action meets social media.* Retrieved from http://cmsw.mit.edu/podcast-jing-wang-ngo20/.

Wang Keqin. (n.d.). *In Wikipedia, The Free Encyclopedia.* Retrieved October 28, 2016, from https://en.wikipedia.org/wiki/Wang_Keqin.

Wang, S. (2012). *China's Fifty Cent party.* Retrieved from http://harvardpolitics.com/world/chinas-fifty-cent-party/.

Wang, S. (2015). *20 new facts you need to know about WeChat.* Retrieved from www.shenglidigital.com/blog/20-new-facts-about-wechat/.

Winfield, B. H., & Peng, Z. (2005). Market or Party Controls?: Chinese Media in Transition. *Gazette, 67*(3), 255–270. doi:10.1177/0016549205052228

Xie, G., & Xu, Y. (2011). Weibo de lishi xianzhuang yu fazhan qushi (Weibo: history, current situation, and future trends). *Xiandai Chuanbo (Modern communication), 4,* 75–80.

Xisen27. (2014, September 15). *Wang Keqin Nanfangzhoumo zeren lingxiu nianhui yanjiang yingwen zimu ban [Wang Keqin's lecture at the Social Responsibility Person of the Year award ceremony hosted by Southern Weekly, English captioned version]* [video file]. Retrieved 2015, November 18, from http://v.youku.com/v_show/id_XNzgyMjg3MTA4.html.

Yang, G. (2005). Environmental NGOs and institutional dynamics in China. *The China Quarterly, 181,* 46–66. doi:10.1017/S0305741005000032.

Yang, G., & Calhoun, C. (2007). Media, civil society, and the rise of a green public sphere in China. *China Information, 21*(2), 211–236. doi:10.1177/0920203x07079644.

Yang, A., & Taylor, M. (2010). Relationship-building by Chinese ENGOs' websites: Education, not activation. *Public Relations Review, 36*(4), 342–351. doi:10.1016/j.pubrev.2010.07.001.

Yu, L. L., Asur, S., & Huberman, B. A. (2015). Trend dynamics and attention in Chinese social media. *American Behavioral Scientist, 59*(9), 1142–1156. doi:10.1177/0002764215580619.

Yuan Li Wang Keqin shoupin chengwei yunxixian chenfeibing fangzhi gongzuo guwen [*Yuan Li and Wang Keqin appointed consultants of pneumoconiosis prevention in Yunxi county*]. (2015, July 16). Retrieved 2015, August 1, from http://politics.people.com.cn/n/2015/0716/c14562–27315182.html.

4 The 'Making' of an Online Celebrity

A Case Study of Chinese Rural Gay Couple An Wei and Wu Yebin

Lianrui Jia and Tianyang Zhou

Introduction

According to the 2016 China Internet Network Information Centre's *Internet development report* (CNNIC, 2016), the total Chinese internet user population reached 688 million at the end of 2015. The rural internet population also experienced impressive growth over this period, surging from 19.31 million to nearly 195 million and today constituting 28.4 percent of the total internet population (Table 4.1). The internet has been appropriated for more diverse uses as it reaches more rural population, from information seeking, to much more diverse social and entertainment uses. Although there exists a divide between rural and urban internet usage patterns and habits in China, the usage of online communication software and web pages such as instant messaging and blogs is more universal than other uses, as Table 4.2 shows.

It is within such a context of Chinese internet development that this chapter presents a unique case of internet and social media use by a rural gay couple from Hebei province in Northern China – An Wei and Wu Yebin. An and Wu are both from rural villages in China and shot to fame in 2014 due to a photo gallery on Ifeng.com entitled the 'Rural gay couple' (乡村同志). In one of the most widely circulated photographs

Table 4.1 Rural Internet Population in China, 2005–2015

Year	2005	2006	2007	2008	2009	2010	2011	2012	2013	2014	2
Rural internet user (in millions)	19.31	23.11	52.62	84.6	106.8	124.8	135.8	155.7	176.6	178.5	1
% of total internet population	17.4	16.9	25.1	28.4	27.8	27.3	26.5	27.6	28.6	27.5	
Penetration rate	N/A	N/A	7.4	11.6	14.8	17.5	20.2	23.7	27.5	28.8	N

Source: Author's compilation of CNNIC annual report.

Table 4.2 Rural and Urban Internet Usage Comparison, 2013

Purposes	Categories	% of Rural Uses	% of Urban Uses	Differences
Info seeking	Search	70.5	82.8	–12.2
Entertainment	Online music	66.9	77.3	–10.4
	Online video	55	74.4	–19.4
	Online games	46.7	58.4	–11.7
	Online literature	37.5	47.6	–10.2
Commerce	Online shopping	31.1	55.2	–24.1
	Online payment	25.7	47.9	–22.2
	Banking	25.4	45.8	–20.4
	Booking	22.1	31.8	–9.6
	Group buying	15.2	25.4	–10.3
	Financial investment	1.1	6.9	–5.8
Communication	Instant messaging	86	86.3	–0.3
	Blog	70.5	70.9	–0.4
	Weibo	35.2	49.1	–13.8
	Email	23	48.6	–25.6
	BBS	14.4	21.3	–6.8

Source: Author's compilation of CNNIC annual report.

taken in a cornfield near where they live, Wu is closing his eyes and leaning against An with a contented smile on his face. The original post on Ifeng.com attracted more than 100,000 participants and their story was picked up and reported by *CNN* and the *Global Times*, the English-language Chinese news outlet under the *People's Daily*, making this couple one of the most iconic symbols for the gay rights movement in China. Moreover, by harnessing new media technologies like online messaging software QQ and the microblog Sina Weibo (the Chinese counterpart of Twitter), An and Wu's Weibo account has attracted more than 7,000 followers (as of May 2016). Their story has made them online celebrities, and has revealed the life and struggle of homosexuals in rural China. As Inglis (2010, p. 10) argues, "celebrity... is the product of culture and technology", because media such as film and radio offer or restore sense of immediacy and intimacy. The same can be said about prevalent uses of social media. Using a narrative account of An and Wu's story, this chapter critically investigates the role of the internet and social media in empowering An and Wu, their online fame, and the social implications for LGBT rights in China.

French sociologist Pierre Bourdieu's concept of symbolic capital provides a theoretical framework in our understanding of An and Wu's case. Bourdieu's theory acknowledges individual agency while also taking into consideration the social and political structures in analysing social changes. As An and Wu's case demonstrates, the internet as a liberator provides key resources for them, as individuals, to garner support from the online gay male community. Born and raised in the countryside, where traditional family values hold strong and societal tolerance is low for homosexuality, An Wei and Wu Yebin's love story carries much significance and inspires many. This chapter argues that social media use did in part transcend the barriers to participation and empower An and Wu with more symbolic capital. However, the internet, as with other forms of media that have emerged and developed in Chinese society, also carries the limitations of the deep-rooted structural, social, political factors that entrench Chinese society, not to mention gay politics, in the country. Therefore, this chapter counters the rosy claims of technological determinism and argues that we must take into consideration the idiosyncratic characteristics of Chinese non-for-profit organisations, the non-oppositional, family-centric orientation of the gay rights movements in China and traditional family values in assessing the role that social media has played in social changes.

Through employing an in-depth interview with An Wei and Wu Yebin and mapping the key social forces at play in their experiences of coming out, being together and gaining publicity, this study parses out the role of the internet and social media in empowering these two individuals from a marginalised social group (rural gay male communities) in China, especially in helping them to obtain symbolic and cultural capital, while also arguing that although social media use played an important role, they are nevertheless embedded in and shaped by the power relations of contemporary Chinese society and the distinct characteristics of Chinese gay politics.

Bourdieu's Social Theory and Online Media

Bourdieu's social theory has informed a wide range of research in media studies. Bourdieu (1993) argues that social life must be understood in terms that do justice to both the objective material, the social and cultural structures and the constituting practices and experiences of individual and groups (p. 3). His theory aims to overcome objectivism, which centres the role of social structures and economic conditions in determining social actions and subjectivism, and which sees the individual as the agent of social change. Social life, to Bourdieu, is a mutually constituting interaction of structures, dispositions and actions whereby social structures and the embodied knowledge of those structures produce enduring orientation which, in turn, are constitutive of social structures.

In other words, the advantage of Bourdieu's theory is that it does not over-empower the individual yet also acknowledges the agency of the individual in social changes. As such, Bourdieu pays special attention to the social–historical context of cultural production and the interplay between the symbolic aspect of social life and the material, structural conditions, without one being reducible to the other. With this focus on historical and social context, Bourdieu endorses a reflexive science of society and aims to reveal the way that taken-for-granted social practices ultimately tend to serve the interest of the dominant class (Hesmond-halgh, 2006, p. 216). As Johnson (1993) writes:

> Bourdieu's theory of the cultural field might be characterised as a 'radical contextualization': it takes into consideration not only works themselves, seen relationally within the space of available possibilities and within the historical development of such possibilities, but also producers of works in term of their strategies and trajectories, based on their individual and class habitus, as well as their objective position within the field.
>
> (p. 9)

However, it should also be noted that the reaction to Bourdieu's theory of culture by media scholars has been sometimes ambivalent – scholars point out in criticism its lack of attention paid to media, such as modern electronic media (Garnham, 1990), the increasingly commercialised cultural industry (Couldry, 2003) and the role that advertising plays in cultural production (Hesmondhalgh, 2006).

In this chapter the key concept that we employ is Bourdieu's symbolic capital. Symbolic capital refers to the degree of accumulated prestige, celebrity, consecration or honour and is founded on a dialectic of knowledge and recognition (Johnson, 1993, p. 7). Bourdieu's theory expands on the Marxian concept of capital, which denotes, first and foremost, a monetary sense, to the notion of capital that captures symbolic, social and cultural capital. The convertibility between economic and cultural capital is key for Bourdieu because through time, education and cultural consumption, the more powerful economic class appropriate the symbolic and cultural sphere to reinforce, reproduce and legitimise class divisions (Garnham, 1990). In this case, the dynamic conception of power offers powerful explanatory capability in terms of understanding why An and Wu, a couple from rural China and from a relatively disadvantaged economic position, possess symbolic capital in the field of gay politics.

The Internet and the Chinese Gay Male Community

The popularisation of the internet in China seems to offer new opportunities to Chinese gay men who have previously been marginalised and underreported by Chinese mainstream media (e.g. Jiang, 2005; van de Werff, 2010; Wei, 2012; Zhou, forthcoming). Surfing the internet has become a new form of entertainment and a fashionable way of gaining information for all Chinese young people since the late 1990s, and a staggering number of emails, BBSs, chat rooms and websites have emerged about homosexuality in particular. The first gay-oriented websites such as Gztz.org (广同) and Yangguang didai (阳光地带) emerged in mainland China in 1998 (Jiang, 2005). These new websites, online forums and chat rooms became increasingly popular and seemed to open up a new world for the Chinese gay male community. Users feel less marginalised and repressed online, at least compared with cruising offline in parks and public toilets at the risk of being arrested by the police. Cyberspace therefore soon became a supreme headquarters to resist media ignorance and spread accurate information, report related news and counter homophobia in the media.

There has also been a remarkable growth in the number of online gay communities due to the great demand for mutual emotional support. Chou (2000, p. 134) highlights the technological enhancement of the *tongzhi* space since mid-1997 as a pioneering force in building indigenous *tongzhi* discourses in the Chinese context, arguing that the popularisation of the internet has made a significant contribution to the emergence of "a small but rapidly growing *tongzhi* community". *Tongzhi* is the Chinese translation of the word 'comrade' which literally means 'people with the same intent'. It was first used at the first Lesbian and Gay Film Festival in Hong Kong in 1989 and since the mid-1990s online 'tongzhi-literature' (同志文学) has become increasing popular, describing the experiences of Chinese gay men and contributing to the self-awareness of many gay men (Chou, 2000). By the end of May 2004, there were approximately 360 *tongzhi* websites in China. In addition, as Zhou (forthcoming) points out, more importantly, since 2010, the emergence of both global (Jack'd) and local gay social networking sites (Feizan.com) has generated unprecedented space for the Chinese gay male community. Jack'd is an international gay social networking mobile application run by Lucid Dreams LLC that has been in service since 2010. By using GPS technologies, it allows users to locate other gay men in the vicinity. Feizan.com is a Chinese gay oriented social networking website that was launched in February 2010. It was the first one to introduce the concept of the 'tongzhi non-sexual interaction' and it had more than 200,000 registered members as of 2012. It launched a Chinese gay mobile application, *Zank*, in May 2013.

In the global context, the lives of gay men have been appreciably transformed in the internet era (e.g. Mowlabocus, 2010; O'Riordan, 2007; Wakeford, 2002). Nevertheless, when consideration is given to specific local contexts, the overstatement of technological empowerment in transforming lives on a global scale fails to grasp the complicated and assorted processes of cross-cultural appropriation in cyberspace. As Berry and Martin (2003) argue, it is worth considering how local identities are transformed by these processes, and how globalising processes are indigenised within local conditions.

Within the Chinese context, Ho (2010) highlights the complex and inconstant processes of "state surveillance, commercialisation, and identity reinvention" in Chinese cyberspace, which "ensure the misrepresentation of same-sex identity, but also produce as much homogeneity as diversity" (p. 99). This cultural homogenisation of gay culture in Chinese cyberspace is prevalent and cyberqueer techno-practices have become an integral part of gay men's everyday lives in contemporary China. Foreign news about the gay pride parades and same-sex marriage can be seen everywhere on Chinese gay websites (Ho, 2010) as homogenous ideas and symbols implanted from Western media coverage and culture to mark gay identity. Yet this cultural globalisation results in the production of stereotypes and misrepresentations that worship the Western gay scene and reduce the diversity of same-sex identities; Western society is also consecrated as a gay haven. However, rather than being "a simple mimicry of patterns", the cyberqueer techno-practices between global and local identities generate and promote a "melange of cultural categories", through which gay netizens and activists strategically appropriate the ideas of identity and gay rights activism from Western sources (Ho, 2010, p. 106). For example, leading Chinese e-commerce company Alibaba, in conjunction with Danlan.org, sent seven gay couples from its online contest "We Do" to "tie the knot" in Los Angeles (Morris, 2015, June 10), in part to promote Alibaba's brand and corporate image. Danlan.org is the biggest LGBT news website in China and was launched in 2000. It developed a gay dating application, *Blued*, in 2012, which is the most popular gay mobile application in China with respect to its user numbers. As of November 2014, *Blued* had 15 million users, was valued at $300 million and had raised $30 million in investments (Agomuoh, 2014, November 6). It is these types of alliances – in this example between Alibaba, Danlan.org and Chinese LGBT NGOs, particularly, PFLAG China (同性恋亲友会) – which indicate the interplay of the appropriation of a Western identity-based gay rights activism strategy and the commercialisation of same-sex marriage.

Overall, the internet does bring positive changes to gay and lesbian communities in China, especially in terms of social visibility. However, as Hung (2011, p. 379) argues, new media is, on the one hand, "transforming into one of the most potent catalytic agents of sexual liberation, revolution and rights protection for LGBTQ in China", yet on the other hand, it also suffers from the malaise of commercialisation, featuring eye-catching posts on sexual encounters as a spectacle to attract eyeballs and clicks. Likewise, in his analysis of the representation of Chinese gay men in two online reality shows developed by local gay social networking mobile application *Zank*, Luo (2016) argues that leading Chinese gay new media groups are promoting a young, urbane, middle-class Chinese gay male image in a desexualised private domain – comprising consumption, love and intimacy, as well as family relationships – which subscribes to a 'homonormative' ideology perhaps more acceptable to society at large. In this vein, gay Chinese couples' weddings in Los Angeles, as a crystallisation of the alliances between Chinese LGBT NGOs and Chinese internet companies, greatly contributes to gay rights promotion within a larger Chinese society, whereas it also reveals a rise of gay consumerism in the internet era, linking identity and consumption. As Charlie Gu, the spokesperson of the co-organiser of the wedding, Chinese Luxury Advisors, a global consultancy that counsels luxury brands and retailers on their China consumer strategy, said, 'for a company like Alibaba there is also a strong business interest in this … When you look at companies like Google and Apple all stepping up their game to embrace marriage equality and support this cause, Alibaba as a publicly traded company in the United States certainly wanted to elevate their status and their participating in the global business community and be part of it – do the right thing' (Morris, 2015, June 10). Clearly, Chinese internet giant Alibaba is trying to squeeze into the gay-friendly 'global business community' with the help of Chinese new media groups and LGBT NGOs, co-contributing to a new Chinese gay and lesbian world of marriage, love and consumerism. More studies are needed at this point for a better understanding of 'who' is in and 'who' is out within the collaborations between business and civil society in improving social visibility of Chinese sexual minority. We need to be careful with the tendency of gayness to become a consumerist identity.

Case Study: An and Wu

It can therefore be argued that in terms of the commercialisation of Chinese gay male culture, with its regulatory restrictions and self-censorship, the spread of An and Wu's love story remains a unique case. Other than the photo album posted on Ifeng.com, there was little coverage on mainstream Chinese language media. The story was only perfunctorily tossed around by official news organisations as a token of social progress in China to broadcast to the Western world; the *Global Times* featured the story in English as a conjunct to Apple's CEO Tim Cook's public announcement of his gay identity. However, although An and Wu's story was not widely reported on new media, their photo album posted on Ifeng.com resulted in a surge of public attention through tweets and retweets on social media. On Sina Weibo, An and Wu's social media presence gained popularity almost overnight. Figure 4.1 shows the sudden surge in the discussion of An and Wu's pictorial coverage, using the keyword research 'rural gay couple' as generated through the Sina Weibo data; to date their Sina Weibo account has attracted 7,000 followers.

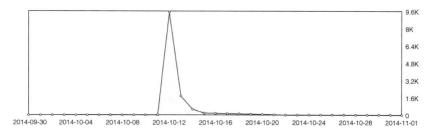

Figure 4.1 Frequency of discussion of the key word "Rural Gay Couple" Over Time.

Nevertheless, An and Wu's story is not one that follows the rosy script envisioned by technological determinism. Focusing on the *process* that led to An and Wu's online publicity, we look at the non-incidental socio–cultural forces at work in the 'making' of An and Wu as a cultural symbol for gay rights in contemporary Chinese identity politics. Given that harmony is a traditional and highly respected value in Chinese families, same-sex attracted Chinese tend to reconcile their sexual identity with the cultural and familial structure of the community (Hu & Wang, 2013). Kong (2011) points out that gay men from rural areas of China face more difficulties than those from urban areas regarding the issue of coming-out due to the deeply-entrenched and strong-held family pressure to get married. An and Wu's case, therefore, remains significant in enriching the understanding of Chinese gay male culture along the lines of the rural–urban divide.

It is apparent that social media alone does not liberate the lives of the under-represented and suppressed lives at the margin. We must take into consideration the distinct social, political and economic contexts, especially the development of 'working class ICT', traditional family values, neoliberal development of non-profit organisations and politics in China. Technological determinism has given us much false hope without consideration of the social context. In this case, we turn to Bourdieu's social theory because it provides an important inroad to conceptualising the underlying social conditions and power relations in the 'making' of An and Wu as public figures for the Chinese gay rights movement.

After conducting two sessions of semi-structured in-depth interviews with An and Wu, complemented by their postings on Sina Weibo, an assemblage of three important factors emerged as the trigger to their online visibility and fame – An and Wu's new media literacy, the contacts they established, and issues they faced, with PFLAG China and the traditional family values as inculcated and widely articulated in mainstream Chinese culture.

Media Literacy

As Zhou (forthcoming) argued, ICTs provide "a freer platform where Chinese gay men can gain support and see that they are not alone". Indeed, social media did play an instrumental role in seeking information and emotional support throughout An and Wu's personal struggles. Before meeting each other, An and Wu had both engaged in heterosexual relationships; the internet became a space where they met people who had experienced similar struggles for identity when they both lived in rural parts of China, where there was barely anyone to turn to for help and understanding. In this sense, the internet offered An and Wu a sense of community. Moreover, An met Wu through the most popular online messaging programme, QQ, owned by Tencent, one of the biggest internet businesses in China. Wu stated in the interview:

> When An Wei came out as gay, he was under a lot of pressure from his family to get married. So he turned to the internet for help. And someone suggested him to contact PFLAG China's regional convener in Hebei, Langman Mama (浪漫妈妈), and then we got in touch with the organisation.

After An and Wu got in touch with PFLAG China, the organisation quickly offered help and asked them to film their daily life together and post those short videos on the internet as promotional materials to support people who are undergoing similar struggles. It was their postings on the video streaming site that attracted journalists from Ifeng.com, who shot the widely-circulated photo album entitled the *Rural gay couple* later in 2013. "The internet", according to Wu, "helps me to get to know more gay men and navigate my life as a gay man".

The internet not only assisted An and Wu in seeking emotional support, but was also the means through which the couple obtained their main source of family income. Initially, An and Wu ran a small grocery store near a highway but after the highway was re-routed in 2013 they had to close their business. PFLAG China's associated staff *Ouyi* (藕姨) suggested that An and Wu run an e-commerce shop online. Through building on the circle of friends and supporters that they had accumulated through years of online exposure, particularly though PFLAG China, they created their main customer base, and the revenue from the e-shop is now the main source of their family income. Their daily routine, according to the couple, includes attending to the e-shop, interacting with customers and assembling the packages ordered online. In this sense, the internet constitutes an important means to convert the symbolic capital that An and Wu have accumulated through media exposure to economic capital.

Currently living in a village near Shijiazhuang, Hebei, with limited economic resources and a busy schedule attending their small e-commerce shop, An and Wu said that they only travel to other parts of the country once or twice every year. Yet the internet also provides them with much entertainment aside from work. They stated: "when we are free, we sometimes do some farm work and when there is not much work left to do, we will watch some movies and listen to music on the internet". An and Wu are also avid users of social media and are active on Sina Weibo as they often post and re-tweet news about marriage equality and gay rights, interact with customers from their e-shop or just share pictures of their everyday life.

Coming from a lower strata of the social class, An and Wu are very open and conscious about their socio–economic status, as they said in a post on Sina Weibo on 2 October 2015:

> What you don't know when people are sending wishes for us and envying us, we really do not have anything comparable to others. We look up to you (their Weibo followers): you have a nice job, a good education, skills, good brain, communication skills… you are good at everything, we don't have any of this. The only resource we have is our dearest friends.

Even though they are from the lower strata of the society, An and Wu are avid social media and ICT users – this is illustrative of the social and technological transformation on a macro scale that is going on with the introduction and popularisation of the internet in China. As Qiu (2009) contends, "the most pivotal change in urban and urbanising areas of China has been the rise of the working-class network society" (p. 3). One of the fundamental changes is that ICT is becoming less expensive, more widespread and more closely integrated with the lives of working-class people. A new social category of 'information have-less' is emerging, which is constituted by low-end ICT users who possess limited income and limited influence in policy processes compared to the upper class.

Even though social media did play an instrumental, or, to a certain extent, indispensable role in transcending An and Wu's life, it is still hard to argue that the internet has changed their life completely. In an honest personal disclosure, Wu stated that the online shop they maintain only brings them 2,000 yuan per month (approximately 315 USD) and that "the business was not looking good". This is due to the fact that the symbolic capital they have accumulated through media exposure is only limited or, at best, temporary, and, more importantly, that the celebrity status that An and Wu have gained almost overnight has been orchestrated by and built on the symbolic capital of PFLAG China. PFLAG China, its capacity and limitations and how the construction of An and Wu as a symbol for gay rights constitutes and is constituted by the overall dispositions and political orientation of the organisation is therefore now considered.

The Role of PFLAG China

Clifford Bob (2005) states in the *Marketing of rebellion* that it is never easy or automatic for a non-for-profit organisation to gain popularity and publicity in the "global morality market". They fight through fierce competition with each other to obtain resources, mobilise the media to raise awareness and lobby potential patrons. Furthermore, they magnify their appeal by framing parochial demands and particularistic identities and portraying their conflicts as righteous struggles to match the interests and agendas of their audience. Harbouring such a conception, NGOs in China have to deal with a peculiar context, where the tolerant and supportive attitude towards civil associations is by no means unconditional and the government is carefully guiding and managing how much public initiative should be allowed. Therefore, as Wang (2004) poignantly points out, all NGOs in China, whether they are registered or not, assume a "semi-autonomous" position in relation to the state and maintain a decent and sometimes cordial relationship with the state in order to remain in the game.

As former Ford Foundation Beijing chief Anthony Saich states, for NGOs to exert the impact they want to achieve and to gain a louder voice in policy-making discussions, as a strategic measure, they voluntarily subordinate to the existing state structure in order to manipulate the official and semi-official institutions for their own advantage (Saich, cited in Wang, 2004, p. 139). This power relation between NGOs and the state therefore preconfigures the non-conflictual characteristic of Chinese NGOs (Lu, 2009). Chinese grassroots NGOs understand this anti-binary thinking intuitively because undertaking consciousness-raising and triggering small change, which often means nothing more than bringing relief to the disadvantaged in the communities they serve, is what they can do and what they do best. Using social media to engage in oppositional politics is not on their agenda (Wang, 2004, p. 28). Rather, the majority of Chinese NGOs serve as informal social services or welfare relief organisations that are compelled to work within the system.

Hong (2010) argues that in China the development of NGOs and charity organisations are subscribing to the neoliberal characteristics and that rather than confronting institutional causes of injustice, these organisations mobilise individual efforts and participation in order to ease social tension. PFLAG China is a telling example of this neoliberal trend of NGO development. It was established in 2008, and was originally staffed by four full-time workers, one part-time worker and 200 volunteers. After eight years, PFLAG China has become a hierarchically structured organisation that is somehow bureaucratic. It has more than 1,200 volunteers, 13 regional branches and eight local working groups (a subordinate unit below a local branch) that cover not only major metropolises but also small cities in China. Its programmes, such as the leadership camp for PFLAG China supporters, the PFLAG China annual conference and the PFLAG China regional sharing sessions, earn high recognition domestically.

It is worth noting that although the name PFLAG China automatically reminds us of the largest family and ally organisation PFLAG (Parents, Families and Friends of Lesbians and Gays) in the United States, PFLAG China does not have a formal affiliation with PFLAG and its focus is also different from that of PFLAG. While PFLAG "commits to advancing equality and full societal affirmation for LGBTQ people through its threefold mission of support, education, and advocacy", PFLAG China aims to "improve the living conditions of LGBT with the joint efforts of families and friends".

Another difference between PFLAG China and PFLAG is that in contrast to the supportive and logistical role of parents involved in PFLAG in the United States, the Chinese parents associated with PFLAG China have become "stars" and play a leading role in the Chinese gay right movement (Wei, 2015). PFLAG China's parent-led and family-centric strategy guarantees its existence as a legitimate NGO in China and also preconfigures the non-oppositional characteristics of its politics; these issues are discussed further below.

Traditional Family Values

An and Wu's story can also be considered in its approach to traditional Chinese family values, values seen as a vital part of everyday, accepted, life. Lending legitimacy from traditional values of family and kinship discourse, the struggle for legitimatisation for gay rights and same-sex marriage is being fought from the standpoint of family, both seeing family as the supreme imperative of gay love, and in treating parental approval as the key reason for whether one can come out and claim their gay identity or not. In this regard, the success of PFLAG China in the competition with other Chinese gay rights NGOs is not haphazard. It is the result of many factors, with the most important one being its non-confrontational, parent-led and family-centric approach. Rather than adopting the Western confrontational act of "coming out", Chou (2000) proposed an indigenous alternative for Chinese queers, namely, "coming home", emphasising the uniqueness of "family" in the negotiation of an individual's sexuality in the Chinese context. As Chou (2000, p. 259) argued, "coming home can be proposed as an indigenous lexicon of *tongzhi* self-confirmation" as "*jia* (home/family) is a culturally unique category that does not have an equivalent parallel in Western languages". PFLAG China's parent-led movement strategy accords with the idea of "coming home" which addresses the historical and ideological importance of family in the Chinese society. Various promotional documentaries and short videos such as *Mama rainbow* (彩虹伴我心) and *Coming home* (回家) of PFLAG China have attracted the attention of the Chinese mainstream media, which has greatly increased gay men and lesbians' public visibility.

However, the essentialists' construction of Chineseness as a 'normal' Chinese family has been subjected to much criticism (e.g. Huang, 2011; Kong, 2011; Lee, 2016; Liu and Ding, 2005; Martin, 2014). Lee (2016, p. 985) argues that "cultural relativists assume the moral infallibility of culture – the impossibility of moral learning or social adaptation except within a specific culture, which often confuses what people have been forced to tolerate with what it values". Liu and Ding (2005, p. 39) questioned the construction of "an allegedly healthy, liberated, diverse and non-homophobic, traditional Chinese utopian space and time", arguing that the idealisation of "coming home" reinforces "the suggestion that the imagined tolerance extends from the past into the present"; moreover, it reduces the complexities of queer experiences and settles the conflict between "queerness" and "family" at the cost of the subjection of queer individuals to the hegemony of the familial system. In a similar way, Huang (2011) points out that the power of Chinese family values has defined the "normative" and "non-normative" sexualities in the Taiwanese queer community. Picking up on queer critiques on family and the marriage institution and combining them with his own observations within PFLAG China, Wei (2015) points out that although some Chinese gay men have "come out" to their parents, their parents are still doing a "matchmaker" job, which limits the individual space for Chinese gays and lesbians and, as a result, places new pressure on them.

With this approach in mind, PFLAG China has harnessed An and Wu's image and constructed the couple as loving, committed, faithful and parents approved and supported. This image not only serves as the ideal image of a long-term, stable, gay monogamous relationship but also inscribes the discipline of how to 'behave' as a gay couple in China. As Bourdieu (1993) argues, power is diffused and often concealed in broadly accepted, and often unquestioned, ways of seeing and describing the world. The system of domination, in this sense, the imperative of family, marriage and the expected family obligations, is reproduced and reaffirmed.

Family is identified by An and Wu as the most important value they uphold. First of all, An and Wu think that family support and approval has been the most important factor in supporting them to come out and start a life together. An Wei stated in the interview: "[among all other factors] … family support is the most important. I do not really care about other people's support. It is the support from my family that gave me the confidence to live and enjoy life as a gay man". On Sina Weibo, An and Wu do not shy away from their longing for long-term, stable, gay monogamous relationships. For example, they have re-tweeted posts and news stories related to same-sex marriage and commented:

> Too many gay people judge others by the look. They only realise the mismatch between personalities and temperaments after engaging in

sexual relations two or three times. This is probably why many gay people complain that they cannot find the 'right one'.

An and Wu's image further fits with the dominant political discourse of 'stability maintenance' promoted by the Communist Party of China. The ideal of a committed relationship, family life and the longing for the idyllic, peaceful life in rural China where people only care about their personal life presents no challenge to the dominant social institution of heterosexual marriage. As long as they set their eyes on their own life, they can and are still allowed to dream the dream of same-sex marriage. However, at the same time, it is noteworthy that there are also gay men who are under-represented by PFLAG China's parent-led and family-centric movement strategy.

Conclusion

The penetration of the internet and the blooming use of social media platforms present a favourable context under which An and Wu's story was able to be circulated and heard by many. As Inglis (2010) argues:

> celebrity is also one of the adhesives which, at a time when the realms of public politics, civil society, and private domestic life are increasingly fractured and enclosed in separate enclaves, serves to pull those separate entities together and to do its bit towards maintaining social cohesion and common values.
>
> (p. 4)

This is exactly why An and Wu's story matters – they are a case where gay politics and domestic life are tightly knitted together under the aegis of technology.

Through investigating a host of social forces in the process of how a gay couple in rural China gained online fame, this chapter reveals that the rise of working-class ICT, social media use and skills played an instrumental role in empowering and overcoming limited mobility for An and Wu, who are from a relatively disadvantaged class in the society. Social media provided the means and connectivity for the couple to stay in touch with the online and offline gay community and solicit emotional support when there was a vacuum of social services and support in remote rural areas of China. Furthermore, the internet can also be seen as a platform upon which An and Wu accumulated social and symbolic capital and later converted such social recognition and support into economic capital.

Social media is an enabler. Yet social media does not exist in a vacuum. Rather, it is always embedded in the larger socio–political imprints of the society and in class relations. In Bourdieu's (1993) words, social life is a mutually constituting interaction of structures, dispositions and actions whereby social structures and the embodied knowledge of those structures produce enduring orientation, which, in turn, are constitutive of social structures. In this sense, An and Wu becoming online celebrities is in no way incidental. Although social media use and skills did play an indispensable role, the offline institutional support offered by PFLAG China was equally important. As an institution, PFLAG China carries its own agenda and has its own organisational goals and limitations. To this end, PFLAG China eventually built a mutually beneficial relationship with An and Wu by harnessing their commitment to each other and to the imperative of family – PFLAG China helped to magnify An and Wu's celebrity and symbolic capital, with its convertibility to economic capital, which allowed the couple an alternative when their business was forced to shut down. Yet, the limitation of PFLAG China and its exclusionary gay rights movement strategy cannot be attributed to the organisation itself but to the political environment of contemporary China and the regulation of NGOs by the state.

Considering these elements, the social practices of PFLAG China and An and Wu in particular, ultimately tend to serve the interests of mainstream culture which promotes social harmony centred around the institution of family and its reproduction. The so-called liberating social media ingrained with dominant ideology, and the overall characteristics of Chinese gay politics, will therefore eventually reproduce these existing social orders, underpinned by the institution of family and marriage in Chinese society.

References

Agomuoh, F. (2014, November, 6). Chinese gay dating app 'Blued' eyes public offering after $30 million investment. *The International Business Times.* Retrieved from www.ibtimes.com/chinese-gay-dating-app-blued-eyes-public-offering-after-30-million-investment-1720033.

Berry, C., & Martin, F. (2003). Syncretism and synchronicity: queer 'n' Asian cyberspace in 1990s Taiwan and Korea. In C. Berry, F. Martin, & A. Yue (Eds.), *Mobile cultures: New media in queer Asia* (pp. 87–114). Durham, UK: Duke University Press.

Bob, C. (2005). *The marketing of rebellion: insurgents, media and international activism.* New York: Cambridge University Press.

Bourdieu, P. (1993). *The field of cultural* production (edited and introduced by Randal Johnson). Cambridge, UK: Polity Press.

China Internet Network Information Centre (CNNIC). (2016). *The 37th Survey Report.*

Chou, W-S. (2000). *Tongzhi: politics of same-sex eroticism in Chinese societies.* London, UK: Routledge.

Couldry, N. (2003). *Media, symbolic power and the limits of Bourdieu's field theory.* Media@lse. Retrieved from www.lse.ac.uk/media@lse/research/mediaWorkingPapers/pdf/EWP02.pdf.

Garnham, N. (1990). *Capitalism and communication: Global culture and the economis of information*. London, UK: Sage Publications.

Hesmondhalgh, D. (2006). Bourdieu, the media and cultural production. *Media, Culture & Society*, 28(2), 211–231.

Ho, L. W. (2010). *Gay and lesbian subculture in urban China*. London, UK: Routledge.

Hong, Y. (2010). The politics of socialist harmonious society in the aftermath of neoliberalism. *Chinese Journal of Communication*, 3(3), 311–328.

Hu, X., & Wang, Y. (2013). LGB identity among young Chinese: The influence of traditional culture. *Journal of Homosexuality*, 60(5), 667–684.

Huang, T-M. (2011). *Queer politics and sexual modernity in Taiwan*. Hong Kong: Hong Kong University Press.

Hung, C-F. (2011). The politics of electronic social capital and public sphere in Chinese *Lala* community: Implications for civil society. *International Journal of China Studies*, 2(2), 369–388.

Inglis, F. (2010). *A short history of celebrity*. Princeton, NJ: Princeton University Press.

Jiang, H. (2005). *ICCGL: Cultural communication via the internet and GLBT community building in China*. Paper presented at Sexualities, Genders and Rights in Asia: 1st International Conference of Asian Queer Studies. Retrieved from https://digitalcollections.anu.edu.au/handle/1885/8687.

Kong, T. S. K. (2011). *Chinese male homosexualities: Memba, tongzhi and golden boy*. London, UK: Routledge.

Lee, P.-H. (2016). LGBT rights versus Asian values: De/re-constructing the universality of human rights. *International Journal of Human Rights*, 20(7), 978–992.

Liu, J.-P., & Ding, N. (2005). Reticent poetics, queer politics. *Inter-Asia Cultural Studies*, 6(1), 30–55.

Lu, Y. (2009). *Non-governmental organizations in China: The rise of dependent autonomy*. London, UK: Routledge.

Luo, M. (2016). 悖论的可见性:《9个gay》与《一屋赞客》对同性恋的再现 [Paradoxical visibility: an analysis of homosexuality representation in *The Nine Gay* and *A House of Zanker*]. *Chinese Journal of Sociology* (社会), 36(2), 215–241.

Martin, F. (2014). Transnational queer sinophone cultures. In M. McLelland & V. Mackie (Eds.), *Routledge handbook of sexuality studies in East Asia* (pp. 35–48). New York: Routledge.

Morris, R. (2015, June 10). Gay Chinese couples marry in Los Angeles. *BBC News*. Retrieved from www.bbc.co.uk/news/world-us-canada-33074682.

Mowlabocus, S. (2010). *Gaydar culture: Gay men, technology and embodiment in the digital age*. Farnham, UK: Ashgate.

O'Riordan, K. (2007). Queer theories and cybersubjects: Intersecting figures. In K. O'Riordan & D. J. Phillips (Eds.), *Queer online: Media technology & sexuality* (pp. 13–30). New York: Peter Lang Publishing Inc.

Qiu, L. (2009). *Working-class network society: Communication technology and the information have-less in urban China*. Cambridge, MA: MIT Press.

van de Werff, T. (2010). The struggle of the tongzhi: Homosexuality in China and the position of Chinese 'comrades'. In I. Dubel & A. Hielkema (Eds.),

Urgency required: Gay and lesbian rights are human rights (pp. 172–180). Hague, Netherlands: HIVOS.

Wakeford, N. (2002). New technologies and cyber-queer research. In D. Richardson & S. Seidman (Eds.), *Handbook of lesbian and gay studies* (pp. 115–144). London, UK: SAGE.

Wang, J. (2004). The global reach of a new discourse: how far can "creative industries" travel? *International Journal of Cultural Studies, 7*(1), 9–19.

Wei, W. (2012). 公开: 当代成都" 同志" 空间的形成和变迁 [*Going public: The production and transformation of queer spaces in contemporary Chengdu, China*]. Shanghai: Shanghai Joint Publishing Company.

Wei, W. (2015). 酷儿中国社会: 城市空间, 流行文化和社会政策 [*Queering Chinese society: urban space, popular culture and social policy*]. Guilin: Guangxi Normal University Press.

Zhou, T. (Forthcoming). Jack'd, Douban Group, and Feizan.com: The impact of cyberqueer techno-practice on the Chinese gay male experience. In J. T. Grider & D. van Reenen (Eds.), *Exploring erotic encounters: The inescapable entanglement of tradition, transcendence and transgression*. Leiden: Brill.

5 Populist Sentiments and Digital Ethos in the Social Media Space

Revelations of Weibo Celebrities in China

Zixue Tai, Jing Liang, and Xiaolong Liu

Introduction

Soaring social media use worldwide as manifested in the expanding variety of platforms and applications of social networking services (SNSs) has fundamentally transformed the landscape of information production, dissemination and consumption. Commonly known as "Web 2.0" (O'Reilly, 2005) or the "participatory Web" (Madden & Fox, 2006), these variegated tools have thrived by allowing the instantaneous, pervasive and ubiquitous exchange of a vast array of user-generated content among mass user bases about mundane events and everyday life. Alongside the innovative technologies, creative uses and unprecedented data availability, it comes as no surprise that waves of scholarly efforts have emerged in recent years to come to grips with the various aspects of social media usage and its ramifications.

Like everywhere else, the penetration of social media into every aspect of Chinese society has dramatically redefined China's communication environment. Built exclusively on user-generated content and grassroots participation, social communication has been a leading force in recent years in engendering a brand new public sphere in China's online space. At the forefront of China's social media revolution are the big three behemoths – QQ Zone (QQ), WeChat and Sina Weibo (commonly known as Weibo – http://weibo.com) – with each serving niche needs of different user cases and interactive dynamics.

The purpose of this chapter is to scrutinise a special genre of microbloggers on Weibo –the top 50 Weibo celebrities, as they are often called – in terms of the thematic alignments and rhetorical invocations as revealed through their Weibo postings. Our analysis is grounded in the Chinese cyber ecosystem, and sheds light on the populist sentiments and overarching ethos dominating the evolving social media landscape in China. The chapter is organised as follows. It starts with a brief overview of Weibo in China, and then lays the groundwork by applying Goffman's dramaturgical framework of self-presentation to impression management on social media. Next, the top 50 Weibo celebrities are profiled in the comparative lens of their Twitter counterparts. We then present a typology of these top 50 Weibo celebrities and critically analyse their diverse thematic alignments and rhetorical invocations. The chapter concludes with a deliberation on the implications for Chinese social media and its ecological system.

Weibo in China

It is useful to foreground social media in the broader context of China's media and information ecology. The Chinese media has been a direct part of the state marketisation drive in the past three decades, and journalists have gained more breathing space in responding to societal demands and audience interests in their day-to-day reporting. Nonetheless, subtle and coercive control of the media business by the state remains in place in different manifestations to ensure the "mouthpiece" instrumentality of the press (Stockmann, 2013).

Due to the highly controlled conventional media environment, user-generated content over the internet plays a particularly important role in fulfilling user needs and defining use patterns (Tai, 2006). As the most popular microblogging platform in China, Weibo closely emulates its global counterpart Twitter in terms of both technical features and functionalities. Inspired by the quick success of Twitter in the United States, Sina, China's most popular portal site, debuted its own brand of microblogging in July 2009, and its user base has experienced exponential growth since then. Just like Twitter, Weibo allows users to send out short messages limited to 140 characters or less to followers via internet and wireless application protocols (WAP) to computers, cell phones and other mobile devices.[1] Subscribers can forward messages to other recipients, and they can also mark particular Weibo authors or messages as 'favourites'. Additional features include the embedding of graphic images, music files and video links within textual messages as well as enabling users to post comments in response to messages. Unlike QQ and WeChat – which are more closed systems in that social networks are formed following a mutually selective process between connected end users – Weibo is very much open-ended. That is, most Weibo accounts are publicly accessible and can be subscribed to by any user, and content propagated therein is defaulted for public view unless defined otherwise. Twitter's publicity-driven nature (Murthy, 2013) is therefore prominently noticeable on Weibo.

In order to assess barometers of public sentiments and populist ethos on Weibo, we picked the top 50 Weibo microbloggers for our analysis (as of September 2015).[2] The list is ranked based on Weibo's algorithm combining metrics incorporating the number of times Weibo posts are read, forwarded, commented on and favoured during a certain time frame.[3] Popular Weibo authors are typically called Big Vs – a play on the letter V appearing next to their screen names (indicating account owner identity has been Verified by Weibo) with the popular slang word VIP – by Chinese netizens to signify their level of impact in influencing online chatters and swaying public sentiments on social media. We follow this popular designation, and classify these top 50 microbloggers as Weibo celebrities to acknowledge their status of being well-known and followed by a large base of users.

Self-Presentation and Impression Management on Social Media

People take on multiple senses of self, or personas, on different occasions in their lifeworld. Academic deliberations of impression management on social media have been usefully informed by Goffman's dramaturgical model of everyday interaction. Goffman (1956) distinguished between bounded areas called "back region" (backstage where a performativity is prepared) and "front region" (front stage where the performance takes place in front of an audience). The backstage is where "the capacity of a performance to express something beyond itself may be painstakingly fabricated … [and] illusions and impressions are openly constructed" (p. 69) whereas the frontstage offers the area where a public impression is fostered through "expressive coherence of the reality that is dramatized by a performance" (p. 87). User-centred production on social media platforms has the potential to redefine the hitherto clearly marked boundaries separating the front and back regions, and may bring backchannel activities to the frontline. From time to time, happenings in the hallway connecting the front and back regions, which used to stay outside of the purview of audience interest, can now take centre stage in online chatters.

The celebrity culture guided by the logic of consumerism necessitates that only a small number of highly selective individuals will climb up to the public spotlight availed by the limited stage space via the commercial media (Cashmore, 2014). The evolving environment empowered by Web 2.0 media, however, has led to what Turner calls the "demotic turn" in which "the explosion of celebrity, reality TV, and user-generated content on the Web and so on … has generated … new visibility of ordinary people in the media as performers and producers" (Turner, 2010, p. 4). This ritualisation of DIY celebrities has signified a profound shift in the social media landscape, and is worth scrutinising in cross-national settings.

Profiling the Top 50 Microblogging Celebrities: Weibo versus Twitter

A side-by-side comparison of the top 50 microblogging celebrities on Weibo and Twitter can shed comparative light on overall audience tastes and public pulses in China and the United States.[4] Both Weibo and Twitter, of course, have an enormous reach in terms of their respective user bases. Coincidentally, the top brand names on Weibo and Twitter both belong to two actresses/singers who have a glaringly successful career in China and the United States respectively. It is also remarkable that the most-followed Weibo celebrity, Yao Chen (姚晨), boasts over 78.1 million fans, while her Twitter counterpart, Katy Perry (@katyperry), owns 77.5 million followers – closely comparable numbers (as of November 2015).

As testimonial to the global infatuation with the celebrity culture (Cashmore, 2014), the top 50 celebrities on Weibo and Twitter are both dominated by real-world celebrities – 64 percent (32 out of 50) of Weibo celebrities originate from the entertainment industry (movie actors/actresses, singers, TV hosts) whereas an overwhelming 84 percent (42 out of 50) of Twitter celebrities hail from accounts owned by pop stars in similar categories. The remainders, however, are drastically different. For Weibo, nine microblogging celebrities have exclusively built their fame via their writings on Weibo. As we discuss next, they each establish a niche ethos by specialising in selective issues of public interest, and create their own brand through unique content. Two conventional writers/authors also make the top 50 list, and they achieve eminence through effectively bridging their microblogs to their published literary works. Streams of discussion on financial and business perspectives find sufficient representation in four Weibo celebrities. We-Media (or Citizens Media) as an emerging genre of grassroots digital publication in China also has a notable presence (three on the top 50 list).

Twitter celebrities display different dynamics. Most interestingly, President Obama, who has been known for his presence first on MySpace and later via Facebook (Johnson & Perlmutter, 2010), also has a prominent voice in the Twittersphere – his Twitter account is ranked No. 4 in the most-followed list. This comes in sharp contrast with the Weibo space, within which very few top-level Chinese officials directly participate. Obama's Chinese counterpart, President Xi Jinping, stays away from Weibo, and his views and whereabouts are consigned to the various official mouthpieces and venues. One sports superstar (LeBron James) makes the top 50 Twitter celebrities list, while the lone corporate representative goes to Bill Gates. Five organisations and established media outlets – ESPN Sports Center, New York Times, NBA, NFL and NASA, most of which are sports-related – have prominent presence on Twitter. On the other hand, sports-related topics are minimal in the Weibo chatter, either through the identities of the Weibo celebrities or via their conversations. None of the Chinese national media venues even comes close to the top 50 list. It bears mentioning that all individuals and organisations in the United States that fare well on Twitter are all attached to a pronounced offline existence in society. By contrast, quite a few individuals and citizen media venues on the top 50 list on Weibo exist almost exclusively through their microblogging charms. We elaborate on this distinct aspect of the Weibo culture in the discussion that follows.

Populist Ethos among Weibo Celebrities

In this section, we present our analysis of how the top 50 Weibo celebrities construct their respective ethos in terms of rhetorical invocations and thematic alignments. In the former, we are looking at specific strategic approaches in mobilising linguistic, visual and other persuasive devices in getting the message across, while the latter pertains to salient topical areas and content materials. We employ ethos in its commonly accepted sense to refer to "the need for rhetors to portray themselves in their speeches as having a good moral character, 'practical wisdom', and a concern for the audience in order to achieve credibility and thereby secure persuasion" (Cherry, 1998, p. 253; see also Sattler, 1947).

S. Michael Halloran traces ethos to the term in the Greek lexicon as "a habitual gathering place", and associates it to the "image of people gathering together in a public place, sharing experiences and ideas" (1982, p. 60). In this regard, Weibo provides a virtual "gathering place" where microbloggers, who otherwise would not be accessible to the vast bases of fans and followers, can construct and maintain their ethos through a continuous stream of updates and postings combining text and audio-visual symbols. Ethos building on Weibo is better conceptualised as a habitual, process-oriented practice. We therefore analyse the discourses of these Weibo celebrities as a dynamic, fluid arrangement. Specifically, we chose the most recent 100 microblog posts with each Weibo celebrity and tried to detect repeated, persistent thematic salience as well as recurring linguistic cues and semantic reinforcements in the texts. In other words, isolated utterances and speech acts that do not fit within the consistent patterns are de-emphasised in identifying thematic streams and tactical cues. The results of our analysis are grouped into five sections clustered on the specific types of these celebrities as stipulated on Weibo.

Virtually Entertaining

Entertainment pop stars comprise the vast majority of the top 50 Weibo celebrities. Gender makeup is 19 males versus 12 females, and areas of specialisation pertain to two TV hosts, 21 actors/actresses and eight singers. The great vantage point these microbloggers have over most other people is that their fame in the mortar world may help their Weibo accounts in recruiting followers. Because they constantly stay in the limelight, it is therefore natural for their popularity to spill over to the virtual world. Notably, all these entertainers are in their prime, and are among the most likely targets of adoration by the youth-led culture that pervades the social media landscape. Nonetheless, prestige and fame in the entertainment business cannot be an automatic guarantee for success on Weibo. These celebrities still have to earn the spotlight on Weibo through prolific and engaging posts.

Entertainers, by nature, are master communicators, as their jobs directly involve interacting with the audience. Their fame mostly originates from their constant exposure on the front stage, and that aspect of their life is likely to be widely known by the general public. It is then unsurprising that their primary focus on Weibo would be on their routine, mundane everyday life. While mundane conversations are a regular part of social media use in general (Lomborg, 2013), they hold special significance for celebrities, whose public images portrayed in the commercial media are shrouded in a mixed sense of mystery and intrigue for the average consumers. Weibo feeds from these celebrities naturally fill this niche void for the general public by offering glimpses of perspectives and life stories centring on these celebrities that are unavailable from other venues. In that sense, Weibo provides a much-needed platform to interconnect entertainment superstars with their fan bases through unfiltered chatter streams.

Across the board among all these celebrities, the most common type of topical themes pertains to regular updates on daily routines, covering a range of topics including 'How I dress today' (attire), 'How I feel' (mood), 'Where I am' (whereabouts), 'What I am eating' (food) and 'What I am seeing' (sightseeing). These mundane activities add personable touches to the screen images of these entertainers, and intermingle everyday life with theatrical performance. While similar topical lines permeate most celebrity microbloggers, how they are articulated speaks volumes for their individual creativity and personal style.

A commonplace practice, especially among performers known for their good looks, is to let selfies do the talk, supplanted with succinct textual cues. A picture may be indeed worth a thousand words on Weibo, particularly considering the limited capacity of microblog chatter. Nobody is doing better than actress Lin Chiling (@林志玲). Touted as the most beautiful actress by many fans in China, Lin has developed a consistent style of letting photos lead the content on her Weibo postings. As an example, in her Weibo message dated 16 October 2015 (weibo.com/1312412824/CFpPfu7dQ), which adroitly combines news update within an eye-catching image, posted a selfie featuring the flower she grabbed while attending the highly publicised wedding between Peter Huang and Angelababy (the latter is also one of the top 50 Weibo celebrities). In another post (weibo.com/1312412824/CD5G7bt0U) dated 1 October 2015, Lin conveys her wishing-well message to her Weibo fans for the National Day holiday break, acting out 'sincerity' through what she calls a "Las Vegas pose".

Another Weibo celebrity, Roy Wang (@TFBOYS-王源, born in November 2000, and one of the trio members of the popular TFBOYS Band) focuses on a lifestyle that typifies a school-age teen – birthday celebrations, presents, school work, parties, pets and so on. Almost all posts are prominently accompanied by pictures. Two entries that best illustrate his style were posted on 11 November 2015 (weibo.com/2812335943/D22BY9otA) and 11 October 2015 (weibo.com/2812335943/CEE2uhSEG) respectively. Both relate to life routines – the first is posted right before he goes to bed where he urges fans to "go to bed early and get up early", the second one notes "this is the state of me after finishing homework".

For those who rely more on text than visual appeals, it is easy to detect the light-hearted, good-natured, casual mode of communicative style to engage the audience. This is aptly shown in a post by Yao Chen on 6 November 2015 (weibo.com/1266321801/D2DA57), the No. 1 followed Weibo microblogger (@姚晨), forwarding a Weibo release by the Tourism Bureau of Fujian Province promoting a local breakfast cuisine. Sidelined by the original message are Yao's own comments: "Come on, pals from Fujian – isn't Guobianhu [the name of the local specialty] the best breakfast in the world?" As she hails from Fujian, nothing can beat talking about a local food specialty in this amicable way as an effort to build rapport with local fan bases.

Humour, in most circumstances, connects well with the audience and adds wit to the chitchat. This is therefore often found in Weibo messages from quite a few of these celebrities, some of whom are particularly fond of poking fun at themselves. This is perfectly demonstrated by Xie Na (@谢娜), a famed TV host. In a message published on 3 November 2015 (weibo.com/1192329374/D28qmCHUP), she shows herself riding a bike supposedly on her way to the studio, in a black facial mask that is typically used in the makeup room, sidelined by the text "Some people like to wear [breathing] masks when they go out; I don't think it is necessary". Another post (weibo.com/1192329374/D23wIgtja) makes happy reference to her attractiveness, with a photo of her headlined "This is taken in Beihai Park; I know it is hard to figure out [it *is* Beihai in the background] because the foreground is too dazzling".

For a significant number of celebrities, a common thread of Weibo prattle revolves around various aspects of family life – carefully crafted images of a good husband/wife and/or loving parent, family events, child raising, exposing good-natured skeletons in the closet and so forth. Comical tones, exaggerating expressions and funny touches typically inhere in the content. A prominent master of this practice is Deng Chao (@邓超), who assumes multiple roles of being an actor, director, producer and singer. One post that speaks well for his communicative style was sent out on 12 November 2015 (weibo.com/5187664653/D3qCQieA), which effuses love on his son's fourth birthday. The layers of heart-touching words – including "thank you for making my life complete" – resonated the most with his audience, and this Weibo post became viral both on Weibo and with the online entertainment media outlets.

Quite a few celebrities have developed an ethos through sustained conversation threads promoting charity causes, social welfare programmes or raising public awareness about vulnerable and disadvantaged groups in society. This fits in well with the repeated call on Chinese citizens to focus on radiating and spreading "positive energy" (正能量) by the Chinese authorities and the official media. We have noted three types of representation in these efforts. The first is to formally serve as a spokesperson for highly regarded domestic and global charity organisations. A leading activist in this category is Yao Chen, who is a designated Chinese Goodwill Ambassador for the United Nations High Commissioner for Refugees (UNHCR) and constantly circulates updates about news and events, and issues calls for public participation. The second type of involvement is to register their 'own' charity funds and use Weibo as a platform of publicity and mobilising mass participation. As a prime example, Zhao Wei, an actress, maintains a constant presence on Weibo rallying participation in the V Leukaemia Charitable Fund she co-sponsors that undertakes surgical costs for selected children aged 3 to 14 years old. The third type of attachment manifests in voluntarily circulating charity information and openly calling for contribution. A leading example in this category is Yang Mi (@杨幂), an actress/singer/producer, who makes it a habit to promote charity information, as demonstrated in one Weibo post (http://weibo.com/1195242865/CFN5MkQdx) dated 19 October 2015, in which Yang Mi reposts a message about the World Breast Cancer Day and calls on her fans to participate.

Finally, it is quite common to see entertainment celebrities discuss their regular jobs in the forms of new releases, studio routines and ongoing productions. A noticeable strategy employed in these discussions is that the commercial entertainment projects are carefully rendered incidental or ancillary to give way to friendships (with directors, performers starring in the film and teledrama productions), personal reflections (on taking part) and buffooneries (poking fun at fellow entertainers and self). Great caution is exercised to avoid turning these threads into blatant brags or outright advertorials. This is understandable – most popular entertainment productions are already advertised excessively in commercial or sponsored messages, and any act of directly marketing these shows further on Weibo runs the risk of alienating fans.

Enamouring Content

The nine niche microbloggers in this category have accumulated their respective fan bases exclusively through blogging. Unlike the previous genre of entertainment celebrities, they do not have the luxury of a widely-known offline identity or fame. As a matter of fact, for almost all in this group, their offline identities are well-guarded secrets. For the fans, the offline identities do not matter or are irrelevant, and what truly gravitates fans is the online content. Seven of the nine show similarities in many ways – we discuss these seven first, and will cover the two outliers at the end of this section.

The first thing to note among these niche microbloggers is they are prolific posters – they constantly propagate their Weibo sites with new content, very often multiple posts every day. Another outstanding commonality is that they rarely contribute original content of their own, and instead thrive in aggregating specialised third-party materials and sharing them with followers. Their own contribution lies in sugarcoating, annotating, relevantising or sometimes repurposing content from existing sources in pitching the content to subscribers. Operationally, they are very much like popular content aggregators in the West such as Reddit, Digg and Feedly, but the main difference is that these Weibo sites rely on the diligence and intelligence of these individual microbloggers in curating external materials while content aggregators mostly depend on algorithms.

More importantly, the Weibo model of distributing aggregated content is prompted by the necessity to adapt to the online publishing environment in China. Current state regulations stipulate that any individual or institution that intends to publish online must obtain a license from the local authorities[5]; in addition, an Internet Content Publishing (ICP) license is required from the Ministry of Industry and Information Technology (MIIT) for any site to engage in distributing allowed types of content.[6] This dual licensing scheme (a license to publish online *and* a license for specified content) makes it virtually impossible for individuals or groups to start web publishing of their own the way that many startup entrepreneurs have done in the West. Therefore it is natural for individuals interested in pursuing such a path to migrate to popular venues such as Weibo to establish their surrogate presence.

A particular point of note is that there is little overlap in the subject matter with regard to the content these niche bloggers each specialise in. In other words, each is able to carve out a highly particularised area of content publishing that has won over a steady fan base. Amazingly, the content that is promoted under each name quite accurately reflects what is branded in the site slogan. Specifically, @Happy张江 labels herself as "hardcore, satirist, news & anecdotes, pranks & humor mongering"; @技能大叔 uses "pranks, DIY, handicraft, jokes, satirist" to brand himself; @嘴巴笑抽筋了owns up to nine labels that pertain to various aspects of "搞笑" (literally meaning laughter-making), an emerging online culture that uses wordplay to create hilarious, humorous and funny content. Three V-microbloggers cater specifically to female fan bases – @文摘精选 uses ten labels for self-branding that revolve around various aspects of the so-called "petty-bourgeois taste", a popular term in China today referring to the lifestyles of the rising middle class with regard to cultural, emotional and consuming preferences; another (@搭配师林欣) – who self-classifies as a fashion freelancer – uses a single label "fashion", and stays truthful to this proclamation in her postings; the third one (@笙南)

develops a focus on love and family, with a special twist to young and newly-wed women. The last one, @我没钱可我想旅游 – the screen name literally meaning "I don't have money but I want to travel" – faithfully practises what he brands himself as in the screen name, and focuses on sharing insightful tips and information as well as captivating photographs on various tactics of money-saving tourism-related activities and events. It is no accident that microbloggers that excel in these thematic pursuits hit the top 50 list on Weibo – they satisfy the surging needs for particular types of informational consumption among the fast-expanding affluent middle class in Chinese society.

While they differ greatly in content, these microbloggers share a lot in how they navigate the Weibo sphere – light-hearted language often interwoven with contagious punchlines that resonate well with the youth-dominated Weibo audience. Furthermore, a dramatic departure from the other Weibo celebrities in the top 50 by this group is the conspicuous but carefully controlled presence of commercial messages ranging from sponsored events to services to consumer products. A common strategy by all the bloggers is to calculatedly fit the commercials within the overall flow of message posts so that they do not appear to be overly obtrusive to the readers.

The two remaining microbloggers in this group stand in stark contrast to the above seven. One (@招财小天使) functions like a digital marketing channel, and mostly circulates commercial messages and business promotions. Despite its commercial orientation, it still manages to garner over 334 K followers thanks to its regular use of cash drawing to encourage public participation. It also issues coupon-like incentives to its followers. As clearly marked on the page logo, it vigorously solicits business sponsorships. The other (@iG 电子竞技俱乐部) is actually the Weibo face of the e-sports club associated with Invictus Gaming (IG), a video game company specialising in organising player participation in domestic and global e-sports competitions. It is used to communicate news and IG-sponsors events to followers. Its popularity indicates the elevated level of popular enthusiasm over e-sports in China.

Everything but Businesslike

Four microbloggers classify themselves as businessmen/entrepreneurs under their Weibo accounts, and we aggregate them into the same category accordingly. In terms of similarities, they all share the status of being super-rich, and their popularity is driven by the originality and outspokenness of their Weibo speech. In opposition to the above category of niche bloggers, all four use their true names and real-life identities in their Weibo branding. They have all built a virtual reputation for their unorthodox and non-conformist comments, often running counter to official doctrines and government-endorsed positions. But their perspectives, more often than not, resonate well with the populist pulse and find support with the commoners. Their Weibo posts read like revelations of their genuine, unfiltered thoughts, and cover a wide range of issues and topics. Noticeably, their focal points are not actually business-related (unless it is framed in relevance to the average citizens), but more aligned with social and everyday life. Moreover, they are never hesitant to chime in on trending topics and hot-button issues.

The highest ranked among them is Ren Zhiqiang (@任志强, ranked #10, with over 35 million followers and nicknamed Big-Mouth Ren for his no-nonsense style), who made his fortunes through real estate development – his business interests now extend to banking, insurance, dining and tourism. His recent comment – made on 31 October 2015 in response to the newly announced state move of relaxing its long-time birth control policy to allow each couple to have two children – smacks well of his rhetorical style: "Allowing two children comes as good news. But this should not be the end goal. What humanity strives for is the freedom to birth and the right to subsistence, which is perhaps more important". In another instance that took place in September 2015, Ren openly proclaimed that what the communist ideology preaches is a utopian dream, as it could never be actualised in any society. This made him the target of denunciation by the Central Committee of the Communist Youth League of China, along with multiple official media publications. But his popularity on Weibo substantially rose in the wake of official tirade, as indicated by the addition of millions of followers to his account. In a recent turn of events, Ren's Weibo account was forced to be terminated by Tencent under a directive from the State Internet Information Office (affiliated with the State Council) in February 2016 for openly challenging the state media's claim that they belong to the Chinese Communist Party (Huang, 2016).

The next microblogger, Hou Ning (@侯宁), registered himself as an "independent financial observer, current affairs commentator, social scholar, and professional investor" on Weibo, and publishes profusely with personal opinions on the financial and stock markets. As more and more average citizens are investing in these markets, an independent voice can provide an important barometer for them. For that, Hou has earned a trustworthy spot on the public pulse.

Wang Sicong (@王思聪), the third one in this category, is an anomaly in a lot of ways. Albeit registered as a businessman (he's the Chairman of a Beijing-based investment firm), he is better known among the general public as the sole son of Wang Jianlin (Chairman of Wanda Group), the richest man in China. Born in 1988, Wang Sicong's extravagant lifestyle has been keeping him in the constant public spotlight. He rarely touches upon business topics on Weibo. Instead, the main topic for his Weibo chat centres on entertainment circles (through outrageous comments on performers and big-name entertainers), which may not be surprising considering that Wanda is the biggest investor in the creative industry (including the film business) and it also owns the largest number of movie theatres in Asia. He also uses Weibo to showcase his ritzy lifestyle.

The last microblogger in this category, Jumei Chen Ou (@聚美陈欧), owns his success to the cosmetics and beauty business. Chen is the founder and CEO of Jumei, one of the leading online vendors specialising in beauty and makeup products. The fact that he brands his Weibo identity starting with the company name suggests an intentional effort to associate him with the corporate entity – precisely what he has been doing on Weibo through content publishing. His Weibo posts mainly fall into two categories, work-related and personal life. There is a consistent effort to promote the Jumei brand across most threads.

From Individual Microbloggers to Self-made Media

Three of the top 50 celebrities are classified as "Weibo-contracted self-publishing media", a category of microbloggers that can only be granted by Weibo upon authentication and approval. This privilege is only extended to microbloggers who have earned a solid reputation in the Weibo sphere through an extended period of publishing and have garnered a steady follower base, much like the niche bloggers we discussed above. Once microbloggers are elevated to the status of self-publishing media, they must agree to churn out a certain quota of content on Weibo in return for technical and financial favours. They also agree to allow Weibo to advertise in their space and, besides the regular followers, Weibo will maximise the reach of their content to potential audience whose profiles match the content area. Individuals in this category are most avid contributors to original content specialising in a niche area, and a revenue-sharing scheme with Weibo earns them monthly income commensurate to the traffic and impact generated by their Weibo output. Microblogging for these individuals has turned from a voluntary activity to an incentivised undertaking. As a result, most individuals in the self-publishing media category encourage audience participation in the process through submitting original content, suggesting story ideas and other feedback.

Of the three media publishers, one (@猪猪爱讲冷笑话) specialises in comical sketches, concocting jokes and finding humour in everyday life – videos are used profusely in his posts. The second one (@逗比, meaning funny dumbhead) also aims at creating content that may lead to laughs, but with different styles – he uses a lot of cartoons and graphic materials. As an example, a recent post runs like this, "We are told that tap water is not fit for direct drinking, and apples cannot be eaten before being washed. But then we are supposed to believe that apples are edible after being washed by tap water". The third one (@艾克里里) features a photographer – his Weibo site makes extensive use of photos (many of which are selfies) to discuss everyday life and drive points home.

Fame, They Write

Two of the top 50 are registered in the author/writer category. They are the least productive in terms of output, but their posts are also the most unique. The first one (@Old先) is a cartoonist and mostly uses his own cartoons in his Weibo posts – he also often provides background information and storylines (e.g. online games, ads) in relation to the cartoons. The other one (@刘同) is an award-winning writer and also the Vice President of EnlightPictures, a Beijing-based movie studio. His Weibo posts radiate the brilliant and penetrating style of his literary writing, and quotes from his published works are common, usually interlaced with annotations and flashing inspirations. Photos and videos are very rare. Albeit less frequently, he also discusses new productions and releases from his studio from time to time.

Conclusion

Social media has been seamlessly ingrained into various aspects of Chinese society. Because all major social media platforms (e.g. Twitter, YouTube, Facebook, Instagram) are blocked out of Chinese cyber territories by the state authorities, home-grown counterparts have thrived to create hugely popular domestic brands of social media venues such as QQ, WeChat and Weibo. Alongside the popularisation of social communication, we have witnessed the emergence of a unique style of social media culture that continues to propel Chinese cyberspace to new terrains. In light of the discussions in this chapter, a few points are worth highlighting here.

The tightly controlled media and information ecology in China has channelled audience interest to online information production and consumption, and Chinese netizens are among the most active in contributing to user-generated content online (Tai, 2006). The recent social media revolution serves to solidify that overall trend by diversifying bases of participants and types of content. Compared with Twitter, the spectacular absence of two types of names – politicians and mainstream media – on the top microblogger list in China is highly indicative of the nature of the social media space in the country. There are still stringently defined boundaries to political discussions on social media, and it is going to be extremely challenging for politicians to migrate conventional propagandist indoctrination to the social media platforms. It is not without strenuous attempts from either the government or the state media, however. Many state agencies, including their representative arms, and all major state media have established a conspicuous presence on Weibo, but none of them has won the love of the general audience. At the moment when content is king, state-sponsored materials may not enamour the average users easily. This does not mean, however, that Chinese social media users are not interested in politics. As Rauchfleisch and Schäfer (2015) observe, multi-layered public spheres where political debates dominate do exist on Weibo. Meanwhile, social media has also turned into a hotbed of collective action and contentious activities in China. The deviation from politics by top microbloggers may suggest tactical moves on their part to minimise the risk of controversial topics to turn them into easy targets by state censors. Being in the spotlight also incurs microscopic scrutiny, as indicated in the recent forced closure of the Weibo account by vocal critic Ren Zhiqiang. On the other hand, the fact that the state has to resort to brutal suppression of targeted individual dissenters through account termination speaks volumes for the challenge of the state in propagating content on social media that conforms to official doctrines.

Blossoming social media space also bodes well and creates unique opportunities for certain types of individuals. As we have seen in the discussion, a sizable number of individual microbloggers have earned celebrity-like prestige and recognition on Weibo through their creative contribution either as niche writers or self-made media. In his account of popular media's infatuation with celebrities, Cashmore (2014, p. 63) notes that "people preferred to read about everyday events in the lives of fantastic people rather than fantastic events in the lives of everyday people". This certainly rings true on Weibo where chatters by pop stars attract significant followings. In that sense, Weibo and other social media communication is a fruitful area of deliberation in re-evaluating Goffman's (1958) theory of self-presentation, because we often no longer see a clearly differentiated public self and inner (private) self. The boundaries between the "backstage" and "frontstage" are blurring in the carefully constructed ethos on Weibo.

In view of the harsh state regulations over online publishing in China, innovative social media venues like Weibo are liberating and empowering in that they open up a brand new space for individuals to exert a voice, such as venting out public outrage directed at certain transgressors (Tai, 2015). For real-world celebrities, Weibo has become a viable platform for them to form new types of relationships through showcasing diverse aspects of their emotional, family, mundane and everyday activities. Quite a bit of the Weibo conversations revealed by these celebrities pertain to phatic communication (Miller, 2008), and this has injected new dynamics in parasocial relations and the formations of stardom in contemporary China. Our chapter, of course, provides perspectives and practices of Weibo celebrities – how they are perceived by average users will be a fascinating area of enquiry.

Notes

1 This quota was lifted by Weibo in November 2016, and users now can type longer text into their microblog entries.
2 The list is available at http://bang.weibo.com/renwu/month?date=20150901&sudaref=bang.weibo.com.

3 The metrics that are considered in ranking top Weibo authors are reported here: http://bang.weibo.com/rules.
4 The top 50 Twitter celebrities are selected from this link, by narrowing the country of choice to the United States: http://twittercounter.com/pages/100.
5 State Administration of Press, Publication, Radio, Film and Television (SAPPRFT), "Internet publishing license process", available www.gapp.gov.cn/govservice/1966/114209.shtml.
6 MIIT, "Telecommunications business permit approval process", available www.miit.gov.cn/n11293472/n11293847/n11301450/11497081.html.

References

Cashmore, E. (2014). *Celebrity/culture* (2nd ed.) New York: Routledge.

Cherry, R. D. (1998). Ethos versus persona self-representation in written discourse. *Written Communication*, 15(3), 384–410.

Goffman, E. (1956). *The presentation of self in everyday life.* Edinburgh, UK: The University of Edinburgh Social Sciences Research Centre.

Halloran, S. M. (1982). Aristotle's concept of ethos, or if not his somebody else's. *Rhetoric Review*, 1(1), 58–63.

Huang, A. W. (2016, 29 February). *Ren Zhiqiang's Weibo account terminated for criticising the official media.* New York Times Online (Chinese edition). Retrieved from http://cn.nytimes.com/china/20160229/c29chinaren/.

Johnson, T. J., & Perlmutter, D. D. (2010). Introduction: The Facebook election. *Mass Communication and Society*, 13(5), 554–559.

Lomborg, S. (2013). *Social media, social genres: Making sense of the ordinary.* New York: Routledge.

Madden, M., & Fox, S. (2006). *Riding the waves of "Web 2.0": More than a buzzword, but still not easily defined.* Pew Internet Project. Retrieved from www.pewinternet.org/~/media/Files/Reports/2006/PIP_Web_2.0.pdf.pdf.

Miller, V. (2008). New media, networking and phatic culture. *Convergence: The International Journal of Research into New Media Technologies*, 14(4), 387–400.

Murthy, D. (2013). *Twitter: Social communication in the Twitter age.* Malden, MA: Polity.

O'Reilly, T. (2005). *What is Web 2.0: Design patterns and business models for the next generation of software.* Retrieved from www.oreilly.com/pub/a/web2/archive/what-is-web-20.html.

Rauchfleisch, A., & Schäfer, M. S. (2015). Multiple public spheres of Weibo: A typology of forms and potentials of online public spheres in China. *Information, Communication & Society*, 18(2), 139–155.

Sattler, W. M. (1947). Conceptions of ethos in ancient rhetoric. *Communications Monographs*, 14(1/2), 55–65.

Stockmann, D. (2013). *Media commercialization and authoritarian rule in China.* Cambridge, UK: Cambridge University Press.

Tai, Z. (2006). *The internet in China: Cyberspace and civil society.* New York: Routledge.

Tai, Z. (2015). Networked resistance: Digital populism, online activism, and mass dissent in China. *Popular Communication*, 13(2), 120–131.

Turner, G. (2010). *Ordinary people and the media: The demotic turn.* Thousand Oaks, CA: Sage.

Part II
Chinese Social Media and (Re)Presentation

6 Framing Food Safety Issues in China

The Negotiation between 'Official Discourse' in Newspapers and 'Civil Discourse' on Weibo

Yang Wang

Introduction

On 16 May 2013, large stocks of rice and rice products in Guangzhou were detected by the Food and Drug Administration (FDA) of the local municipality to contain excessive levels of cadmium, a heavy metal which has been proved as a predisposing factor of pathological changes in the kidneys and other organs (Duan, 2013). This food safety scandal served as another reminder of painful memories about the many food safety disasters in China over the past decade such as melamine-contaminated baby formula, sewer oil and clenbuterol-tainted pork (Foster, 2011; Mou & Lin, 2014) and immediately attracted intensive public attention and media exposure.

In contemporary Chinese society, food safety problems, as a typical form of modern risk (Beck, 1992), have increasingly become part and parcel of people's everyday life, and have brought about a pervasive sense of insecurity and uncertainty (MacLeod, 2012). All kinds of stakeholders – from the government, commercial institutions, social elites, to the relatively 'powerless' general public – are striving for the most favourable positions in a risk environment. In this context, the representation and solution of food safety incidents are largely shaped by the negotiation of multiple social discourses, and the media sphere, including both traditional news media and emerging digital media platforms, serves as the main arena of diverse social discourses.

Traditionally, mass media like newspaper and television have played a crucial role in defining and interpreting risk issues (Beck, 1992; Hansen, 1991). In Chinese society, mainstream mass media organisations are under the control of the party–state (Esarey, 2005; Stockmann & Gallagher, 2011), and thus tend to represent the voice of dominant official discourses (Yang, 2013). With the rapid proliferation of information and communication technologies (ICTs), especially social media platforms, the top-down ideologies propagated by mass media are now faced with unprecedented challenges from bottom-up narratives created in the digital media sphere (Hu, 2008; Yang, 2009b; Zheng, 2007). In this context, this chapter seeks to provide novel insights into this dichotomy between top-down 'official discourses' and bottom-up 'civil discourses' through a comparative framing analysis of a case study of mainstream newspaper reports and public expressions on the most popular microblogging site, Sina Weibo, during the cadmium-tainted rice incident.

The empirical data revealed that newspaper articles mostly followed the authoritative standpoints of the government and constructed an official frame of 'risk under control', while online public expressions drew on everyday experiences and moral judgments to deconstruct the official discourses and develop a civil frame of 'risk out of control'. During this process, the top-down 'grand narratives' of social stability are gradually losing legitimacy and being challenged by the bottom-up 'small narratives' of daily life, basic human rights and personal emotions. However, the dominance of fragmented and sometimes irrational expressions in the latter has rendered them vulnerable to the invisible control of the mass media agenda.

The Dichotomy of 'Official Discourse' and 'Civil Discourse' in China

The mass media system in China has long been viewed as the 'tongue and throat' of the party–state (Pan, 2008) which serves to produce public consent and consolidate the political power of the government (Esarey & Qiang, 2011; Yang, 2013). Through multiple forms of propaganda and censorship, the Chinese government makes restrictions on the range of facts and interpretations that citizens are exposed to (Brady, 2008; Sullivan, 2013), hence shaping their opinions about particular social problems. Nowadays this information control has become more problematic due to the increasing prevalence of advanced ICTs. The emergence of these new technologies has challenged the existing hierarchy of social power, and given rise to the prosperity of alternative civil voices in the public sphere – voices which are sometimes in conflict with the official standpoint of the state (Hu, 2008; Yang, 2009b).

Previous studies have identified two distinct yet closely related types of discourses in current Chinese society – the top-down official discourse and the bottom-up civil discourse (He & Chen, 2010; Hu, 2008; Zhao, 2008). The former usually appears in mainstream mass media, such as newspaper coverage and television programs, and primarily represents the dominant values of authoritative ideology. The latter mostly takes the form of public expressions on digital media platforms, and reflects the multiple, fragmented and sometimes conflicting values in society (Shi, 2009; Wang, 2013a).

Official discourses disseminated by mass media and civil discourses developed on digital media platforms usually play different roles in the development of social events. Specifically, information provided by mass media assumes crucial significance in defining and interpreting certain events due to its advantaged social position and historical social influence (Stockmann & Gallagher, 2011; Wang, 2013b). However, in the current public arena, the process and solution of problems are no longer monopolised by official discourses – the rise of social media empowers the marginalised general public to reflect on, resist and deconstruct the top-down dominant frames (Hu, 2008; Yang, 2009b; Zheng, 2007). The constant gaze and challenges from the public online exert considerable pressure on the authorities, and therefore shape the results of social events (Hu, 2008). In specific cases, official discourses and civil discourses often interplay with each other in dynamic manners, ranging from sharp conflict, to subtle balance, to reciprocal collaboration (He & Chen, 2010).

Compared with the relatively stable and homogenised official discourse, civil discourse is more flexible and heterogeneous, characterised by sporadic outbreaks of public discussions and fluid relationships between participants (Rauchfleisch & Schäfer, 2015). The heterogeneous 'cacophony' online on the one hand serves as a powerful outlet for ordinary citizens to freely express their opinions and exert pressures on political authorities (Fu, Chan, & Chau, 2013; Hu, 2008; Yang, 2009b), while, on the other hand, it also falls short of substantial and long-term social influences. In particular, a considerable proportion of participants in online public discussions are 'event public' (Xu, 2005) – those who assemble with the outbreak of a 'hot issue' and melt away immediately when the issue cools down. These participants usually do not have stable values and clear objectives, and thus can easily be mobilised by emotions such as anger and sympathy (Yang, 2009a). As a result, expressions by these short-term participants sometimes are reduced to irrational quarrels rather than offering substantial contribution to the solution of social problems.

Case Study: Media Analysis of the Cadmium-Tainted Rice Incident

Methodology

Framing Analysis

In this study, framing analysis was conducted to identify different characteristics of, and interactions between, mainstream newspaper reports and public expressions on Sina Weibo during the cadmium-tainted rice incident. Framing is an appropriate theoretical and methodological approach to understand the media representation of public issues. In journalism and communication studies, frames are viewed as tools for media and individuals to convey and interpret information (Neuman, Just, & Crigler, 1992). According to Entman (1993), to frame is to "select some aspects of a perceived reality and make them more salient in a communicating text, in such a way as to promote a particular problem definition, causal interpretation, moral evaluation, and/or treatment recommendation for the item described" (p. 52). In this sense, frames can shape how people understand, evaluate and act upon specific problems (Reese, 2001), and thus serve to help prioritise some social issues or opinions over others (Gamson & Modigliani, 1989).

There are two types of media frames, namely the generic frame and the issue-specific frame, which correspond to the deductive and inductive approaches of framing analysis (De Vreese, 2005; Semetko & Valkenburg, 2000). Generic frames are pre-defined sets of themes which can be employed to identify similarities and differences across the media coverage of different social problems. Issue-specific frames are more flexible and subjective in that they are detected from specific contents, and vary according to the issues being analysed.

Sametko and Valkenburg (2000) further identified five prominent generic frames in political news coverage – conflict, human interest, economic consequences, morality and responsibility. The conflict frame places emphasis on the conflicts between individuals, groups or institutions; the human interest frame brings an emotional angle to the presentation of an event or issue; the economic consequences frame reports certain problems in terms of the economic consequences it brings to a specific individual or group; the morality frame puts a particular event or issue in the context of religious tenets or moral prescriptions; and the responsibility frame often attributes the responsibility of causing or solving a problem to the government, a certain individual or a group.

Research Sites

For this study, *People's Daily, Southern Metropolitan Daily* and Sina Weibo were chosen as the main sites of sampling for framing analysis. *People's Daily* is the major mouthpiece of the Chinese Communist Party since the establishment of People's Republic of China (PRC) – it represents the official ideology of the Chinese government and serves to shape public opinions.[1] During significant social events, *People's Daily* usually acts as the main source of information for other Chinese newspapers and news websites because of its timeliness, large circulation and high authority.[2] *Southern Metropolitan Daily* is the most competitive and influential metropolitan newspaper in contemporary Chinese society.[3] It emphasises in-depth reporting and diversified viewpoints, and is particularly popular among relatively young-aged and well-educated social groups.[4] Both newspapers are published on a daily basis.

Weibo, the Chinese microblog, has dramatically transformed the traditional patterns of public discussion in China, and has made itself the new centre of public opinion since its first launch in 2009 (Xie & Rong, 2011). As is revealed by China Internet Network Information Center (CNNIC), Weibo had attracted a total of 204 million users by 2015, covering 30.6 percent of internet users in China (CNNIC, 2015). Among all the microblogging platforms, Sina Weibo is the most popular and influential, and serves as the cradle of many public events and the main channel of civic participation for ordinary citizens (Chan, Wu, Hao, Xi, & Jin, 2012; Huang & Sun, 2014).

Sampling and Research Process

News articles in *People's Daily* and *Southern Metropolitan Daily*, as well as microblog messages in Sina Weibo published between 16 May 2013 and 30 July 2013 were sampled. After July 2013, the newspaper coverage and public discussion concerning this incident become very scarce, so 31 July was chosen as the end point of sampling. The articles and messages were retrieved using keywords of 'cadmium-tainted rice' (*ge da mi/ge mi*) and 'rice with excessive levels of cadmium' (*da mi ge chao biao*). Only the articles or messages that are original and directly related to the specific food safety issue were included in the analysis.

For news reports, all the resulting articles from keyword search were included in the sample.[5] Weibo messages were sampled via the 'real-time retrieval' (shi shi jian suo) function provided by the Weibo platform and gathered according to different stages of the incident (Wang, 2013b), namely latent stage, outbreak stage, diffusion stage and retrospective stage. The stages of the event were divided on the basis of previous research on crisis communication (e.g., Fink, 1989; Li, 2007; Sturges, 1994). In the latent stage, relevant Weibo messages were too few to constitute a sample; in the outbreak stage (when online discussion was the most active), ten messages were randomly sampled every day; in the diffusion stage (when online discussion began to cool down), five Weibo messages were sampled every day; in the retrospective stage (when online discussion had become very inactive), five Weibo messages were randomly sampled every week. In all, 32 newspaper reports and 280 Weibo messages were analysed.

This study combined the deductive and inductive approach of framing analysis, and drew on both the generic frame and issue-specific frame to examine the chosen texts (De Vreese, 2005; Semetko & Valkenburg, 2000). The 'fact frame' was added to Semetko and Valkenburg's (2000) framework to better locate news articles that were purely factual statements about the event, without any form of implications, judgements or emotional appeals.

Besides examining the general frame preferences of mass media reports and social media expressions, this study also conducted inductive framing analysis to identify dominant themes involved in the representation of the specific food safety issue. All the news articles and Weibo messages were categorised according to 10 themes – governmental actions, role of media and journalists, role of experts, knowledge introduction and policy interpretation, responsibility of the government, economic impacts, social impacts, everyday life impacts, reflection on the incident and satires.

Results

Grand Narrative – 'Risk Under Control' in Mass Media Coverage

The generic frames of newspaper articles are shown in Table 6.1. Of all the selected articles, nearly half (46.9 percent) fell into the fact frame, which indicated a strong objectivist orientation across the mass media contents. The responsibility frame and human interest frame were the next two frequently used frames, which made up 21.9 and 15.6 per cent of the articles respectively. Only three (9.4 percent) articles employed the morality frame, and even fewer used the conflict and economic consequences frames, each accounting for only 6.1 percent of the total sample.

The issue-specific frames of newspaper articles are reported in Table 6.2. Among the selected articles, 34.3 percent focused on the actions of the government in the incident ('governmental actions'), followed by media comments on the governmental actions ('responsibility of the government') which accounted for 18.8 percent of the sample. This means that more than half (53.1 percent) of all the articles revolved

Table 6.1 Generic Frames of Newspaper Articles

Frame	People's Daily	Southern Metropolitan Daily	Total	
	n	*n*	*n*	%
Conflict	0	1	1	3.1
Human interest	0	5	5	15.6
Economic consequences	0	1	1	3.1
Morality	1	2	3	9.4
Responsibility	3	4	7	21.9
Fact	4	11	15	46.9

Table 6.2 Issue-specific Frames of Newspaper Articles

Theme	People's Daily	Southern Metropolitan Daily	Total	
	n	*n*	*n*	%
Governmental actions	4	7	11	34.3
Role of media and journalists	0	2	2	6.3
Role of experts	0	3	3	9.4
Knowledge and policy interpretations	2	1	3	9.4
Responsibility of the government	1	5	6	18.8
Economic impacts	0	1	1	3.1
Social impacts	0	3	3	9.4
Everyday life impacts	0	1	1	3.1
Reflection of the incident	1	1	2	6.3
Satires	0	0	0	0

around the government. In addition, journalists and experts also showed some discursive power in framing the food safety risk. Specifically, the themes of 'role of experts' and 'knowledge introduction and policy interpretations' made up 9.4 percent of the articles respectively; 'role of media and journalists' and 'reflection of the incident' made up 6.3 percent respectively. However, the impacts of the food safety risk on the economy ('economic impacts') as well as individual citizens ('everyday life impacts') attracted scant attention from mass media (3.1 percent each). The theme of 'satires' did not appear in any of the news articles selected.

Generally speaking, mass media coverage on the cadmium-tainted rice incident constructed a grand narrative of 'risk under control' through disseminating reassuring yet superficial announcements and highlighting the positive role of the government. Most of the newspaper articles focused on the factual information about the process of the incident, such as results of official investigation, proposed solutions and social responses to administrative actions. The government remained as the focus of these articles, and performed active roles of 'problem solver' and 'public interest protector'. For example, the first news report about the cadmium-tainted rice on *People's Daily* paid primary attention to the 'large-scale investigation into, and punishment of, related individuals and institutions in the rice industry' conducted by the Guangzhou provincial government and Hunan Youxian county government (He, Hou, & Li, 2013) Although it was titled 'Where did cadmium come from, who is responsible for the incident', the article did not emphasise the accountability of the food safety problem, but rather highlighted the determination and efficiency of the local governments in handling the emergency. In addition to the government, social elites such as journalists, entrepreneurs, related experts and public intellectuals also managed to present a voice, while the general public who bear the brunt of food safety risks were rendered invisible in mass media coverage.

Apart from imparting factual information, newspaper reports on the food safety problem also manifested a certain degree of reflection and accountability. As is shown in the empirical data, both the generic frame of 'responsibility' and the issue-specific frame of 'responsibility of the government' accounted for a relatively large proportion of all the articles. However, close examination revealed that these reflections were mostly descriptive summaries of the particular incident which did not touch the fundamental cause and long-term solution of food safety crises. In these media articles, pollution from heavy industries, weak supervision of local governments, profit-driven behaviours of businessmen and so on were all blamed for the contaminated rice (Pan, 2013), but none of them were expected to be responsible for the incident, nor make changes to alleviate the problem.

Small Narrative – 'Risk Out of Control' in
the New Media Sphere

As is shown in Table 6.3, the human interest frame was the most frequently used generic frame across the selected Weibo messages and made up nearly half (43.9 percent) of the sample. In contrast, the fact frame – the dominant frame in newspaper reports – accounted for only 5.4 percent. This indicates that public expressions place more emphasis on emotional elements and human concerns than mere facts. The responsibility frame and morality frame also had a significant place in Weibo public discussions, with the former accounting for 20.7 percent of the sample and the latter 16.8 percent. Moreover, only 27 out of 280 (9.6 percent) messages were conveyed in terms of conflict frame, and even fewer (3.6 percent) employed the economic consequences frame.

Table 6.3 Generic Frames of Weibo Messages

Frame	*n*	%
Conflict	27	9.6
Human interest	123	43.9
Economic consequences	10	3.6
Morality	47	16.8
Responsibility	58	20.7
Fact	15	5.4

As for issue-specific frames used by Weibo messages, statistics in Table 6.4 show that the category of 'satires', which did not appear in newspaper articles, made up the largest body of the sample (40.7 percent). The satires mostly took the form of short ironic stories and doggerels – commonly referred to as *duanzi* in China – about the overall situation of food safety risks in China, as well as the irresponsible remarks or behaviours of relevant officials. The second most common theme was the 'everyday life impacts', which accounted for 17.1 percent of all the Weibo messages. Comments on the performance of the government ('responsibility of the government') served as another important theme, and accounted for 11.8 percent of the messages. Apart from these three prominent categories, 'knowledge introduction and policy interpretations', 'governmental actions', 'role of experts' and 'reflection of the incident' also attracted a certain degree of attention, and made up 8.6, 6.1, 5.4 and 5.0 percent of the messages respectively. The themes of 'role of media and journalists', 'economic impacts' and 'social impacts' were seldom mentioned across the messages.

It can therefore be argued that in the cadmium-tainted rice incident, public discussions on Weibo challenged the top-down grand narratives of 'under control', and constructed small narratives of 'out of control' on the basis of everyday life experiences, emotional expressions and moral interrogations. That is, compared with the factual information disseminated by mass media coverage, public discussions on Weibo tended to focus more on the potential consequences of the food safety risks on individuals' life and health than the development of the incident itself. As is shown in the empirical data, the majority of Weibo users drew on everyday experiences and emotions to express their dissatisfaction with the status of food safety in Chinese society. For example, some people were anxious about the existence of cadmium-tainted rice around them, and asked "how to distinguish between contaminated and uncontaminated rice", or "what are the brands of those substandard rice products".

Table 6.4 Issue-specific Frames of Weibo Messages

Theme	n	%
Governmental actions	17	6.1
Role of media and journalists	2	0.7
Role of experts	15	5.4
Knowledge and policy interpretations	24	8.6
Responsibility of the government	33	11.8
Economic impacts	8	2.9
Social impacts	5	1.8
Everyday life impacts	48	17.1
Reflection of the incident	14	5.0
Satires	114	40.7

Others expressed the desperation about food safety problems as a whole, and claimed that "the only way to avoid eating poisoned rice is to grow rice by ourselves", or even "do go abroad if you do not have the privilege to eat special-supplied food".

Apart from emotional expressions, public discussions on Weibo also showed strong moral concerns. The food safety risk was constantly related to broader social contexts, especially the phenomena of corruption, economic inequality and moral crisis. For example, many people viewed the food safety incident as another proof of the "long-standing collusion between corrupt government officials and unscrupulous businessmen". The problem of social inequality was also highlighted repeatedly in terms of "the privileged stratum can eat special-supplied food, while our ordinary people only deserve poisoned food".

The emotional and moral discourses in the Weibo public sphere regarding this incident often also took the form of sarcasm and irony. A typical example was the irony of the "invincible Chinese" which asserted that, after surviving more and more poisoned food, the Chinese would "finally evolve and become the strongest ethnicity in the world". Many people joked that they "kept learning chemistry through food safety incidents", and were expected to "memorize the entire periodic table of elements in the near future". Some creative users even composed *duanzi* to satirise a series of food safety problems.

Negotiations between Official Discourse and Civil Discourse According to the Stage of the Incident

In the trajectory of the cadmium-tainted rice incident, official discourses disseminated by mass media and civil discourses produced by public expressions on Weibo manifested distinct characteristics during different stages, and interacted with each other in a dynamic manner. The issue-specific frames of newspaper articles and Weibo messages at different stages of the event are shown in Table 6.5.

As a long-standing food safety problem, the cadmium-tainted rice had attracted scant public attention before the outbreak of the specific event and the appearance of extensive mass media coverage. During this 'latent stage', the food safety issue was almost invisible in both news reports and online discussions. On Weibo, for example, real-time search with the keywords of 'cadmium-tainted rice' (*ge da mi/ge mi*) on a random date (5 May 2013) before the outbreak of the incident retrieved only eight posts. Within the limited messages, four were posted by the same user and three were the same ironic *duanzi* repeated by different users.

The outbreak of the specific food safety incident transformed the invisible social problem into the focus of public concern. The outbreak stage was the shortest yet most active stage during the process of the incident, which was characterised by sharp contradictions between official

Table 6.5 Issue-specific Frames of Newspaper Articles and Weibo Messages during Different Stages of the Event

Theme	Outbreak Stage		Diffusion Stage		Retrospective Stage	
	Newspaper	Weibo	Newspaper	Weibo	Newspaper	Weibo
Governmental actions	9 (52.9%)	8 (18.2%)	2 (18.2%)	6 (6.0%)	0	3 (33.3%)
Role of media and journalists	0	2 (2.2%)	2 (18.2%)	0	0	0
Role of experts	1 (5.9%)	5 (5.6%)	1 (9.1%)	4 (4.0%)	1 (25.0%)	6 (6.7%)
Knowledge and policy interpretations	0	10 (11.1%)	3 (27.3%)	7 (7.0%)	0	7 (7.8%)
Responsibility of the government	3 (17.6%)	16 (17.8%)	1 (9.1%)	12 (12.0%)	2 (50.0%)	5 (5.6%)
Economic impacts	1 (5.9%)	1 (1.1%)	0	4 (4.0%)	0	3 (3.3%)
Social impacts	1 (5.9%)	5 (5.6%)	1 (9.1%)	0	1 (25.0%)	0
Everyday life impacts	1 (5.9%)	15 (16.7%)	0	21 (21.0%)	0	12 (13.3%)
Reflection of the incident	1 (5.9%)	4 (4.4%)	1 (9.1%)	5 (5.0%)	0	5 (5.6%)
Satires	0	24 (26.7%)	0	41 (41.0%)	0	49 (54.4%)
Total	17	90	11	100	4	90

discourses and civil discourses. Specifically, more than half of the news reports in this stage focused on active actions of the government in solving the food safety crisis as well as positive progresses of these actions ('governmental actions', 52.9 percent). In contrast, public expressions on Weibo laid more emphasis on the ineptitude of the government in preventing the incident ('responsibility of the government', 17.8 percent) and negative impacts of the contaminated food on their daily lives ('everyday life impacts', 16.7 percent). More often than not, official discourses propagated by mass media, such as government's promises of food safety during the next few years, were precisely the targets of criticism and deconstruction in the online public sphere.

When the food safety event moved into the diffusion stage, the frequency of relevant news reports and online expressions dropped significantly, while range and depth increased. Compared with the outbreak stage, in the diffusion stage the radical contradiction between official discourses and civil discourses were largely replaced by an emerging relationship of collaboration. On the one hand, information provided by mass media still constituted a large proportion of online expressions, and served as the main centre of debate. On the other hand, expressions on Weibo were also included into mass media coverage as the reflection of public opinions. For example, the *Southern Metropolitan Daily* published an article on 18 May 2013 to question the government for concealing information, wherein related Weibo comments were listed to represent prevalent social responses to government's actions (Liu, 2013).

In the last stage of the incident, the retrospective stage, the intensity and diversity of news reports and online expressions continued to drop as the specific incident faded out of media agenda and the focus of public discussion. In particular, the food safety issue became invisible again in mass media coverage unless significant progress was made or similar incidents happened. At the same time, online discussions became dominated by repeated *duanzi* ('satires', 54.4 percent) about a series of food safety problems which lacked substantial contribution to the improvement of food security situations in China.

Conclusion

According to Bourdieu (1998), mass media is not a mirror of objective facts, but rather a tool of creating reality. The news coverage in the cadmium-tainted rice incident created an 'official reality' in which everything was under control and well organised. Specifically, the government paid high attention to the food safety problem and carried out immediate solutions; at the same time all sectors of the society fully supported and cooperated with the government to satisfactorily solve the crisis. This grand narrative of 'risk under control' actually masked the panorama of the incident, and obstructed alternative interpretations of and critical reflections on food safety problems.

With the rapid proliferation of digital media, however, top-down official discourses as well as the one-way information dissemination paradigm have increasingly been destabilised and deconstructed by bottom-up civil discourses emerging in the online public sphere. During the cadmium-tainted rice incident, a small narrative of 'out of control' was developed on the basis of emotional and moral expressions, wherein the unitary official ideology of social stability and economic development had become marginalised and replaced by everyday life experiences, a sense of insecurity as well as requirements for basic human rights.

In different stages of the incident, official discourses disseminated by mass media and civil discourses produced on the social media platform Weibo interacted with each other in a dynamic manner, ranging from sharp contradiction, to intensive negotiation to interpenetration. Despite the increasing discursive power of civil discourses, the dominance of fragmented and sometimes irrational expressions rendered them vulnerable to the invisible control of mass media agenda. In the trajectory of the food safety incident, the ups and downs of public discussions were actually determined by the intensity and diversity of media exposure.

Specifically, the long-standing food safety problem was beyond the focus of public concern before the appearance of extensive mass media coverage. Similarly, when the media attention decreased in the later stages of the incident, the intensity and diversity of public discussions also dropped immediately.

Notes

1 Quoted from "Introduction of *People's Daily*", www.people.com.cn/GB/50142/104580/index.html.
2 Quoted from Baidu Encyclopedia of *People's Daily*, http://baike.baidu.com/view/38274.htm.
3 Quoted from official introduction of *Southern Metropolitan Daily*, http://corp.oeeee.com/nfdsb.html.
4 Quoted from Baidu Encyclopedia of *Southern Metropolitan Daily*, http://baike.baidu.com/view/1611.htm.
5 News reports of *People's Daily* were retrieved from the search function of the newspaper's official website (http://search.people.com.cn/rmw/GB/bkzzsearch/index.jsp); news from *Southern Metropolitan Daily* were retrieved from 'Baidu News' (http://news.baidu.com/).

References

Beck, U. (1992). *Risk society: Towards a new modernity*. London: Sage.
Bourdieu, P. (1998). *On television*. New York: The New Press.
Brady, A. M. (2008). *Marketing dictatorship: Propaganda and thought work in contemporary China*. New York: Rowman and Littlefield Publishers.
Chan, M., Wu, X., Hao, Y., Xi, R., & Jin, T. (2012). Microblogging, online expression, and political efficacy among young Chinese citizens: The moderating role of information and entertainment needs in the use of Weibo. *Cyberpsychology, Behavior and Social Networking*, 15(7), 345–349.
CNNIC (China Internet Network Information Center) (2015). Statistic report on the internet development in China – the 36th survey report. Retrieved from www.cnnic.net.cn/hlwfzyj/hlwxzbg/hlwtjbg/201502/t20150203_51634.htm.
De Vreese, C. H. (2005). News framing: Theory and typology. *Information Design Journal + Document Design*, 13(1), 51–62.
Duan, W. (2013, May 20). Guangzhou finds cadmium-tainted rice. *Global Times*. Retrieved from www.globaltimes.cn/content/782736.shtml.
Entman, R. M. (1993). Framing: Toward clarification of a fractured paradigm. *Journal of Communication*, 43(4), 51–58.
Esarey, A. (2005). Cornering the market: State strategies for controlling China's commercial media. *Asian Perspective*, 29(4), 37–83.
Esarey, A., & Qiang, X. (2011). Digital communication and political change in China. *International Journal of Communication*, 5, 298–319.
Fink, S. (1989). *Crisis management: Planning for the inevitable*. New York: American Management Association.
Foster, P. (2011, April 27). *Top 10 Chinese food scandals*. The Telegraph. Retrieved from www.telegraph.co.uk/news/worldnews/asia/china/8476080/Top-10-Chinese-Food-Scandals.html.

Fu, K., Chan, C., & Chau, M. (2013). Assessing censorship on microblogs in China: Discriminatory keyword analysis and the Real-Name Registration Policy. *IEEE Internet Computing, 17*(3), 42–50.

Gamson, W. A. & Modigliani, A. (1989). Media discourse and public opinion on nuclear power: A constructionist approach. *American Journal of Sociology, 95*(1), 1–37.

Hansen, A. (1991). The media and the social construction of the environment. *Media, Culture and Society, 13*(4), 443–458.

He, Z., & Chen, X. (2010). Shuang chong hua yu kong jian: Gong gong wei ji chuan bo zhong de zhong guo guan fang yu fei guan fang hua yu hu dong mo shi yan jiu [Dual discourse context: The interaction model of China official discourse and unofficial discourse within public crisis communication]. *Guo ji xin wen jie [Journal of International Communication], 8*, 21–27.

He, L., Hou, L., & Li, G. (2013, May 23). Ge lai zi na li, ze ren you shui dan? [Where did cadmium come from, who is responsible for the incident?]. *Ren Min Ri Bao [People's Daily]*, p. 4. Retrieved from http://finance.people.com.cn/n/2013/0523/c1004-21584918.html

Hu, Y. (2008). *Zhong sheng xuan hua: Wang luo shi dai de ge ren biao da yu gong gong tao lun [The rising cacophony: Personal expression and public discussion in the internet age]*. Guilin, China: [Guang xi shi fan da xue chu ban she [Guangxi Normal University Press].

Huang, R., & Sun, X. (2014). Weibo network, information diffusion and implications for collective action in China. *Information, Communication & Society, 17*(1), 86–104.

Li, X. (2007). Stages of a crisis and media frames and functions: US television coverage of the 9/11 incident during the first 24 hours. *Journal of Broadcasting & Electronic Media, 51*(4), 670–687.

Liu, Z. (2013, May 18). Ge da mi cha le bu gong bu, cha lai gan ma? [Investigated cadmium-tainted rice but refused to publish, why bother investigating?]. *Nan Fang Du Shi Bao [Southern Metropolitan Daily]*, p. GA02. Retrieved from http://epaper.oeeee.com/epaper/G/html/2013-05/18/content_2111467.htm?div=-1

MacLeod, C. (2012, May 28). *Chinese despair at endless food-safety scares.* USA Today. Retrieved from http://usatoday30.usatoday.com/news/world/story/2012–05–28/china-food-safety/55252482/1

Mou, Y., & Lin, C. A. (2014). Communicating food safety via the social media: The role of knowledge and emotions on risk perception and prevention. *Science Communication, 36*(5), 593–616.

Neuman, W. R., Just, M. R., & Crigler, A. N. (1992). *Common knowledge: News and the construction of political meaning.* Chicago, IL: University of Chicago Press.

Pan, Z. (2008). Chuan mei gong gong xing yu zhong guo chuan mei gai ge de zai qi bu [The publicity of media and the restart of China's media reform]. *Chuan bo yu she hui xue kan [Journal of communication and society], 6*, 1–16.

Pan, S. (2013, June 1). Ji ran mei wu ran, wei he ge chao biao? [If there is no pollution, why there are excessive levels of cadmium?]. *Ren Min Ri Bao [People's Daily]*, p. 9. Retrieved from http://opinion.people.com.cn/n/2013/0601/c1003-21697129.html

Rauchfleisch, A., & Schäfer, M. S. (2015). Multiple public spheres of Weibo: A typology of forms and potentials of online public spheres in China. *Information, Communication & Society*, 18(2), 139–155.

Reese, S. D. (2001). Framing public life: A bridging model for media research. In S. D. Reese, O. H. Gandy, & A. E. Grant (Eds.), *Framing public life: Perspectives on media and our understanding of the social world* (pp. 7–31). Mahwah, NJ: Erlbaum.

Semetko, H. A. & Valkenburg, P. M. (2000). Framing European politics: A Content analysis of press and television news. *Journal of Communication*, 50(2), 93–109.

Shi, Z. (2009). Gou tong yu dui hua: Gong min she hui yu mei ti gong gong kong jian – wang luo qun ti xing shi jian xing cheng ji zhi de li lun ji chu [Communication and dialogue: Civil society and media public space]. *Guo ji xin wen jie [Journal of International Communication]*, 12, 81–86.

Stockmann, D., & Gallagher, M. (2011). Remote control: How the media sustains authoritarian rule in China. *Comparative Political Studies*, 44(4), 436–467.

Sturges, D. L. (1994). Communicating through crisis: A strategy for organizational survival. *Management Communication Quarterly*, 7(3), 297–316.

Sullivan, J. (2013). China's Weibo: Is faster different? *New Media & Society*, 16(1), 24–37.

Wang, W. Y. (2013a). Weibo, framing, and media practices in China. *Journal of Chinese Political Science*, 18(4), 375–388.

Wang, Y. (2013b). Mei ti shi jian zhong de gong min can yu: Quan li, guan xi yu ce lue de dong tai bo yi [Civic participation in media events: The dynamic game of power, relationship and strategy]. In Z. Shi & J. Jin. (Eds.), *Xin mei ti fu quan: Guo jia yu she hui de xie tong yan jin [New media empowerment: The Co-evolution between state and society in China]* (pp. 133–174). Beijing: She hui ke xue wen xian chu ban she [Social Sciences Academic Press].

Xie, Y. & Rong, T. (2011). Wei bo yu lun sheng cheng yan bian ji zhi he yu lun yin dao ce lve [The generative and evolutionary mechanism of Weibo public opinion]. *Xian dai chuan bo [Modern Communication]*, 5, 70–74.

Xu, B. (2005). *Chuan mei gong zhong he gong gong shi jian can yu [Media public and participation in public affairs]*. Retrieved from www.aisixiang.com/data/4850.html.

Yang, G. (2009a). Bei qing yu xi xue: Wang luo shi jian zhong de qing gan dong yuan [Sorrow and sarcasm: Emotional mobilization in internet events]. *Chuan bo yu she hui xue kan [Journal of Communication and Society]*, 9, 39–66.

Yang, G. (2009b). *The power of the Internet in China: Citizen activism online*. New York: Columbia University Press.

Yang, G. (2013). Contesting food safety in the Chinese media: Between hegemony and counter-hegemony. *The China Quarterly*, 214, 337–355.

Zhao, Y. (2008). *Communication in China: Political economy, power, and conflict*. Lanham, MA: Rowman & Littlefield.

Zheng, Y. (2007). *Technological empowerment: The internet, state, and society in China*. Stanford, CA: Stanford University Press.

7 Face-work on Social Media in China

The Presentation of Self on RenRen and Facebook

Xiaoli Tian

Introduction

The internet has become an essential component in the daily lives of Chinese urbanites. According to the China Internet Network Information Center, 61.7 percent of Chinese netizens use social networking services (SNSs) such as QQ, MoMo and WeChat (CNNIC, 2015, p. 4). Given the popularity of social media in China, much inter-personal interaction takes place online. It is a sociological truism that the way people act or behave is influenced by those who stand before them, that is people present themselves in different ways with different audiences in order to achieve a desirable self-image (Goffman, 1959). However, social media usually involves interacting with others who are not physically visible. These "undetectable others" undoubtedly influence self-presentation on social media in China (Tian & Menchik, 2016).

Scholars of new media argue that social media encompasses different audiences from various networks who are situated together in one place, a scenario better known as "context collapse" (Davis & Jurgenson, 2014; Marwick & boyd, 2011). Without a physical co-presence, potential audiences can only be mentally constructed when determining how information is shared (Litt, 2012; Marwick & boyd, 2011). Therefore, online disclosures are usually oriented by the "imagined audience" (regular respondents), who often do not resemble the actual audience (including both regular respondents and other unaccounted readers during posting) (Tian & Menchik, 2016). As a result, interactions can involve unsolicited observers when the discourse is initially composed online (boyd, 2008; Davis & Jurgenson, 2014).

This problem of context collapse and its impacts on self-presentation online are especially salient in the Chinese context because the Chinese culture places much importance on maintaining 'face' (*mianzi*) and doing 'face-work' in front of others within the same social network (Hwang, 1987). Face is the respect or deference received from one's social network (Ho, 1976). Face-work involves the projection of self-image and impression management, with the goal to shape and instil a favourable image. Face is gained by successfully performing one or more specific social roles that are well recognised by others (Hu, 1944); the loss or gain of face leads to changes in social prestige (Yang, 1945).

Social face is a powerful force and is often used to explain findings such as the tendency of the Chinese to avoid conflicts (Tse, Francis & Walls, 1994). However, little empirical work has been done on how social face influences online interactions with a physically invisible audience. In this article, I shall therefore examine how the Chinese culture of face influences self-presentation on social media. I discuss how Chinese users present themselves online, and how this is related to the Chinese face culture, as well as whether face is still important in online interactions even though there is a physically invisible audience. Consequently, the findings reveal that while students use both RenRen and Facebook social media platforms, they are much more frequently and intensely engaged with the former. Although the two platforms are technically similar, the students present themselves in very different ways on the two sites. They are very mindful of using Chinese on RenRen and English on Facebook. They share personal news, pictures of travel abroad and pictures of a social nature on Facebook. However, fewer personal experiences are shared on RenRen – pictures of travel usually only show mainland China, and there are minor everyday complaints or gossip, and a sharing of practical information.

The findings also show that although the other parties in online interactions may not be physically or immediately present, face-work is still essential. The strategies that the students use for face-work are based on their careful weighing of their own perceived relative status, and that of the other parties involved. Consideration of the nature of the relationship and the relative status between the user and the perceived audiences determine the amount and type of information disclosed.

In the following, I will first discuss the background to how self-presentation is influenced by different others, why the culture of face is so important in the Chinese context and how this is reflected when interacting on social media. I will then provide a brief introduction of the methodology used in my research of mainland Chinese students in universities in Hong Kong. I will consider the students' ideas on self-representation and their perceived audiences on both Facebook and RenRen. Finally, I will compare how these students present themselves differently on these two platforms.

Self-presentation and the Culture of Face Online: A Background

It has been shown that the presence and response of others affect the formation of our self-images (Cooley, 1922; Mead, 1965). How we present ourselves largely relies on our definition of our audience and the degree of their involvement in our interactions (Goffman, 1959). Many factors contribute to how we perceive our audience, including the physical distance between the speakers, visible manners, audible tonal inflections and the socio-cultural background of the audience (e.g. Bell, 1984; Labov, 1966).

In face-to-face interactions, Goffman (1967) posited that one acts out a line, or a certain pattern of verbal and non-verbal expressions, that establishes one's identity and how one considers him/herself to relate to others who are present (p. 5). This in turn, affects "face", which Goffman defined as "the positive social value a person effectively claims for (her) himself by the line others assume (s) he has taken during a particular contact" (p. 5). Goffman (1967) therefore indicated that face is situationally defined by the immediate respect that one expects others to show in each specific social encounter. Face-work is calculated to avoid personal embarrassment and maintain self-respect.

The phenomenon of face is found in all societies, but academics have argued that face is more important in China due to its hierarchical structure of status inequality (Blau, Ruan, & Ardelt, 1991) and that the self is defined through relations with others (Chu, 1985; Fairbank, 1991). Although not restricted to East Asians, protecting social face is especially valued in Chinese society to promote interpersonal relationships (Bond & Lee, 1981; Brunner & Wang, 1988; Earley, 1997). It has been argued that Chinese people strongly emphasise interpersonal harmony more than Westerners (Bond & Lee 1981; Markus & Kitayama, 1991; Ting-Toomey, 1988) and place great importance on the maintaining of relationships. Chinese people are particularly motivated to protect the face of others and are equally concerned that their own face is accepted (Boisot & Child, 1996).

However, in doing so, Chinese individuals are expected to use different standards and different degrees of intimacy to interact with people (Fei, 1948; Hwang, 1987) because face gain or loss is related to the ingrained inequality in the Chinese hierarchical structure (Blau et al., 1991). For example, one must be obedient to superiors, considerate to friends and authoritative to lower social status individuals. "In the context of Chinese culture, these principles are much more emphasised than elsewhere" (Hwang, 1987, p. 949). During social interaction, Chinese people therefore carefully consider the nature of the relationship to determine their appropriate moves. If they do not behave as expected, they may then lose face. Based on empirical research, Gao (1998) found that the need and concern for face and regard for the "other" have an important role in what, as well as how and why, something is communicated in a particular context among the Chinese. Indeed, the pursuit of gaining face and the avoidance of losing face have been generally recognised as priorities of the Chinese to gain respect in front of their peers; they do not only represent reputation and prestige, but they also have social value (Barbalet, 2014; Yang, 1945). Face-work is also therefore carried out with the goal to achieve social status or prestige (Hu, 1944).

Face can be confirmed or disconfirmed. The confirmation of face leads to a gain in social status and prestige, the latter, a loss of face or lower status. The mutual confirmation of social face is personally rewarding and strengthens relationships (Hwang, 1987). Disconfirmation of face as a resource loss might motivate individuals to withdraw from the relationship. People are expected to both prevent disconfirmation and make restitutions after they have suffered an affront to their face (Goffman, 1967).

The impact of social face is considered powerful and often used to explain findings such as the tendency of Asians to avoid conflict or open-minded discussion of diverse views (Tse et al., 1994). However, little empirical work has directly studied social face, especially how the consideration of face influences self-presentation or interpersonal interaction. To fill this gap, this paper therefore examines how the characteristics of interactional venues of social media and the Chinese face culture influence self-presentation on social media.

Social media is a compelling field site for studying interpersonal interactions and the presentation of self as much of these take place online, especially for youths (see Holmes & Choudhury, Chapter 8 in this volume). However, online settings have different technical affordances than conventional face-to-face interactions. Constraints are imposed that ultimately influence whom interactants perceive their audience to be, and also specify the meaning assigned to messages (Menchik & Tian, 2008). These constraints mean that the audience can be ambiguous, and social media users have a limited awareness of it. Consequently, they may post content online that does not take their relationship with some of the readers into consideration which could cause problems during interpretation (Tian & Menchik, 2016). Also, interaction and presentation of the self on social media largely depends on text or pictures, which are more difficult to interpret meaning from as opposed to face-to-face interactions, since paralinguistic cues, gestures and body language are absent (Menchik & Tian, 2008). The audience is forced to rely on their own interpretations of the postings.

In considering the uniqueness of interaction in virtual encounters, I explore how technical settings influence self-presentation on social media in the Chinese context. In particular, I examine the interplay of technological affordances and the Chinese face culture, its influence on the way that users present themselves on social media and the unintended consequences of their attempts at self-expression.

Study Results

Methodology

To understand how the Chinese face culture influences self-presentation online, I conducted in-depth interviews in Mandarin Chinese with mainland undergraduates at three Hong Kong universities. Since 1997, mainland Chinese students have been permitted to enrol in Hong Kong universities. There were 11,376 mainland students enrolled in the academic year of 2013–2014, and the number continues to increase (UGC Statistics, 2016). I recruited 23 females and 19 males, 42 students in total, through a non-random quota sampling method.

I asked for basic demographic information as well as information on the use of different social media services, including social network composition and online activities. The interviews provided details on how the students personified themselves online and why they chose that personification, and on their imagined audiences and how their perception of their audiences influenced the contents posted and posting style.

I also conducted online observations on both RenRen and Facebook from March 2011 onwards.[1] I asked for permission to add the respondents as 'friends' so that I could observe their online activities on a daily basis, including the contents of their profile, messages, pictures, language used, etc. The interview data and online ethnographic information provided an understanding of both the online self-presentation style of the respondents in the broader context of the specific online platform as well as the underlying reasons for their online behaviour.

Self-representation and Perceived Audiences

Although the respondents used both RenRen and Facebook, their engagement was very different with the two platforms. They spent much less time on the latter, and posted on the two social media sites with very different styles because the perceived audiences are different. They individualised themselves on Facebook, but focused on shared experiences on RenRen. The students tended to use Facebook for contact with local Hong Kong or international students, and RenRen with other mainland students:

> The Mainland students use both Facebook and RenRen and... don't use Facebook that often. Sometimes I add... local and international students, such as my classmates or hallmates. But since I'm not a committed Facebook user, I don't add too many people.
>
> (Case 8, male)

Students also did not actively interact with local and international friends on their Facebook because they did not use the account very often:

> I use Facebook probably twice a month... use RenRen more often, daily perhaps. If something comes up, I would post it on RenRen and ask for help. I wouldn't use Facebook to do that.
>
> (Case 11, female)

The audiences of the respondents on RenRen were high school friends who were still in mainland China and other mainland students in Hong Kong, especially those who were attending the same university. High school friends were considered important, especially those who were enrolled in different universities in mainland China, because many of the respondents still considered them as their reference group:

> Heard a girl complain that her high school roommate, who is not as good-looking and smart as her, is now interning at Goldman Sachs. Our parents also tell us these things; they like to compare us with other kids.
>
> (Case 31, male)

Here, the student observed that mainland students in Hong Kong still think of their hometown peers as one of their important reference groups. This is because their parents in their hometowns would exchange recent updates about the students. Many of these students studying in Hong Kong and their parents believed that they were more privileged as they were pursuing an education at a Hong Kong university, or at least as elite as those enrolled in the top universities in China. Students in mainland universities also recognised this status differential, but were reluctant to admit it to their former classmates who were studying in Hong Kong because it disadvantaged them. This is because mainland students who wish to study in Hong Kong must also take the national college examination like other students who want to attend universities in mainland China, but are recruited through a special enrolment programme. If accepted, they pay a much higher tuition fee of over HK$ 140,000 (around US$ 18,000) per year (Tian, 2016). Also, many Hong Kong institutions only use English for instruction, and the curriculum and school schedules are also quite different from those in mainland China.

The following student demonstrated this clear awareness of his relative status and the expectations of other people. Indeed, many were mindful of their audiences on RenRen, and admit that their RenRen postings were very different from their Facebook postings due to the different audiences:

> I know that I am more privileged than my high-school friends because I am in Hong Kong for university. But they think that our status is the same. So I have to be careful not to say anything that might look like I am showing off, so that I don't come across as snobby.
>
> (Case 25, male)

The most obvious difference was the language used on the two sites – only simplified Chinese was used on RenRen and English on Facebook.

In the latter, this was due to their audience of international friends. When the respondents were further asked about why English was not used on RenRen they indicated that they did not want their hometown friends to feel that they had changed after leaving for Hong Kong. They strived to 'be equals' with their hometown friends.

However, despite the fact that they may only have had a few international friends who couldn't read Chinese on Facebook, and many other friends who were mainland or local Hong Kong students with the ability to read Chinese, they were still reluctant to use Chinese on Facebook because "it's better to show that I have confidence in my English skills and feel comfortable posting in English" (Case 3, female). Facebook was therefore a place to demonstrate that their English skills were comparable to those of the local students.

The contents of their postings on RenRen and Facebook were also quite different due to their careful consideration of their relationship with their imagined audiences and their relative status. Many consider RenRen to be 'Chinese' so they followed Chinese cultural norms, for instance, they "do not shout private issues out loud". Facebook is considered 'Western' so it was acceptable to be more upfront. In other words, RenRen was a platform to express commonality for bonding purposes, but Facebook was a venue to compete and show off. This was better reflected in the contents of the postings, which will be discussed in the following sections.

Self-presentation Online: A Comparison

Self-presentation on RenRen

The student respondents were very sensitive to their different audiences and knew that others were viewing their postings.[2] As their contacts on RenRen were mainly mainland Chinese, they avoided using English and mentioning holidays or school breaks in Hong Kong because their mainland counterparts had different and usually fewer school breaks. They also avoided commenting about going abroad, securing an internship position or obtaining a job offer. One of the student respondents elaborated:

> I use RenRen to keep in touch with my old friends. I graduated from a Mainland high school, and now I'm here, so this is my way of connecting... I post... neutral things... nothing controversial. Say that I get a job offer, I wouldn't post it on RenRen... The Mainland has a competitive culture, so if we post anything that we do in Hong Kong or abroad, some people may be uncomfortable, and think that I'm just trying to show off.

> (Case 27, female)

This respondent was aware that if she posted anything that reflected her privileged status in Hong Kong, she would be disconfirming the face of her hometown friends. Therefore, she was careful to ensure that her postings would not "upset" other people. Showing off is considered inappropriate or inconsiderate in the Chinese face culture because the face of other people is hurt when it is implied that they are less successful. When one hurts the face of other people, one's own face is also lost. That is why the students were so concerned with whether they had upset other people.

Another student indicated that to maintain an "equal" status with his hometown friends, he avoided posting finance-related information:

> I'm a finance major and have always been interested in keeping track of this kind of information, but I won't circulate it... on my RenRen account... It's not a good idea to have others think that I'm all about business, otherwise, they're all going to avoid me. My high school classmates talk about games, TV dramas... So it's not a good idea for me to discuss something that makes me seem pretentious...
>
> (Case 40, male)

Similar to this respondent, many of other students also indicated that the safest topic of discussion was related to entertainment because there was no demonstration of privilege and therefore it would not affect nor disconfirm the face of others. Other 'safe' topics included complaints about daily life or gossip about relationships. These were considered safe because they presented a low-profile and unthreatening image of the user.

RenRen was also a popular place to share various practical information with mainland students who sought advice related to their daily tasks and practical problems (e.g. visa applications); such advice was rarely found on Facebook. Also, RenRen users were more likely to seek help and favours than those posting on Facebook, for example such as borrowing textbooks. This was also seen as effective – most of the time, someone lent assistance (Tian, 2016).

The students considered RenRen "their own" (*ziji ren*) highly intimate community with contributing members. Most importantly, they felt they could use RenRen and still take the feelings of other people into consideration, as well as confirm and avoid hurting the face of others, and, in so doing, gain face as well.

Self-presentation on Facebook

In contrast, the student respondents did not consider Facebook as their own community because the perceived audiences were international *and* local Hong Kong students. While they tended to want to bond with other mainland students who were still studying in the mainland (i.e. their high school friends), and considered them as peers – albeit lower in status, although they avoided emphasising this superiority to give face to their mainland peers – they considered other international and local students who are also studying in Hong Kong as their competitors whom they desired to outperform. Therefore, Facebook was a place to flaunt and compete for attention or higher status, as expressed by the following female student:

> Facebook has too much stuff going on, such as postings of funny videos, vacation pictures that are photo-shopped, current news, and debates. A random posting won't get anyone's attention. It's kind of like a public bulletin board where everyone posts to show off and look their best.
>
> (Case 22, female)

In contrast to RenRen Facebook was considered a good venue to broadcast personal news, for example, when the mainland students had a job offer or secured an internship position:

> My Facebook posts are different from my RenRen posts. I would post about things that happened (to me) in Hong Kong or abroad. If I got a job offer or secured an internship position… go abroad for an exchange program… I would post on Facebook but rarely or not on RenRen.
>
> (Case 19, male)

Travel pictures are an interesting type of posts because while the students would post them on both SNSs, they tended to post domestic travel on RenRen and international travel on Facebook:

> I definitely update my Facebook more often when I go overseas. Like for an exchange program or a vacation abroad. But I usually don't post overseas travel pictures on RenRen. The first time I went overseas, I posted quite a lot on RenRen because I was a newbie then… But… my posting caused conflict between me and some of my old friends (in Mainland China), (so) I stopped doing that… My friends on RenRen… share pictures of their travel around China. If I go to Xinjiang province, I'll post those pictures on RenRen, because others (who are studying in Mainland China) can afford to go there too.
>
> (Case 2, male)

In general, mainland students who are studying in Hong Kong have more opportunities to travel abroad in various programmes, and it is also easier for them to obtain visas. This student indicated that he changed his posting contents on RenRen after they aroused conflict.

However, international and local students commonly travel around the world and post pictures on Facebook. Therefore, the mainland students in Hong Kong also take part in this practice to show that they are equally global and well-travelled, perhaps to counteract the usual impression that mainland Chinese students have minimal opportunities to travel abroad.

The presentation of the self in front of international and especially local Hong Kong students has further increased in complication given the current political climate in Hong Kong. In recent years, the Hong Kong–mainland conflicts have led to discrimination towards the mainland Chinese in Hong Kong. Indeed, nearly 17 years after the reunification of Hong Kong with China, tension between the two continue to mount (Lai, 2012; Tharoor, 2014). Such tensions can be seen in the anti-national education movement (Ko, 2012), protests against mainland tourists who visit Hong Kong to shop (Shadbolt, 2014) and the social media fuelled controversies around a mainland child being allowed to urinate in Hong Kong streets (Tharoor, 2014). These incidents have attracted wide media coverage and online discussions in Hong Kong (Adorjan & Yau, 2015). Related to the increasing tensions is the identity issue. In recent years, more Hong Kongers recognise themselves first and foremost as Hong Kong citizens instead of Chinese (Ko, 2012). Some hold negative stereotypes of the mainland Chinese. As a result, the latter have been accused of violating social rules in Hong Kong (Chow, 2012), and some mainland Chinese tourists have encountered discrimination because of language and social norm differences (Ye, Zhang, & Yuen, 2013).

Mainland students who study in Hong Kong are situated within this context of conflicts. Although attitudes may greatly vary at the individual level, the respondents tended to have different viewpoints on the various events related to Hong Kong–mainland conflicts. This is why some also shared particular information on China on their Facebook account to counter the negative opinions of local youth in China and the mainland Chinese in general:

> I mainly share information on China on Facebook, because I mainly use it to connect with local and international students... I might post an article from the Financial Times on China so that they have more information... if I read something that would create misunderstandings about China, I will post... on my Facebook page and correct the information. For example, I saw a picture of a Chinese antique that was mistaken by foreigners for a cup and they used it for drinking. But it is actually used for spitting out phlegm... I posted this on Facebook... it's my responsibility to show them things that they do not know about China.
>
> (Case 5, male)

The student quoted above felt that he was providing knowledge and demonstrating diligence. Many of the other respondents also indicated that their Facebook account served this purpose.

To further counter the discrimination in Hong Kong, many of the respondents also admitted that they have flaunted their achievements on Facebook, such as academic performance, successful internships or penchant for high culture or fashionable items and sometimes even for luxury (such as staying in five-star hotels), to show that they were well-off, hard-working, open-minded and academically inclined. Their intentions were to demonstrate superiority to the local students, and gain status and face in the context of discrimination against the mainland Chinese in Hong Kong.

In summary, online self-presentation is closely related to the perceived audiences. The student respondents are modest and low profile individuals on RenRen as the main audiences are hometown friends and other mainland students in Hong Kong. They attempt to conform and avoid being seen as competitive or overly serious, and also downplay their privileged status so as to avoid harming the face of their hometown friends. However, their perceived audiences on Facebook are international and local students, and consequently, the opposite is true.

Conclusion

I have shown here that students present themselves in very different ways on RenRen and Facebook due to differences between the two imagined audiences. Although the other parties of the interaction may not be physically or immediately present, considerations of face are still essential in determining the style and content of their postings. The strategies on self-presentation are based on careful determination of perceived relative status – both their own and that of the other parties involved – because even though the latter may not be physically or immediately present on the social media, face-work is still essential.

Due to this evaluation of relationships, the relative status of others and avoidance of disconfirmation of face, RenRen users rarely post items that underline privilege and status; consequently, trivial daily life updates, complaints, domestic travel photos and practical information dominate the postings. Anything more would be inconsiderate of the feelings of others and arouse controversy. However, the opposite is true on Facebook. Additionally, many have found that the best way to maintain or gain face on RenRen is a low profile and alignment of emotions and actions. Conversely, the best strategy on Facebook is a relatively high profile to compete with their international counterparts.

Although this study focuses empirically on mainland Chinese students in Hong Kong, the research findings on the importance of the perceived audience on social media, as well as how people present themselves differently on different online platforms, can be also applied to other forms of online interactions. When people present themselves online, their perception of the potential audience, and evaluation of their relationship and relative status with them, still have key importance. That is why they present themselves in very different ways on the two technically similar platforms. Based on this line of thinking, on online platforms with a wider and more anonymous audience (such as Twitter and Weibo) or those more closed networks (such as WeChat), we might expect users to behave in different ways.

This research affirms the resilience of cultural influence on interpersonal interactions, even online, where people often interact with undetectable others. The Chinese face culture, that is the emphasis placed on gaining face and confirming the face of others, extends to the online sphere. Yet because social media offers a wider and less predictable arena for face-work, the consequences of misjudgment are different from those of face-to-face interaction, in which all interactants immediately feel the embarrassment caused by the loss of face. On social media, for example, sometimes it takes time for the user to realise that s/he has posted information that has led to the loss of face. Whether social media has any reverse impacts on the face culture can be the direction of future research.

Funding

This work was supported by the Public Policy Funding Scheme of the Central Policy Unit of the HKSAR Government. The project number is 2014.A8.027.15B.

Notes

1 Since 2013, RenRen has been largely replaced by WeChat. However, the data in this chapter were collected during 2011-2012 as at that time, RenRen was still the dominating social media for Chinese students. Now, even though students prefer WeChat, the self-presentation strategies are very similar, at least as shown in my recent study on its use. Therefore, the theoretical argument that I have made in this chapter still holds.
2 Both male and female mainland Chinese students in different majors and from different hometowns tend to act in very similar ways on RenRen and Facebook. This is probably because the mainland Chinese students who are studying in Hong Kong are a highly homogeneous group in terms of social class background and orientation (Tian, 2016).

References

Adorjan, M., & Yau, A. (2015). Resinicization and digital citizenship in Hong Kong: Youth, cyberspace and claims-making. *Qualitative Sociological Review, XI*, 2.

Barbalet, J. (2014). The structure of guanxi: Resolving problems of network assurance. *Theory and Society, 43*, 51–69.

Bell, A. (1984). Language style as audience design. *Language in Society, 13,* 145–204.

Blau, P. M., Ruan, D., & Ardelt, M. (1991). Interpersonal choice and networks in China. *Social Forces, 69*(4), 1037–1062.

Boisot, M., & Child, J. (1996). From fiefs to clans and network capitalism: Explaining China's emerging economic order. *Administrative Science Quarterly, 41,* 600–628.

Bond, M. H., & Lee, P. W. H. (1981). Face-saving in Chinese culture: A discussion and experimental study of Hong Kong students. In A. King & R. Lee (Eds.), *Social life and development in Hong Kong* (pp. 288–305). Hong Kong: Chinese University Press.

boyd, d. (2008). Why youth (heart) social network sites: The role of networked publics in teenage social life. In D. Buckingham (Ed.), *Youth, identity and digital media* (pp. 199–242). Cambridge, MA: MIT Press.

Brunner J. A., & Wang, Y. (1988). Chinese negotiating and the concept of face. *Journal of International Consumer Marketing, 1,* 27–43.

Chow, V. (Feb. 1, 2012). Anger at mainland visitors escalates with 'locust' ad. *South China Morning Post.*

Chu, G. C. (1985). The changing concept of self in contemporary China, In A. J. Marsella, G. DeVos, & F. L. K. Hsu (Eds.), *Culture and self: Asian and western perspectives* (pp. 141–166). New York: Tavistock Publications.

CNNIC (China Internet Network Information Center). (2015). Di 36 ci Zhongguo hu lian wang luo fa zhan bao gao *(The 36th report on the development of internet in China),* July 2015, online report, accessed 10 October 2015.

Cooley, C. H. (1922). *Human nature and the social order.* New York/Chicago, IL: Charles Scribner's Sons.

Davis, J. L., & Jurgenson, N. (2014). Context collapse: Theorizing context collusions and collisions. *Information, Communication & Society, 17*(4), 476–485.

Earley, P. C. (1997). Doing an about face: Social motivation and cross-cultural currents. In P. C. Earley & M. Erez (Eds.), *New perspectives on international industrial organization psychology* (pp. 243–275). San Francisco, CA: Jossey-Bass.

Fairbank, J. K. (1991). The old order. In R. F. Dernberger, K. J. DeWoskin, J. M. Goldstein, R. Murphey, & M. K. Whyte (Eds.), *The Chinese* (pp. 20–26). University of Michigan, MI: Center for Chinese Studies.

Fei, H. T. (1948). *Peasant life in China.* London, UK: Routledge and Kegan.

Gao, G. (1998). An initial analysis of the effects of face and concern for "other" in Chinese interpersonal communication. *International Journal of Intercultural Relations, 22*(4), 467–482.

Goffman, E. (1959). *The presentation of self in everyday life.* New York: Anchor Books.

Goffman, E. (1967). *Interaction ritual: Essays in face-to-face behavior.* Chicago, IL: Aldine Publishing.

Ho, D. Y. (1976). On the concept of face. *American Journal of Sociology, 81*(4), 867–884.

Hu, H. C. (1944). The Chinese concept of face. *American Anthropologist, 46,* 45–64.

Hwang, K. K. (1987). Face and favor: The Chinese power game. *American Journal of Sociology*, *92*, 944–974.

Ko, V. (2012, July 30). Hong Kong divided over plans for patriotic lessons in schools. *Time*. Retrieved from http://world.time.com/2012/07/30/hong-kong-divided-over-plans-for-patriotic-lessons-in-schools/.

Labov, W. (1966). *The social stratification of English in New York City* (2nd ed.). Cambridge, UK: Cambridge University Press.

Lai, A. (2012, February 8). Hong Kong newspaper ad rails against Chinese 'invasion'. *CNN*. Retrieved from http://edition.cnn.com/2012/02/01/world/asia/locust-mainlander-ad/.

Litt, E. (2012). Knock, knock. Who's there? The imagined audience. *Journal of Broadcasting & Electronic Media*, *56*(3), 330–345.

Markus, H. R., & Kitayama, S. (1991). Culture and the self: Implications for cognition, emotion, and motivation. *Psychological Review*, *98*, 224–253.

Marwick, A. E., & boyd, B. (2011). I tweet honestly, I tweet passionately: Twitter users, context collapse, and the imagined audience. *New Media & Society*, *13*(1), 114–133.

Mead, G. H. (1965). *Mind, self and society from the standpoint of a social behaviorist*. Chicago, IL: Chicago University Press.

Menchik, D., & Tian, X. L. (2008). Putting social context into text: The semiotics of email interaction. *American Journal of Sociology*, *114*, 332–70.

Shadbolt, P. (2014, March 7). Hong Kong protests take aim at 'locust' shoppers from mainland China. *CNN*. Retrieved from http://edition.cnn.com/2014/03/07/world/asia/hong-kong-china-visitors-controversy/.

Tharoor, I. (2014, April 30). Chinese toddler pees in Hong Kong street, stirs online firestorm. *Washington Post*. Retrieved from www.washingtonpost.com/blogs/worldviews/wp/2014/04/30/chinese-toddler-pees-in-hong-kong-street-stirs-online-firestorm/.

Tian, X. L. (2016) Network domains in social networking sites: Expectations, meanings, and social capital. *Information, Communication & Society*, *19*(2), 188–202.

Tian, X., & Menchik, D. A. (2016). On violating one's own privacy: N-adic utterances and inadvertent disclosures in online venues. *Studies in Media and Communications*, *11*, 3–30.

Ting-Toomey S. (1988). A face negotiation theory. In Y. Y. Kim, & W. B. Gudykunst (Eds.), *Theory and intercultural communication* (pp. 47–92). Thousand Oaks, CA: Sage.

Tse, D. K., Francis J., & Walls, J. (1994). Cultural differences in conducting intra- and inter-cultural negotiations: A Sino-Canadian comparison. *Journal of International Business*, *24*, 537–555.

UGC Statistics. (2016). General statistics on UGC-funded institutions/programmes. University Grants Committee, Hong Kong SAR. Retrieved from http://cdcf.ugc.edu.hk/cdcf/searchStatSiteReport.do.

Yang, M. C. (1945). *A Chinese village*. New York: Columbia University Press.

Ye, B. H., Zhang, H. Q., & Yuen, P. P. (2013). Cultural conflicts or cultural cushion? *Annals of Tourism Research*, *43*, 321–349.

8   RenRen and Social Capital in Contemporary China

David Holmes and Naziat Choudhury

As the Facebook of China, RenRen has been a popular networking site in that country for a decade. Since the renaming of Xiaonei.com to Ren-Ren in 2009 it has grown from having 83 million users to 228 million in 2015 (Statista, 2016). In China, RenRen, like Facebook, grew out of a university context of young users, but quickly broadened out to a general urban demographic. Alexa.com (2016) shows that non-college background users of the site are comparable with non-college users generalised to the Chinese internet. Further, the usage prohibition of international social networking sites (SNS) in China has attracted users of all demographics to home grown sites like RenRen.

In more recent times, RenRen, as with other dedicated online SNS, has led many users to integrated apps like WeChat that emphasise a messaging function. This situation is similar to Facebook in the USA; however, Facebook has retained users by anticipating the shift to messenger apps and simply buying these apps like WhatsApp. RenRen seemed to have failed to take such steps which may have led to its decline in popularity. Recently, RenRen witnessed a decrease in the number of monthly active users – falling from 54 million in 2013 to 44 million in 2014 (China Internet Watch, 2014) and then to 41 million users in 2015 (Ren-Ren, 2016).

Social media demographics in China are rapidly responding to changing urban conditions. Economic development has led to much greater urbanisation and we argue that these changes have created the conditions for online social media to flourish. Whyte and Parish (1984) argued that the Cultural Revolution and the economic reform led people to isolation and to remain confined to a small number of close friends. In today's world, however, social capital in urban areas based on face-to-face interaction is declining. There are many studies – albeit all non-China based research – which point to the way social capital in urban life has migrated to SNS. (Ahn, 2012; Ellison, Steinfield, & Lampe, 2007; Miller, 2011; Valenzuela, Park, & Kee, 2008; Vitak, Ellison, & Steinfield, 2011). Without investing time in physical interaction, SNS offer a platform to maintain existing and newly built relationships.

In the case of China, the study of social media is underdeveloped, and has had little exposure to western media studies traditions. This paper investigates how Chinese urbanisation has created the conditions for the popularity of RenRen. Through RenRen as a case study and meta-analysis of secondary sources (such as articles, books and theses) we examine the ways in which RenRen is an instance of how social capital has, like in other countries, migrated online in China. We argue that the decline of social capital in the institutional and street life of the large Chinese mega-cities has led to compensatory forms of assembly online. It is also argued that RenRen was a pioneering site in this regard and that what began on RenRen has spread to other social media in China. But what is distinctive about RenRen, we argue, is that it is most suited to a particular form of social capital known as 'bridging social capital'. The benefit of this type of capital is the ability to maintain low intensity relationships across very large groups. An explanation of this difference is set out in a discussion of the role of the Confucian principal *guanxi* in the migration of social capital to RenRen.

Online Social Capital Research

RenRen offers its users platforms for social interaction. As for what might cause people to assemble on RenRen, social interaction is the focal point. Studies suggest a close link between social interaction on Facebook and social capital (Bruke, Kraut, & Marlow, 2011; Ellison et al., 2007; Valenzuela et al., 2008); however, the research on Facebook predominantly looks at individual behaviour in relation to online SNS. This study proposes to shift from individual centric to social centric. To the extent that the urban settings of social capital have moved online in China, RenRen is a paradigm case because it was the first SNS to demonstrate this trend.

The maintenance of relationships on RenRen is best explained through the theory of social capital. To study the social capital aspect of RenRen, we explore, as a starting point, the applicability of Robert Putnam's (2000) theory of social capital to Chinese social media. Putnam, a political scientist, conceptualised social capital from the civil society and civic engagement perspective. While explaining the term more elaborately Putnam (2000) states:

> Whereas physical capital refers to physical objects and human capital refers to the properties of individuals, social capital refers to connections among individuals – social networks and the norms of reciprocity and trustworthiness that arise from them. In that sense social capital is closely related to what some have called "civic virtue". The difference is that "social capital" calls attention to the fact that civic virtue is most powerful when embedded in a sense

network of reciprocal social relations. A society of many virtuous
but isolated individuals is not necessarily rich in social capital

(p. 19)

Psychologists, also in the USA tradition, tend to associate social capital with the concept of "social support" (Burke et al., 2011). Social capital refers to the benefit that one attains through their social relationships. These benefits may include sharing information and emotional support and other forms of benefits including economic benefits (Ellison, Steinfield, & Lampe, 2011). The form of benefits depends upon the relationships and the individual's status in their social network. Hence, social capital is divided into two categories – bridging and bonding social capital. Here, bridging social capital is referred to as benefits attained through weak ties such as acquaintances. Bonding social capital is related to strong ties where benefits are obtained through close-knit relationships.

In USA literature, the main elements of social capital are rooted in traditions of classical sociology. The most common concepts that can be found in social capital analyses of Facebook are used as parameters to measure social capital – these concepts are community, social interaction and social relationships, trust and reciprocity. To these we add the concept of *guanxi* in our discussion of RenRen. What RenRen has in common with social networking around the world is that it became popular as a response to users overcoming the volume of relationships and interactions that characterise settings of large scale integration – that is in large cities and metropolises. In China, as with other highly urbanised or urbanising nations around the world, SNS exhibit their highest per capita density. This idea is supported by older studies on Facebook and MySpace which have identified both as overwhelmingly urban networking services (see Bumgarner, 2007; Van Doorn, 2010).

What is also distinctive about social networking is that participation is grounded in external contexts wherein online relationships reproduce and reinforce offline connections between the same groups of people. This is a departure from early experience of online platforms which are characterised by more anonymous and avataristic form of use (see Holmes, 2011). That is, wherever new platforms appear, there is a higher incidence of anonymity. In western nations, anonymity, typified the early years of internet use across platforms, whereas in China, there is often a 'surveillance lag' in the ability of the state to monitor communications in new platforms.

Urbanisation and a Sense of Community on RenRen

As mentioned above, in many respects any consideration of online social capital cannot be separated from the extraordinary scale of urbanisation in China. As Greenspan (2014) has observed in her recent book, Shanghai Future:

> Nowhere is the global transformation from rural to urban life more intense than in China. Here urbanisation is faster and larger than ever before. In 1980 under 20 percent of China's population lived in its cities. Today it is over 40 percent. This explosive trend shows no sign of abating. Intense high-speed urbanisation is a central tenant of the Xi Jinping/Li Keqiang regime. Government officials predict that the urban population will surpass 700 million in the next 5 years, exceeding the number of rural dwellers for the first time. McKinsey Global forecasts that by the year 2030 there will be a billion people living in Chinese cities
>
> (p. 9)

The massification of urban dwellers, the disruption to existing neighbourhoods and constant movement of new migrants to the cities as they find jobs and connections, makes online life an option that can often be more anchoring for people. As Read and Chen explain, "City residents commonly speak of the coldness and anonymity of interpersonal relations among neighbors in the new apartment complexes, compared to older neighborhoods they remember" (cited by Zhuo, 2012, p. 125). The rapid economic development in Chinese society has raised threats of social isolation (Cook & Powell, 2007) and this in turn has influenced the popularity of RenRen which is seen to help to connect social gaps that this urbanisation has created. RenRen is considered to be helping to build a sense of community through connection, social support and game playing. The role that different generations play is also considered.

The first idea, that of connection, is an important one. Social media, especially RenRen, is closely associated with the socio-cultural context of its host nation. In big cities like Shanghai and Beijing, middle-class and upper-middle-class families use social media similar to other cities of the world. SNS, like RenRen, has become a tool for them to connect and build community. For example, these cities have a large number of students who migrated from other parts of China – RenRen works as an online bridge for them to connect with those in the cities and in their home towns. Social institutions such as neighbourhood communities, kinship and family relations and working units that once used to be the platform for establishing connections are now on the wane. Online SNS like RenRen are replacing or supporting these social institutions for easier maintenance of social connection. Hence, social and cultural practices that were common in the offline world are evident on these sites as well. For example, rather than always actively engaging in conversations, the users sometimes visit the site simply to view pictures (Jiang et al., 2013; Men and Tsai, 2013).

With regard to social support features, RenRen also makes possible a form of community that provides a place to socialise with others, creating support among its users. Compared to micro-blogging sites like Sina Weibo, RenRen provides an opportunity to sympathise and secure emotional support (Zhang, Lu, Gupta, & Zhao, 2014). It is interesting to find that along with usage, uploaded images also indicate a similar pattern. For instance, photos on Sina Weibo were related to political and news items, and RenRen had images that mirrored inner emotions (Hjorth & Arnold, 2013). Therefore, users gather on the site to share certain personal causes which provide a sense of community within themselves.

Another feature of RenRen that attracts a lot of attention from users is its online games and users create a community through this feature. Online games in China enjoy vast popularity. One of the most popular games is Happy Farm which was launched on RenRen first and is known to have contributed to the increase of users on RenRen and other such online SNS (Millward, 2012). Back in 2012 when RenRen had 26 million daily users, almost half of them played some form of online games and these games contributed to its yearly profit (Hjorth & Arnold, 2013). Users of these games today are mainly the older generation who learned to use the internet to communicate with their children who relocated in another place. The basis of these games is to interact with other users and gain points through such interactions. This has helped to maintain their relationships which, as Hjorth and Arnold (2013) put it, contribute "to alleviate the negative effects of cross-generational class mobility" (p. 55). Thus, through connection, social support and game playing, RenRen helped to migrate offline community to online community.

Finally, it can be argued that the cultural attributes of RenRen, compared to Facebook, are "sharing-oriented, conformity-oriented, hierarchical, and less egalitarian" (Qiu, Lin, & Leung, 2013, p. 112). This confirms the premise above, that social media takes the form and unique culture of locality (Chu & Choi, 2010).

Generational Changes in Urban Life

The extent and nature of social media use are closely linked to changes in generational identity in urban areas since the 1980s (Li, Zheng, & Wang, 2015). During this period China first began to experience the acceleration of its economic changes, which corresponded to cultural and ideological shifts. According to Li (2009), the public moved from being overtly conscious about political engagement to being more concerned about their own personal materialistic gains such as acquiring more property and cars, and having better jobs. The younger generation are in a similar pattern; they are more interested in Korean fashion, television drama, computer games and instant messaging. In regards to the internet, younger people represent the most users and online content creators who are more inclined to upload materials that are light and superficial in nature. The influence of popular culture in every aspect of life is witnessed – it is all about expressing one's self on the internet, "a vehicle of independent self-representations" (Li, 2009, p. 50). Hence Li (2009) concluded that "With the drive to prosperity, public life in China – like that in the West at the same point in its economic development – metamorphosed from political activism to pop culture" (p. 54). Perhaps this led to a different state of mind which is now reflected in their RenRen use. Hence there has been a blending culture of past collectivist tradition and present individualistic tradition which was being transformed to online culture on RenRen.

Social Interaction and Social Relationship

In Chinese society, collectivism is a strong basis of identity. Fei, Hamilton and Wang (1992) compared the traditional social structure of China to "the circles that appear on the surface of a lake when a rock is thrown into it", to the structure of SNS where an individual "stands at the center of the circles produced by his or her own social influence" (Fei et al., 1992, pp. 62–63). RenRen was one of the first online SNS in China to enable a shared interactivity. As with Facebook, RenRen allows users to extend their offline relationships in an online setting on the basis of shared demographics and group affiliation. These users share certain commonality traits based on age, social and educational background and locality. In terms of relationships, RenRen helps to create bridging social capital. Studies have suggested that RenRen users tend to have a large network of friends on the site, often more than 150 RenRen friends (Yan, 2014). Although RenRen-based friends create more of a homogenous group (age, educational background), their large network indicates loose connections. These loose connections help to get access to informational benefits that generate bridging social capital. Therefore, this site creates more of bridging social capital than bonding social capital.

Self-disclosure on RenRen is another feature directed towards bridging social capital. One of the elements of social capital is social relationship and the production of relationships which rely on creating channels to gain information. In other words, in the online context, people need information on others to build interaction that pave the way for relationships (Liu & Brown, 2014). For example, new students expand their network for information and social support by connecting with existing students – based on information published on profiles, new students gather the courage to seek support. Hence, self-disclosure is closely linked to bridging social capital rather than bonding social capital (Liu & Brown, 2014).

Interestingly, and perhaps unlike Facebook, RenRen is used more for the purpose of communication than entertainment. Communicating with other members, especially in institutionally-based contexts, is vital here unlike with other social media in China (Wang, Jackson, Zhang, & Su, 2012). Mobile technology makes keeping connection with others easier for RenRen users. These mobile phones played a role in the expansion of social media, including RenRen, as they offered "new platforms, avenues and contexts for social and locative media engagement" (Hjorth & Arnold, 2013, p. 53). Wallis (2011) added that mobile phones are supporting the concept of "self and autonomy" that exists in Chinese culture (p. 67). Mobile phones (*shouji*) are the only personal media certain sections of the urban society owns. Before *shouji* became popular, they used to be called *dageda* (big-brother-big) (Qiu, 2008). Only the elite could afford such devices back in the 1990s. Competition in the market increased (Qiu, 2008) and now mobile phone usage allows its users to collect and share information and events which involve both "collective and individual experiences" (Hjorth & Arnold, 2013, p. 49). RenRen also offers location-based services which enable many of its users to connect with those nearby (Hjorth & Arnold, 2013, p. 52). So the use of RenRen through mobile phones made creating and maintaining relationships easier and one of the largest beneficiaries of this are the younger generation.

RenRen users build connections more easily with mobile technologies as the social constraints of face-to-face are non-existent. Online SNS provide the platform for those who feel less comfortable engaging in social interactions and, when this access is mobile, users are not even tied to rituals of place. Moreover, as mobile use is characterised by an always on perpetual contact, there is less need for RenRen users to actually meet, as the mobile connection increasingly becomes the relationship. Similar to Facebook on mobile, RenRen offers to minimise "... users' uncertainty about their social contacts and provides common ground for their subsequent communication encounters. Therefore, social information seeking can facilitate future interactions" (Rui, Covert, Stefanone, & Mukherjee, 2014, p. 13). These attributes enhance the reliability of RenRen for establishing connection and relationships. Such reliability has assisted RenRen in gaining popularity among internet users.

Trust and Reciprocity

In relation to an analysis of crime and crime control in China, Zhuo has argued that outside of family and kinship relationships, measures of trust indicate weak social ties (Zhuo, 2012). In that context, RenRen appears to be offering an easier opportunity to establish trust. RenRen is known as a 'real name' SNS which indicates that people cannot use alternative names or personas to be on the site. The real name registration process in RenRen allows its users to trust others and hence have less privacy concerns. In order to be a member of RenRen, users need to provide certain background information and therefore, the architectural design of RenRen has trust built in. As Yan (2014) claims, in order for individuals to trust and reciprocate, information such as name, educational information and hometown are needed. Studies have suggested that the majority of the users on RenRen provide the basic information. Real names, photos and birth dates are provided by more than half of the users (Yan, 2014). Perhaps because RenRen began as an education-based website this allowed for more scope to trust others. Unlike Facebook, where anyone with an email address can open an account, this site offers some form of a trustworthy platform. These features of RenRen allows users to trust others which help to build relationships.

Guanxi

Researchers have observed that social capital in China includes another element known as *guanxi*. Within the discussion of social capital through RenRen, *guanxi* practice demands attention. As mentioned previously, Chinese society put great emphasis on social relationships and within that relationship whether *guanxi* is being taken from offline to online will be discussed here. The meaning of *guanxi* is usually connoted with "social ties", "connections" or "social relationships" but as Bian (2012) points out that these Western concepts fail to justify the inherent cultural meanings associated with it (p. 40). *Guanxi* is a social and cultural practice that has stemmed from three Confucian principles, *li*, *ren* and *xiao* – structure, gentleness and obedience (Hackley & Dong, 2001). Although each are interrelated, *ren* is clearly witnessed in RenRen use, as the users are passive users, expressing inner feelings, maintaining a gentleness in their use rather than actively engaging in exchange of opinions. Hence, *guanxi* practice is visible throughout studies on RenRen, for example users preferring to shield their real emotion to maintain the social cohesion on the site could be explained as *guanxi* practice (See Tian, Chapter 7 in this volume).

Hwang (1997) explains that "...the major goal for an individual to interact with the other party is to utilize their *guanxi* as an instrument to acquire a certain kind of resource" (p. 20). For example, gaining access to job related information easily through RenRen could be seen as a way to maximize *guanxi* through the online SNS.

Bao, or reciprocity, is also regarded as a part of *guanxi* relationships. According to Yang (1957) *guanxi* ties may fall apart due to inadequate reciprocation. Although no major connection was found between reciprocity and RenRen use, it could be stated that RenRen use is based on *guanxi* relationships. Users were united under the assumption that "... the person will be greatly helped in the future should the need arise"

(Chang & Holt, 1991, p. 262). If *guanxi* is understood as a representation of relationships and maintenance of that relationship, then RenRen use supports *guanxi* practices. *Guanxi* through social media has broadened its horizon as these media adds other channels for interpersonal communication along with the offline world. Through these media users meet new people and keep the communication running with their existing friends. In the online world, social media provides the platforms to practice *guanxi* which is to renew or form relationships outside of kinship networks. *Guanxi* plays a role to integrating users who have a connection based on an "intimate public" which avoids "other, less close contacts", a notion Habuchi terms "tele-cocooning" (Hjorth & Arnold, 2013, p. 60).

Conclusion

It has been argued in this paper that there is a strong link between rapid economic growth, the urbanisation of China and the rise of various forms of social media in China. RenRen, being one of the first online SNS in China, in many ways pioneered the shift of social capital to online forms. As this study has shown, elements of community, social relationships, trust, reciprocity and *guanxi* found through RenRen use has led to its high level of acceptability among internet users in China. But what is distinctive about RenRen, we have argued, is the way in which it enables 'bridging' forms of social capital, which expands the social world of users to scales much larger than offline, even though the intensity of those relationships remains weak. Nevertheless, in urban settings of large-scale integration RenRen has pioneered the rise of electronic assemblies in China, that has offered new levels of connection and integration that matter to so many.

References

Ahn, J. (2012). Teenagers' experiences with social network sites: Relationships to bridging and bonding social capital. *The Information Society: An International Journal*, *28*(2), 99–109.

Alexa.com (2016). *Site overview: renren.com*. Retrieved from www.alexa.com/siteinfo/renren.com.

Bian, Y. (2012). Network social capital and civic engagement in environmentalism: Findings from Chinese general social survey. In A. Daniere & H. Luong (Eds.), *Social capital and civic engagement in Asia* (pp. 37–53). London and New York: Routledge.

Bumgarner, B. A. (2007). You have been poked: Exploring the uses and gratifications of Facebook among emerging adults. *First Monday*, *12*(11).

Burke, M., Kraut, R., & Marlow, C. (2011, May). *Social capital on Facebook: Differentiating uses and users*. Paper presented at the Conference on Human Factors in Computing Systems. Vancouver, BC, pp. 1–10.

Chang, H.-C., & Holt, G. R. (1991). More than relationship: Chinese interaction and the principle of Kuan-Hsi. *Communication Quarterly*, *39*(3), 251–271.

China Internet Watch. (2014). Renren's monthly unique log-in users down to 54 Million in Q2 2014. Retrieved from www.chinainternetwatch.com/8454/renren-q2–2014/.

Chu, S., & Choi, S. M. (2010). Social capital and self-presentation on social networking sites: a comparative study of Chinese and American young generations. *Chinese Journal of Communication*, *3*(4), 402–420.

Cook, I. G., & Powell, J. L. (2007). Ageing urban society: Discourse and policy. In F. Wu (Ed.), *China's emerging cities: The making of new urbanism* (pp. 126–142). London: Routledge.

Ellison, N. B., Steinfield, C., & Lampe, C. (2007). The benefits of Facebook "friends": social capital and college students' use of online social network sites. *Journal of Computer-Mediated Communication, 12*(4), article 1. Retrieved from http://jcmc.indiana.edu/vol12/issue4/ellison.html.

Ellison, N. B., Steinfield, C., & Lampe, C. (2011). Connection strategies: Social capital implications of Facebook-enabled communication practices. *New Media & Society*, *13*(6), 873–892

Fei, H.-T., Hamilton, G. G., & Wang, Z. (1992). *From the soil: The foundations of Chinese society*. Berkeley, CA: University of California Press.

Greenspan, A. (2014). *Shanghai future: Modernity remade*. Oxford: Oxford University Press.

Hackley, C. A., & Dong, Q. (2001). American public relations networking encounters China's Guanxi. *Public Relations Quarterly*, *46*, 16–19.

Hjorth, L., & Arnold, M. (2013). *Online@AsiaPacific: Mobile, social and locative media in the Asia-Pacific*. London: Routledge.

Holmes, D. (2011). What's "social" about social media. *Communications and Convergence Review*, *3*(2), 105–115.

Hwang, K.-K. (1997). Guanxi and mientze: Conflict resolution in Chinese society. *Intercultural Communication Studies*, *7*(1), 17–38.

Jiang, J., Wilson, C., Wang, X., Huang, P., Sha, W., Dai, Y., & Zhao, B. Y. (2013). Understanding latent interactions in online social networks. *ACM Transactions on the Web*, *7*(4), 1–39.

Li, H. S. (2009). The turn to the self: From "big character posters" to YouTube videos. *Chinese Journal of Communication*, *2*(1), 50–60.

Li, L., Zheng, S., & Wang, Z. (2015). An exploratory study on social media in China. In I. Tussyadiah & A. Inversini (Eds.), *Information and Communication Technologies in Tourism 2015* (pp. 255–267). Switzerland: Springer.

Liu, D., & Brown, B. B. (2014). Self-disclosure on social networking sites, positive feedback, and social capital among Chinese college students. *Computers in Human Behavior*, *38*, 213–219.

Men, L. R., & Tsai, W.-H. S. (2013). Beyond liking or following: Understanding public engagement on social networking sites in China. *Public Relations Review*, *39*, 13–22.

Miller, D. (2011). *Tales from Facebook*. Malden, MA: Polity Press.

Millward, S. (2012). The rise and fall of China's first hit social game (the one Zynga ripped off as FarmVille). *TECHINASIA*. Retrieved from www.techinasia.com/rise-fall-china-happy-farm-social-game-2012/.

Putnam, R. (2000). *Bowling alone. The collapse and revival of American community.* New York: Simon and Schuster.

Qiu, J. L. (2008). Wireless working-class ICTs and the Chinese informational city. *Journal of Urban Technology, 15*(3), 57–77.

Qiu, L., Lin, H., & Leung, A.K. (2013). Cultural differences and witching of in-group sharing behavior between an American (Facebook) and a Chinese (Renren) social networking site. *Journal of Cross-Cultural Psychology, 44*(1), 106–121.

RenRen. (2016). *Financial Report 2015.* Retrieved from http://phx.corporate-ir.net/External.File?item=UGFyZW50SUQ9MzM4MzQ4fENoaWxkSUQ 9LTF8VHlwZT0z&t=1&cb=635986201122110803.

Rui, J. R., Covert, J. M., Stefanone, M. A., & Mukherjee, T. (2014). A communication multiplexity approach to social capital on- and offline communication and self-esteem. *Computers in Human Behavior, 49*, 1–21.

Statista. (2016). Number of Renren.com users in China from 2009 to 2015 (in millions). Retrieved from www.statista.com/statistics/227059/number-of-renren-com-users-in-china/.

Valenzuela, S., Park, N., & Kee K. F. (2008). *Lessons from Facebook: The effect of social network sites on college students' social capital.* Submitted to the 9th International Symposium on Online Journalism Austin, Texas, April 4–5, 2008.

Van Doorn N. (2010). The ties that bind: The networked performance of gender sexuality, and friendship on MySpace. *New Media and Society, 12*(4), 583–602.

Vitak, J., Ellison, N. B., & Steinfield, C. (2011). *The ties that bond: Re-examining the relationship between Facebook use and bonding social capital.* Paper presented at the 44th Hawaii International Conference on System Sciences, Kauai, HI, USA, 4–7 January 2011.

Wallis, C. (2011). (Im)mobile mobility: Marginal youth and mobile phones in Beijing. In R. Ling & S. W. Campbell (Eds.), *Mobile communication: Bringing us together and tearing us apart* (pp. 61–81). New Brunswick, NJ: Transaction Publishers.

Wang, J.-L., Jackson, L. A., Zhang, D.-J., & Su, Z.-Q. (2012). The relationships among the big five personality factors, self-esteem, narcissism, and sensation-seeking to Chinese university students' uses of social networking sites (SNSs). *Computers in Human Behavior, 28*(6), 2313–2319.

Whyte, M. K., & Parish, W. L. (1984). *Urban life in contemporary China.* Chicago, IL: University of Chicago Press.

Yan, J. (2014). *Understanding Chinese student social networking interpersonal communication at RenRen.com.* (Master's Degree Thesis). Uppsala University, Sweden.

Yang, L.-s. (1957). The concept of "pao" as a basis for social relations in China. In J. K. Fairbank (Ed.), *Chinese thought and institutions* (pp. 291–309). Chicago, IL: University of Chicago Press.

Zhang, H., Lu, Y., Gupta, S., & Zhao, L. (2014). What motivates customers to participate in social commerce? The impact of technological environments and virtual customer experiences. *Information & Management, 51*, 1017–1030.

Zhuo, Y. (2012). Social capital and satisfaction with crime control in urban China. *Asian Criminology, 7*, 121–136.

Part III

Chinese Social Media and Disability

9 WeChat and the Voice Donor Campaign

An Example of 'Doing Good' on Social Media

Mike Kent, Katie Ellis, He Zhang and Danjing Zhang

China has the largest population of people who are blind in the world at 5 million people (World Health Organisation, 2017). While this figure constitutes 18 percent of the total global population of people who are blind, it represents a mere 0.4 percent of the Chinese population (World Health Organisation, 2017). While blindness and vision impairment is recognised as a significant health problem in China, particularly with regards to the prevalence of cataracts amongst the ageing population (Tang et al., 2015), the social model of disability recognises that it is not the impairment that disables a person with disability, but rather inaccessible environments, attitudes, technologies and modes of communication, that determine whether that person is able to fully participate in society. An example of this is the way people with disability including blindness and vision impairments were historically denied access to education in China. Either directly, by being prevented from attending, or indirectly – via pressure to leave by school administrators and/or parents of other children, or due to a lack of access to assistive technology and alternative formats for educational materials (Crouch, 2015; Human Rights Watch, 2013). Indeed, the college entrance exam, the Gaokao, was only made available in Braille and electronic format in 2014. Human Rights Watch (2013) recognises this as a significant social problem; they cite as evidence the explanation provided by the Shandong Provincial Education Bureau for preventing a blind student from accessing the exam that could provide access to higher education:

> Even if [the student] takes the exams, she would be unable to participate in class like normal students and since ordinary universities cannot provide Braille textbooks, she cannot receive a normal education in ordinary schools.

The student was denied access to the Gaokao, under the assumption that universities don't have the capability to provide facilities for people with vision impairments. This assumption severely limits the opportunity to continue in full time education. As a result of these limiting environments and educational opportunities, 90 percent of China's blind and vision impaired population who find work become masseuses or acupuncturists (Osnos, 2013). However, recent moves to recognise functional barriers and the ways society can be adapted to be more inclusive of people with disabilities are gaining traction (Fjeld & Saglai, 2011). The World Report on Disability jointly published by the World Health Organisation and the World Bank (2011) recognises important action by industry in China to address barriers to accessing information and communications technology (ICT). This chapter explores a specific facet of this increasing of ICT access and investigates how social media can be used to better facilitate the inclusion of people with disabilities in China, with a particular focus on people who are blind or with a vision impairment. In doing so it interrogates the emergence and development of corporate social responsibility (CSR) in China, particularly in relation to people with disabilities. Chinese internet and high-tech companies play a notable role in promoting social innovation in enabling greater social inclusions for people with disabilities. In this context, we also explore the understanding of 'doing good to others' drawing the Confucian value of benevolence (*ren*) and how this is applied to an understanding of corporate social responsibility, particularly in relation of Chinese social media companies. To illustrate this, we present the case study of the United Nations and WeChat joint initiative in the Voice Donor Campaign for audio books as both a community and corporate example of 'doing good to others' via social media.

The Social Model of Disability

This chapter proceeds from the social model of disability whereby disability is recognised as existing within the structures and cultures of society rather than within an individual's damaged body (Oliver, 1990). In China protections against discrimination against people with disabilities are recognised in the Law of the People's Republic of China on the Protection of Disabled Persons (1990). This law prohibits discrimination against disabled people and mandates:

> Disabled persons shall enjoy equal rights with other citizens in political, economic, cultural and social fields, in family life and other aspects.

While the social model of disability has been used to argue for accessibility in public space, such as access to schools and university, access to ICT is also increasingly being recognised as a vital form of inclusion (Ellis & Kent, 2011; Goggin & Newall, 2003). As a result, a number of incentives to promote social inclusion have been initiated in China including the prioritisation of ICT access for students with disabilities

(Zhao, 2011). For people who are blind or with vision impairment this would normally revolve around access to a Braille interface or screen reading technology.

However, the availability of both Chinese Braille and screen reading technology has had a problematic history. While a 2013 article in *The Economist* identifies Braille as "the key to literacy" for China's 17 million vision impaired population (The Economist, 2013), Jurgen Grotz describes the lack of connection between Chinese Braille and Chinese characters as a primary reason for "difficulties in participating in education and the job market" (Grotz, 1995). Although a less complicated Braille system was developed in the 1960s and 1970s as part of a suite of social initiatives to facilitate the inclusion of China's blind and vision impaired community in public life, for many "the system never lived up to its potential" (Crouch, 2015). Therefore, with people accessing more online and computer based information, screen readers would perhaps seem to offer more potential, yet the availability of this form of assistive technology has similarly been problematic. In the west, JAWs is the most commonly used screen reader; however, it does not adequately support Chinese characters (Yeh, Tsay, & Liang, 2008). Chinese developed screen readers have also been criticised for various inadequacies. For example, it is difficult for blind people to input Chinese characters into a computer or mobile phone, with the standard input method based on Pinyin, a set of Chinese phonetic alphabets used to indicate pronunciation of Chinese characters (Wang, Wang, Qian, & Lin, 2010). With less than 10 percent of China's blind and vision impaired community able to even read Braille (Wang et al., 2010) and these documented issues with screen reader translation of Chinese characters, access to alternative technologies such as audio books is a crucial social initiative.

Corporate Social Responsibility: An Overview

The notion of CSR began appearing in China's public discourse in the late 1990s and is now a familiar topic in policy forums, academic research and social media. As perceived by chief executives and business owners, Chinese companies have social responsibilities similar to their western counterparts for issues such as environmental protection, staff safety, product quality and charity undertakings (Xu & Yang, 2010). Additionally, they also have responsibilities to provide job opportunities, show good faith in operation and price-setting and ensuring social stability and progress. For people with disabilities this manifests in a quota system for employment – companies who fail to meet a 1.5 percent quota must pay a fee into the Disabled Persons Employment Security Fund which then goes towards supporting disabled people in the community (World Health Organisation & World Bank, 2011, p. 242).

The notion of CSR is also sometimes referred to as 'doing good to others'. Doing good encourages compassion towards minorities and people who may be considered weak or vulnerable. This approach can in part be traced back to the traditional Confucian value of benevolence (*ren*) which espouses putting oneself in the place of another and has been explicitly linked to the notion of corporate social responsibility (Low & Ang, 2012, 2013; Zhao, 2014). While these values are traditionally enacted at an individual level this notion took on a more corporate aspect after China joined the World Trade Organisation in 2001, when the engagement and competition in overseas markets also fuelled the need to adopt CSR for Chinese companies to make them more internationally accepted. International regulations such as import rules of the EU and ISO for supply chains pressured Chinese manufacturers to reform activities such as excessive pollution and child labour (Sarkis, Ni, & Zhu, 2011).

Yet unlike the more market-led practices of CSR in the United States and Europe, in China, CSR has historically been driven by government policy, global engagement and civil society. In addition, while companies in other parts of the world usually adopt CSR on a voluntary basis, CSR is regulated in China. In 2005 the Chinese Communist Party initiated a mission to 'build a harmonious society' (Zheng & Tok, 2007) in a bid to mitigate social gaps and imbalance, the ill effects of the previous concentration on economic growth. In line with this mission, the government initiated legislation, including the assumption of social responsibility in the 2006 revised Chinese Company Law and policy making targeting state-owned enterprises. In 2006, one of the largest of these enterprises, the State Grid Corporation, was the first Chinese company to publish a CSR report. Since 2008, the Shanghai Stock Exchange has required all listed companies to disclose environmental information (Moon & Shen, 2010). Under Xi Jiping's leadership a new slogan emerged – 'to pass on positive energy' and many internet companies, celebrities and ordinary people have subsequently been encouraged to do philanthropy as a response to this.

However, there are signs which indicate both regulation and social awareness of CSR in China is still at an early stage. The policy enforcement involving CSR is often found to be lax because of conflicting incentives for local governments (Epstein-Reeves, 2012a; Sarkis et al., 2011). The development of CSR is uneven – environmental issues are given earliest and strongest emphasis, while the attention paid to human rights issues like internet censorship is limited (Lin, 2010; Moon & Shen, 2010). Further, despite this mandate for CSR, there are still many Chinese managers who do not have any knowledge of CSR (Xu & Yang, 2010) or perceive CSR as philanthropy which is separate from management (Liu, 2015).

The idea of the stakeholder is a recent CSR focus for companies in China due to the rise of a technology-enabled civil society, particularly through the adoption and use of social media. As well as consumers and shareholders, local communities have also become an increasingly informed stakeholder group in business activities. As other chapters in this volume illustrate, people all over China are speaking up through social media and exposing many issues including substandard milk powder, poor air quality and workers' suicides and demanding that these issues be addressed by both companies and authorities. This public scrutiny adds to the pressure upon companies to be both responsive and responsible. A number of companies in China such as Baidu, Jingdong, Alibaba, Tencent, DIDI Taxi, Hangzhou Ancun Technology and 360 Share, not only manage social media accounts to publicise CSR practices, but also try to acquire an informal 'social license' from local stakeholders to ensure positive performance in businesses (Liu, 2015).

Social Media Companies and Corporate Social Responsibility

Social media and internet companies also play a significant role in CSR development in China, especially when the CSR is oriented towards the community of people with disabilities. In 2009 Tencent launched a 'barrier-free' design of its products for people with vision impairment. In 2015 Tencent made this design publicly available by making its code available as open source. Also in 2015, Alibaba joined China's Disabled Persons Federation to develop a service-locating application for people with disabilities. Their affordance of technology for civil society has drawn attention from the government and it has subsequently set out policy frameworks and agreed principles for the IT industry. The Internet Society of China (ISC) organized the second China Internet Enterprises Social Responsibility Forum in Beijing in 2015 and more than 20 technology companies including Alibaba, Tencent and Baidu signed the Internet Enterprises Social Responsibility Declaration. This was a government led push for internet enterprises to have a greater focus on corporate social responsibility. A third forum was held in 2016 where 104 internet and media companies signed an initiative to further develop this incentive.

Almost all social media platforms in China have functions for organising community building – examples include the QQ group, Weibo Group and WeChat group. These spaces create social awareness, sociality, a sense of belonging through social integration and communities and they engage users in politics and civic activities. Social media sites have the advantages of mass users, speed, broad reach, interactivity and low barriers to entry. CSR initiatives, NGOs and grassroots communities have all used the combination of online channels to distribute information and education to change people's social awareness.

In order to meet its CSR obligations, Tencent established the Tencent Public Welfare Department. WeChat, as part of Tencent, enacted its

CSR via a number of philanthropic efforts the company describe as 'charity', including disaster relief efforts, public health announcements and encouragement for users to 'do good to others'. Tencent Public Welfare also joined with the United Nations in 2012 to launch the WeChat Voice Donor campaign in order to provide greater access for the blind community (WeChat, 2016). While the language of 'charity' is problematic in relation to disability this activity should be seen in the context of both WeChat's CSR obligations as well as providing accessible resources for people with disabilities to better engage in society, and as a programme to raise awareness about disability inclusion in the wider Chinese community.

Case Study: The Voice Donor Campaign

The Voice Donor campaign came about as part of Tencent's CSR responsibilities. The company invited Chinese speakers to 'donate' their voices by reading aloud one minute recordings of books which could then be compiled and distributed amongst people who are blind and vision impaired. Its aim is to create a public service and awareness around issues facing the blind and visually impaired community in China. The crowd-sourced Voice Donor campaign has a WeChat official account – ID: voicedonate – where people can follow and donate their voice.

The campaign began by converting the United Nations Convention of the Rights of People with Disabilities, which China had ratified in 2008, into audio. The UN described their motivations:

> By participating in this campaign UNDP hopes to help community groups and the general public better understand the content of the Convention and raising public awareness of disability rights. UNDP works to promote respect for the rights and interests of people with disabilities, eliminating discrimination and prejudice
> (United Nations Development Program, 2015).

The United Nations reported in 2015 that 3 million people had contributed 1 minute audio clips to the programme and produced in excess of 100 audio books. These books were distributed to schools and community groups and had been used by over 3 million people (United Nations Development Program, 2015). The newspaper the Nanjing Daily reported that when the campaign was introduced in 2012 it attracted 500 volunteers – by 2016 the team has expanded to more than 7,000 people (Jiang & Xing, 2016). Participants are selected and trained by Tencent and customer feedback on public social media platforms is used to evaluate the quality of the campaign. WeChat automatically combines the voices of many participants into audiobooks. Spreadable content is actively co-produced and distributed across social media.

WeChat is used as a vehicle for expanding Tencent's CSR to include the United Nations, local NGOs and its own customers, who each in turn are able to embrace the 'doing good to others' ethos that the CSR espouses. Tencent's integrating CSR into its innovation and technology can in part be seen through the lens of the Confucian ideal of the *'junzi'* or superior person, who through constant self-improvement, exhibits exemplary behaviour reflecting the Confucian theory of benevolent leadership. Tencent as a corporation can be seen to be addressing issues of social inclusion and seeking to become a leading example for both Chinese technology companies and the general public. In this context, the Voice Donor Campaign is a successful CSR programme that highlights the importance of being benevolent in relation to developing shared resources for the blind and visually impaired community. However, as Yu explored in chapter two in relation to microphilanthropy this benevolence comes in the form of a patron-client structure of social hierarchy – one in which people who are blind or vision impaired are very much at the lower end. While there are models of charity, particularly around microphilanthropy in China, that utilise social media to enable citizen led and citizen initiated actions (Yu, 2017), in this case it enables a company lead initiative through Tencent's CSR programme that both reflects positively on the company, and also allows individuals to easily contribute and enables other organisational partners to also be involved.

A number of enterprises and institutions have developed their own CSR campaigns for the blind and visually impaired community to collaborate with Tencent's Voice Donor campaign. These include the Shandong Art Institute, Shandong University of Finance and Economics, Shandong Sports Institute of Jinan, Shandong Airline, Wanda Group, Shanghai Pudong Development Bank, Shandong Jinanbaoyue and Shandong Airlines (Qilu Evening, 2015). For example, Shandong Airlines undertook its own CSR programme along with the WeChat Voice Donor campaign. When the number of voice donations reached 95,369 in the Voice Donor campaign in 2015, Shandong Airlines organized charitable donations to Qingdao Blind Institutions, Yantai City Special Education School and Chongqing Special Juvenile Education Center for Blindness (Qilu Evening, 2015).

The affordance offered by social media builds social networks to mobilize resources, volunteers, supporters and partners to participate in the CSR programme. They can share Tencent's CSR posts and materials through their personal page and post. They can circulate information and help companies and NGO's CSR initiatives gain more attention and support. They can also broaden the reach of the campaign through their own social networking. For example, more than 21 celebrity volunteers have led the voice donation campaign. One of the voice donor ambassadors was Yang Lan, television host and media company founder who has 33 million followers on Weibo; she was echoed by more than 50 other celebrities, including supermodel Lin Chi-ling, with their combined social media profiles reaching 210 million people (see also Chapter 5 for further discussion of social media, celebrities and charity in China).

NGOs and philanthropic organizations also engage with the WeChat platform, setting up organizational WeChat accounts to promote their CSR communication and activities, and in this way sidestepping regulation that requires NGOs to be registered offline. Through their organizational WeChat accounts, they can publicise CSR practices and information to attract individual followers, as well as mobilizing social media users to advocate for their initiatives or lobby others to join. For example, the Legal Aid Center of the Ministry of Justice, the China Disabled Persons' Federation and other Disabled People's Organisations (DPOs) partnered with WeChat in this voice donor programme. Tencent compiled voice recordings and provided devices to national libraries, schools for people with vision impairment and DPOs.

The WeChat platform also enables participation in the Voice Donor programme by the private sector, communities and individuals with vision impairments. For example, book shops and blind massage parlours displayed WeChat Voice Donor QR-codes in order to promote the Voice Donor campaign. In book stores QR codes on the back cover of books in the new arrivals sections serve as an invitation for people to donate their voice to the project. In blind massage parlours, customers also receive an invitation to connect to the Voce Donor official WeChat account under the massage couches. An individual donor can also invite more people to take part through the Voice Donor account.

The WeChat Voice Donor campaign also disseminated its public appeals through more traditional main stream media, including China Central Television (CCTV), major newspapers and internet news services. All these services reported positively on the campaign, as Tencent aligned its CSR with both the 'harmonious society' and 'pass on positive energy' social agendas. WeChat also collaborated with the popular reality TV programmes, 'The Voice of China', which reached 200 million individual internet users in 2015 (Keane & Zhang, 2017). Hua Shao, the host, invited the audience to do voice donations together with him during a live broadcast, and challenged everyone to see how fast they could complete a voice book together.

These examples demonstrate how the use of social media allows the facilitation of 'doing good to others' to reach beyond the traditional notion of those directly inspired by the traditional Confucian ideal of benevolent leadership to reach out across society more broadly to both create accessible crowd sourced resources and raise awareness of issues facing the blind and vision impaired community. While these examples often point to leadership from prominent public figures, it is the social media, and the facilitation provided by WeChat's CSR commitment that allowed the broad adoption and success of the programme.

Conclusion

It has been argued that China's integration into the global economic order has brought many opportunities but also responsibilities for Chinese companies. With China's enormous internet and digital communication population size, and rising global importance, the solutions developed and implemented in this country will contribute to the world's knowledge base and provide an opportunity to lead the way for other developing countries.

This chapter argues that technology companies have shown they are able to reach out to people, solidifying their ability to deliver their CSR obligations. Digital communication is crucial in community building, networking and marketing, particularly in the absence of government policy to support disability communities in China. This is exemplified by initiatives such as WeChat's Voice Donor campaign which help facilitate disability inclusion by providing people with vision impairment access to reading materials in an accessible format. The success of WeChat's Voice Donor campaign demonstrates the importance of social media platforms and highlights their role in community networking and facilitating social engagement.

However, there is also a need for further research. There are questions around the agency of the blind and visually impaired as part of this process, and we are unaware of how they view the campaign and what actual benefits it delivers beyond showing Tencent in a good light. The blind and visually impaired are a significantly disadvantaged group in Chinese society with limited opportunities for education, work and broader participation in society. While the production of audio books is a potentially positive step to greater social inclusion for this group, there are still lots of areas that still need to be addressed, and there are questions as to whether relying on corporate charity is not the only, or the most suitable, path to do so.

References

Crouch, E. (2015, 16 July). Sightless in Shanghai – Being blind in a 21st century Chinese megacity. Retrieved from www.thatsmags.com/china/post/10638/ sightless-in-shanghai-being-blind-in-a-21st-century-chinese-megacity-1.

Ellis, K. & Kent, M. (2011). *Disability and New Media*. New York: Routledge.

Epstein-Reeves, J. (2012a, 6 November). *The CSR challenge for companies doing business in China*. Retrieved from www.forbes.com/sites/csr/2012/11/06/ the-csr-challlenge-for-companies-doing-business-in-china/#2bf18af7a53d.

Epstein-Reeves, J. (2012b, February 21). *Six reasons companies should embrace CSR*. Forbes. www.forbes.com/sites/csr/2012/02/21/six-reasons-companies-should-embrace-csr/#269972503495.

Fjeld, H., & Saglai, G. (2011). Disability, poverty and healthcare: changes in the canji ('disability') policies in the history of the People's Republic of China.

In A. H. Eide & B. Ingstad (Eds.), *Disability and poverty: A global challenge* (pp. 31–54). Bristol: Polity Press.

Goggin, G. & Newall, C. (2003). *Digital disability: The social construction of disability in new media*. Lanham, Rowman and Littlefield Publishers Ltd.

Grotz, J. (1995). *Vision-impaired can learn Chinese Braille*. China Daily, Nth American edition, New York.

Human Rights Watch. (2013, July 2013). *"As long as they let us stay in class": Barriers to education for persons with disabilities in China*. Retrieved from www.hrw.org/sites/default/files/reports/china0713_ForUpload.pdf.

Jiang, H. & Xing, H. (2016). *Readers donated voices for the visual disabilities* (trans). Nanjing Daily. 蒋海燕 & 邢虹. (2016) 南京朗读者为盲人"捐"声音 范小青等无偿授权 Retrieved form www.njdaily.cn.

Keane, M. & Zhang, J. D. (2017) Formats, cultural trade and China's going out policy, In J. Chalaby & A. Esser (Eds.) *Many formats: One world*, London: Intellect.

Law of the People's Republic of China on the Protection of Disabled Persons. (1990). Retrieved from www.npc.gov.cn/englishnpc/Law/2007–12/12/content_1383889.htm.

Lin, L.-W. (2010). Corporate social responsibility in China: Window dressing or structural change? *Berkeley Journal of International Law, 28,* 64. doi: 10.15779/Z38F35Q.

Liu, M. (2015). Is corporate social responsibility China's secret weapon? Retrieved from www.weforum.org/agenda/2015/03/is-corporate-social-responsibility-chinas-secret-weapon/.

Low, K. C. P. & Ang, S. L. (2012). Confucian leadership and corporate social responsibility (CSR), the way forward. *Asian Journal of Business Research, 2,* 1.

Low, K. C. P. & Ang, S. L. (2013). Confucian ethics, government and corporate social responsibility. *International Journal of Business and Management, 8,* 4.

Moon, J., & Shen, X. (2010). CSR in China research: Salience, focus and nature. *Journal of Business Ethics, 94*(4), 613–629.

Oliver, M. (1990). *The politics of disablement*. Basingstoke, UK: Macmillan Education.

Osnos, E. (2013, 17 June). *NYU, China and Chen Guangcheng*. Retrieved from www.newyorker.com/news/letter-from-china/n-y-u-china-and-chen-guangcheng.

Qilu Evening (2015, 14 June). 不要钱也不要物!为盲人捐点"声音",你愿意吗? Retrieved November 20, 2016 from http://sjb.qlwb.com.cn/qlwb/content/20161121/PageArticleIndexWZ.htm.

Sarkis, J., Ni, N., & Zhu, Q. (2011). Winds of change: Corporate social responsibility in China. *Ivey Business Journal, 75*(1), 1–4.

Tang, Y., Wang, J., Huang, W., Gao, Y., Luo, Y. & Lu, Y. (2015). Prevalence and Causes of Visual Impairment in a Chinese Adult Population: The Taizhou Eye Study. *Ophthalmology, 122*(7), 1480–1488.

The Economist, (2013, 13 July). *Feeling their way: Chinese Braille*. Retrieved from www.economist.com/news/china/21581761-blind-people-china-struggle-more-just-their-disability-feeling-their-way.

United Nations Development Program. (2015, 17 May). *UNDP and WeChat promote the rights of people with disabilities*. Retrieved from www.cn.undp.org/content/china/en/home/presscenter/articles/2015/05/undp-uses-social-media-to-promote-the-rights-of-people-with-disa.html.

Wang, C., Wang, X., Qian, Y., & Lin, S. (2010). *Accurate Braille–Chinese translation towards efficient Chinese input method for blind people.* Paper presented at the 5th International Conference on Pervasive Computing and Applications, Birmingham City University. Need more details on dates etc.

WeChat. (2016, 17 February). Tag archives: WeChat gives back. Retrieved August 3.2016 from http://blog.wechat.com/tag/wechat-gives-back/

World Health Organisation. (2017). *Blindness as a public health problem in China: Fact Sheet No 230.* Retrieved from www.who.int/mediacentre/factsheets/fs230/en/.

World Health Organisation & World Bank. (2011). *World report on disability.* Retrieved from www.unicef.org/protection/World_report_on_disability_eng.pdf.

Xu, S., & Yang, R. (2010). Indigenous characteristics of Chinese corporate social responsibility conceptual paradigm. *Journal of Business Ethics, 93*(2), 321–333.

Yeh, F.-H., Tsay, H.-S., & Liang, S.-H. (2008). Human computer interface and optimized electro-mechanical design for Chinese Braille display. *Mechanism and Machine Theory, 43*(12), 1495–1518. doi:10.1016/j.mechmachtheory. 2008.01.006.

Yu, H. (2017). Philanthropy on the move: Mobile communication and neoliberal citizenship in China. *Communications and the Public.* 1–15. doi:10.1177/2057047317693634.

Zhao, J. (2011). China special education: The perspective of information technologies. In P. Ordóñez de Pablos, J. Zhao, & R. Tennyson (Eds.), *Technology enhanced learning for people with disabilities: Approaches and applications* (pp. 34–43). Hershey, PA: Information Science Reference.

Zhao, J. (2014) *Corporate social responsibility in contemporary China.* UK: Edward Elgar Publishing Limited Cheltenham.

Zheng, Y., & Tok, S. K. (2007). *Harmonious society and harmonious world: China's policy discourse under Hu Jintao.* China Policy Institute. Briefing Series, 26.

10 Information and Communications Technology and Social Media Accessibility in China

A Peep at a Leopard through a Tube?

Yao Ding and G. Anthony Giannoumis

The title of this chapter comes from the Chinese idiom "a peep at a leopard through a tube – see a spot or two" (管中窥豹, 可见一斑), which means looking at an issue from a single perspective and conjuring up a bigger picture. The chapter considers the accessibility of Chinese social media platforms through a pilot research project.

Introduction

Weeks before the 2016 Chinese New Year, a heated debated emerged on social media over a lawsuit against the China Railway Corporation. Chen Bin, a blind masseur in Beijing, sued the state-owned corporation after finding it impossible to pass through the CAPTCHA system of their ticket buying website. Bin had to take a day's leave from work and take a taxi to the railway station to buy the ticket ("Visually impaired man sues," 2016). Many websites use CAPTCHA to determine whether a user is human by asking them to type the letters of an obscured image. For non-sighted users, websites typically use an audio CAPTCHA, which the train ticketing website failed to offer. Being China's first case on information accessibility, it drew immediate attention. Days later, an article published in the government official media, the People's Daily website, defended the China Railway Corporation stating that "blind or visually impaired passengers, without help from other people, can hardly use the internet independently... so as long as help is available, having no speaking Captcha will not stop blind passengers from purchasing tickets online" ("Without speaking Captcha," 2016). This statement consequently drove thousands of blind people to speak up on social media.

This incident illustrates three overarching themes regarding information and communication technology (ICT) accessibility in China. First, myths and misconceptions about people with disabilities are being circulated in China. For instance, "people with disabilities cannot use technology independently and always need help", or "if people with disabilities can go to a physical store/ticketing place, why do they need online access" ("Without speaking Captcha," 2016). Social media is often used as a means of communication to refute the myths. Second, the fact that blind users are using social media to discuss accessibility issues shows that websites and mobile apps run by private-held companies appear more accessible than those of public services managed by state-owned corporations – this is in spite of the fact that only the latter are obligated to offer full and equal access. Third, people with disabilities are a driving force in demanding accessibility, either by taking legal action against violators or voicing their dissatisfaction on social media.

This chapter explores these accessibility practices in China using qualitative data from a case study of a Chinese social media company. We start by briefly presenting research on ICT and social media accessibility from an international perspective. Next we review Chinese laws and policies on ICT accessibility and analyse the relevant stakeholders involved in social media and accessibility in China. This is supported with the aforementioned case study using policy document analysis and data from semi-structured qualitative interviews with social media developers and users with disabilities. Finally, we discuss potential mechanisms for elevating awareness and promoting ICT accessibility in China.

This chapter draws from international research regarding social media accessibility as a useful basis for examining the implementation of ICT accessibility practices in China (Brown, Jay, Chen, & Harper, 2012; Cooper, 2007; Gibson, 2007; Jaeger, Bertot, & Shilton, 2012; Jaeger & Xie, 2009; Magro, 2012; Rodriguez, 2011). However, limited research exists that specifically examines ICT accessibility in China. In an evaluation of web accessibility from 2009 to 2013, Rau, Zhou, Sun and Zhong (2016) demonstrate the low levels of accessibility for public and private sector websites in China. However, research has yet to examine ICT accessibility in practice in China from an organisational perspective. It is hoped that the research in this chapter – particularly data from the case study – will start to redress that.

ICT and Social Media Accessibility

Research on social media can be seen to relate to broader investigations of web and ICT accessibility for people with disability (Ellis & Kent, 2011; See Kent, Ellis, Zhang & Zhang, Chapter 9; Chen, Bong & Li, Chapter 11 in this volume). For example, Petrie, Savva and Power (2015, p. 37) provide a unified definition of web accessibility stating, "all people, particularly disabled and older people, can use websites in a range of contexts of use, including mainstream and assistive technologies; to achieve this, websites need to be designed and developed to support usability across these contexts". When applied to social media accessibility, this definition stipulates that accessible social media technologies are usable by everyone, including persons with disabilities. However, research by Goggin and Newell (2003) examines how the lack of participation on social media is a barrier to participation in society. The authors argue that social media developers do not typically consider persons with disabilities in market research when developing new products and services. The authors go on to claim that despite the potential for internet and web technologies to enable persons with disabilities to participate in society, "the Internet has been, and remains, a disabling technology for many people" (p. 122).

In research by Ellis and Kent (2011), the authors explore new media and the accessibility and usability barriers experienced by persons with disabilities. According to the authors, new media or "Web 2.0" accessibility involves "the capacity to access information in the format of choice when working within the largely unstructured environment of user-generated content" (p. 25). Ellis and Kent (2011) characterise web 2.0 as the development of dynamic and user-generated web content especially through social media. Ellis and Kent (2011) further explore recent innovations in web and social media technologies and the role that those technologies have in reproducing social barriers that exclude persons with disabilities from participating in society. The authors argue that while social media platforms provide an opportunity for participation on a broader scale than ever before, the design of new media technologies can have the effect of disabling individuals with impairments. The authors additionally argue that only after new media platforms achieve widespread adoption, do developers begin to consider accessibility. Ellis and Kent (2011) suggest that social and political advocacy efforts may provide a useful mechanism for promoting new media accessibility.

Research has also examined the implementation of web accessibility law and policy (Ellis & Kent, 2011; Giannoumis, 2014a). According to Ellis and Kent (2011), "[b]ecause accessibility is a choice, it is inherently a political decision" (p. 150). The authors argue that the legal requirements for web accessibility in Australia may not act as a panacea for promoting web accessibility outcomes. Research in the UK, Norway, USA and European Union has similarly concluded that complex and contravening factors mediate the implementation of web accessibility law and policy (Giannoumis, 2014a, 2014b, 2015a, 2015c). To date, the myriad national and international law and policy efforts have yet to substantively reduce the "digital divide" between persons who can use the web and persons who, due to the design of web content, experience barriers in using the web (Blanck, 2014a; Ragnedda & Muschert, 2013). As Blanck (2014a) points out, issues of auto-personalisation, privacy and security have yet to be resolved in ensuring a "right to the web" for persons with disabilities.

However, other research suggests that principles of universal design may provide a useful basis for ensuring web accessibility in practice

(Blanck, 2014a; Ellis & Kent, 2011; Giannoumis, 2014c, 2015b). According to the United Nations Convention on the Rights of Persons with Disabilities (CRPD), universal design refers to "the design of products, environments, programmes and services to be usable by all people, to the greatest extent possible, without the need for adaptation or specialized design". Research has argued for integrating universal design principles in business processes (Giannoumis, 2015a; Kelly et al., 2007). Ellis and Kent (2011) suggest that a process-based approach may ensure accessibility for everyone. According to the authors (Ellis and Kent, 2011, p. 26) "Toolkits must be better developed in order to anticipate ways to allow for different impairments because there are many web developers and no one single way to ensure accessibility for everyone". The authors go on to consider the role of universal design as a response to the commercial resistance for adopting practices that ensure web accessibility. According to the authors, "what is considered an accessible retrofit in today's web environment, will become increasingly important for the average user" (p. 144). In other words, by focusing on universal design, web developers can "develop better, more flexible, and customisable technology which can be mainstreamed to benefit everyone" (Ellis and Kent, 2011, p. 146).

The research reviewed in this section suggests that despite national and international law and policy efforts aimed at ensuring ICT and social media accessibility, persons with disabilities continue to experience barriers in accessing and using web-based services. Research suggests that the implementation of ICT accessibility law and policy has yet to result in the removal of these barriers. However, research also suggests that expanding the scope of accessibility using universal design principles may provide a useful basis for realising accessibility in practice. This research provides a useful basis for examining the accessibility barriers for social media companies in China.

Chinese Laws and Policies on ICT Accessibility

Recognition of the need for accessible ICT in law and policy came later in China than in neighbouring countries such as Japan, Korea and India. In 1990, 1 year following the introduction of the internet to China, the government passed the first Law on the Protection of the Disabled ("Evolution of internet in China," 2001). However, the Law made no mention of ensuring equal access to ICT.

In 2008, the Chinese government ratified the United Nations CRPD ("United Nations Treaty Collection," 2016), which obligates the government to raise awareness and foster respect for the rights and dignity of persons with disabilities and to ensure access to ICT. Later in the same year, the Chinese president at the time, Hu Jintao, signed an amendment to the 1990 Law on Protection of the Disabled aimed to promote the "gradual improvement and promotion of accessibility of ICT". In 2012, the then Chinese Premier Wen Jiabao signed the State Council Decree of Regulations on Building a Barrier-Free Environment ("Regulations on building a barrier-free environment," 2012). Among the 35 provisions of the Regulations, nine concerned access to ICT. The Regulations require that the government, at various levels, provide accessible formats of, among other things – information, services and statewide exams; accessible reading rooms in libraries; and captioned and sign language on TV programmes.

Since 2008, the Ministry of Industry and Information Technology (MIIT) have published or proposed a series of technical requirements, including requirements for website accessibility (YD/T 1761–2012), requirements for accessible call centres (YD/T 2097–2010) and requirements for compatibility between hearing aids and communication devices (YDT 1643–2007) and between hearing aids and telephone headsets (YD/T 1889–2009). However, despite these efforts to promote ICT accessibility through law and policy, research has yet to examine comprehensively the implementation of ICT accessibility in practice.

Relevant Stakeholders

The China Disabled Persons' Federation (CDPF) is the most important governmental organisation for people with disabilities ("Introduction to CDPF," 2007). The CDPF maintains responsibility for representing the interests and protecting the rights of people with disabilities. In addition, the CDPF is responsible for managing and guiding a variety of organisations for persons with disabilities. In terms of ICT accessibility, the CDPF, in collaboration with the MIIT, participates in relevant research and in the design and implementation of laws and regulations ("MIIT of PRC," n.d.). The CDPF also works with the Internet Society of China to promote compliance with accessibility regulations ("ISC website," n.d.), and, for the first time in 2013, website accessibility was included in the performance metrics of government websites ("2013 China Statistical Communiqué," 2014). Since 2004, the CDPF has also organised the annual Forum on China Information Accessibility in Beijing ("Forum on China Information Accessibility," n.d.).

Non-governmental organisations and the IT industry in China are also emerging as strong promoters for information accessibility. In 2013, leading tech companies in China set up the Chinese Accessible Products Association (CAPA) to promote accessibility internally and externally ("About CAPA," n.d.). Members not only improve accessibility of their own products, but also participate in developing and updating technical requirements. However, despite these efforts, most individuals with disabilities remain invisible on the internet due to the inaccessible design of web content (Lisney, Li, & Liu, 2007; Shi, 2007), and research demonstrates that the situation may be getting worse (Shi, 2006).

Case Study: Chinese Social Media Company

Case studies provide useful evidence for elaborating organisational and implementation models – in this case the implementation of ICT accessibility practices (Yin, 2013). This case study of one of the largest Chinese social media companies with over 200 million users provided a useful basis for elaborating on the role of ICT accessibility practices in China as a component of human rights and antidiscrimination law and policy. To preserve the privacy of our respondents, the company and participants will remain anonymous.

The data was collected from policy document analysis and semi-structured interviews. As a pilot study aimed at producing exploratory research, the data provided a useful basis to begin analysing ICT accessibility practices in China. Policy document analyses provided useful data on the explicit norms, values and procedures in China and focused on primary source policies including national and international laws and policies, regulations, standards, policy proposals and government reports. These policy documents were located via web searches, through referrals and through organisational or governmental public websites. Semi-structured interviews with a purposive sample of three participants were also carried out. The interviews were conducted in-person in Mandarin in 2015. The data were transcribed and analysed by a researcher fluent in Mandarin. These provided useful data on the perspectives involved in implementing ICT accessibility in China. One interview was conducted with a blind user of social media in China and the remaining two were conducted with social media ICT designers including a multimedia content designer and a mobile app designer. Each interview lasted for about 40 minutes. The interviews covered the following topics:

- What accessibility related laws and regulations are you aware of? Are they effective?
- How does the company ensure product accessibility in practice? What should be improved?
- What do you think would help in building a barrier-free environment in general? By whom should they be implemented?

Data from these interviews demonstrated four themes – the role of awareness of ICT accessibility; the perceptions regarding the efficacy of ICT accessibility requirements; the practical considerations for implementing ICT accessibility within an organisation; and the myths and misconceptions concerning the role of ICT in the lives of persons with disabilities.

Awareness of ICT Accessibility

Awareness has been found to be low in terms of need for, and policy of, ICT accessibility among Chinese older adults (Yao, Qiu, Huang, Du, & Ma, 2011). The awareness among ICT designers and developers remains underspecified. When asked if they knew about any legal policies or regulations regarding accessibility, both designers interviewed in this study replied "no". This confirmed our hypothesis that social media designers possessed a low level of awareness about disability and accessibility and that government has yet to enforce legal obligations for ICT accessibility among social media companies. Jia and Wang (2014) contributed part of this low awareness to a rulemaking process that is primarily led by experts without public participation of stakeholders. For example, the aforementioned *Chen v. China Railway* is the first and the only lawsuit of its kind brought to court since the regulations entered into force. The blind social media user interviewed states:

> It's not long since "barrier-free" was introduced to China... Now the regulations are rather general and suggestive... I look forward to detailed rules. The government has started to pay attention [to accessibility], but [policies are] still in their infancy.

Even though they were not familiar with accessibility requirements, the designers were aware of, or had done some work for, improving accessibility. One designer said their website design would be tested with popular screen readers and be adjusted accordingly so that it could be read easily. The blind subject, who used their product for an hour on average each day, said, "it [the social media app] is okay in terms of being 'usable', but far from 'accessible'. Most WCAG requirements are not met". Indeed, while WCAG provides a useful basis for measuring the accessibility of websites, the application of WCAG to mobile apps has yet to be fully examined (Giannoumis, 2015c).

It can therefore be argued that the recognition of accessible design within the company was seen to be sporadic and largely driven from the bottom-up. Both designers confirmed that there were no internal design requirements related to accessibility, nor was any work related to accessibility initiated from an administrative level. On the contrary, accessibility efforts had been propelled by the emerging needs from users with disabilities. One designer stated, "As the user base increases, we are able to analyse, identify, and meet these needs [for accessibility]. It was proposed by the Department of UED [user experience design]".

The results presented in this section suggest that designers are aware of the concept of "accessibility" or "barrier-free design" but have limited knowledge about and how to meet the legal requirements. End users with disabilities, especially tech-savvy users, are more aware of accessibility than the designers, and are eager for more attention from the government and IT companies on ICT accessibility.

Perceptions on the Efficacy of ICT Accessibility Requirements

The designers expressed concerns about the effectiveness of accessibility requirements. One of them said, "It depends on the cost and the severity of punishment. Small companies, especially start-ups, will not spare the man-hours on meeting accessibility requirements if [the] punishment doesn't compare to the cost". This viewpoint stems from a weak enforcement and a lack of clearly defined responsibilities for accessibility requirements in China (Zhang, 2015). The other designer said, "Large companies have the resource and expertise to do that, and have to consider the company's positive image". The blind participant didn't think highly of the efficacy of the requirements, "the non-governmental power is more valuable compared to the government requirements". The designers were also concerned about the timeline and scope of the requirements. "It's almost impossible to do everything right in the beginning. It's better first [to require to] meet part of the requirements, starting from first-tier cities, then expand to second- and third-tier cities".

In summary, the subjects were negative about the efficacy of accessibility requirements. Major concerns centred around the financial burden and required expertise to meet the requirements, as well as the timeline of mandating accessibility for all companies.

Implementing ICT Accessibility

Both designers stated that no one in the company was, in particular, responsible for accessibility of products, and no one on the development team would consider accessibility because it was not in the internal requirements or design guidelines:

> There is not a uniform standard. If there is anything [related to accessibility] done, it's not standardized. Now we require developers to add text descriptions to every control, button, and label, but there are always omissions in the development process.

With regards to the question about how the company gathers user feedback and identifies access needs by users with disabilities, one of the designers stated:

> The User Experience Design Department will consider [accessibility]... For mobile apps, users can make reviews in app stores. Within the app there is built-in feedback function. ... Also, through customer service hotlines, we can collect user feedback. About biannually, we

conduct in-depth interviews with the users... We probably won't [invite disabled users] – we only invite mainstream users, who are not individuals with disabilities.

The designer's response suggested that accessibility had not been part of the standard design and development cycle, and that no one in the company was particularly responsible for product accessibility. That is, instead of considering accessibility upfront, the company only solved access issues after the product had been launched.

Myths and Misconceptions Regarding ICT Accessibility

One of the most prevalent misconceptions about accessibility is that users with disabilities do not need all of the available functions, and should be satisfied as long as the basic functions are accessible. One of the designer subjects remarked, "I think disabled users should be okay with the most basic functions and not able to use 'deep' functions... should not expect themselves to use a product as normal users do, not 100%". This misconception directly contravenes the CRPD's obligation to ensure access to ICT for persons with disabilities on an equal basis with others. Another misconception is that accessibility is extra responsibility, an expensive add-on that brings no business value but may improve a company's public image. Both designers mentioned positive image as a leading motivation for a company to improve product accessibility.

The interviewees also implied that accessibility was understood as being only about blindness and visual impairments, rather than all types, degrees and combinations of disabilities. One of the designers said, "Users with physical disabilities will figure out a way to use touchscreens – unlike cellphones with buttons where you need to consider button size, etc. ... Looking at the entire [IT] industry, I haven't heard of any company that designs for people with physical disabilities".

In summary, many commonly held myths and misconceptions exist among designers and developers regarding the barriers that people with disabilities experience using ICT and the meaningfulness of accessibility. As awareness of accessibility increases, some may be refuted, but this article recommends that efforts promoting disability rights in China focus on breaking down misconceptions about ICT accessibility in any awareness-raising effort.

Potential Mechanisms for Evaluating Awareness and Promoting ICT Accessibility

One of the questions that this case study posed was, "what are the effective ways of promoting ICT accessibility in China?" This section draws implications from the interview results and discusses two potential strategies of advancing accessibility in practice – to integrate accessibility into user experience design and to encourage compliance with accessibility requirements.

Integrate Accessibility into User Experience Design

One of the barriers to effectively implementing accessibility in practice is the lack of a systematic approach to ensuring accessibility – only minimal guidelines exist (e.g., add text descriptions to visual elements), and no monitoring or assessment processes occur. This may account for a common access failure that many blind users pointed out – accessibility regression with updates. That is, what used to be accessible in an older version may become inaccessible in a later update. Heavily relying on user feedback, designers and developers can only solve problems that have become sufficiently prominent and that the users report. Instead, these barriers could have been more easily identified using a set of systematic accessibility guidelines regarding user experiences.

This systematic reporting of user experience could be a possible entry point to improving accessibility in practice. The reason is twofold. First, user experience has been introduced into China for years and has gained great importance in Chinese companies. Both designers thought that user experience was valued in the company:

> We emphasize UE [user experience] a lot. Every week we email the product team user feedbacks, in very detailed datasheets including user ID, feedback content, device, network environment... the problems are described very clearly.

Second, it is natural for most designers to think of accessibility as an extension of user experience – that of people with more diverse needs – so accessibility will not impose undue burden on the expertise of designers. Specifically, it is worth considering whether to integrate accessibility into ICT company design guidelines. As one of the designers said, "We have design guidelines for height of lines, indents and spacing, and many others, but not for accessibility". Integrating accessibility into user experience design may ensure that designers consider accessibility early in the development process – this may also lead to a decrease in development costs which occur when accessibility is retrofitted. It is widely accepted best practice to consider accessibility early and throughout the design and development process (BSI, 2010). Even though additional steps are required, most activities of planning, designing, implementing and checking for accessibility can be fit into a pre-existing process (Thatcher, 2006).

A potential barrier to this user experience design integration approach may be the mentality that characterises user experience as being about average users or representative users, rather than all users and users with a diverse spectrum of physical and cognitive abilities. Users with disabilities are considered to be a totally different group, rather than users with different needs. Universal design may provide a useful basis for countering the "average user" approach as universal design is typically considered a "one-size-fits-one" approach (Blanck, 2014b).

In summary, integrating accessibility into user experience design will be a natural way of introducing accessibility to routine practice. It does not require a radical change to design processes and may also be valued in a user-centred culture in Chinese companies.

Encourage Compliance with Accessibility Requirements

Government policies play an important role in the design and operation of China's social media. As one of the designers pointed out:

> Policies influence our operational strategies... For example, the user comment feature. The original design was that users could see their own or others' comments instantly as posted. But the [State Council] Information Office requires comments be reviewed and moderated prior to being posted, so user comments may take 2 to 3 minutes to appear.

Given the strong governmental control, one may wonder if a top-down, steadfast push would advance ICT accessibility effectively in China. Both designers argued that mandatory compliance would not work in China. One designer said, "Top priority is to survive, to maximise profits. Accessibility doesn't bring any business value". This reflected the hidden assumption that accessibility would not receive as great an emphasis as content moderation, which may lead to a shut-down of the entire platform if not done properly. In addition, accessibility is still deemed to be an "add-on" project for large companies that can afford it, both financially and technically. According to one of the designers, "If very complex, the requirements will be resented. If [financial] punishment is used, small companies may have to consider [compliance to accessibility regulations]".

Given the subjects' negativity towards mandating compliance, another way of enforcing accessibility requirements may be worth considering. There are basically two types of accessibility regulations adopted internationally – "push" regulations that are mandatory to all and whoever fails to comply will be punished; and "pull" regulations that are optional and only those who comply will be rewarded. Examples of "pull" regulations are Section 508 of the USA Rehabilitation Act, which uses the purchasing power of the USA government to financially persuade businesses to ensure accessibility by requiring ICT accessibility in all government procurement. Products conforming to these accessibility requirements may gain a competitive edge, and small companies not intending to compete in the government procurement market may choose not to conform to the requirements.

For IT companies that are mostly profit-driven, mandating accessibility for all may impose an undue burden, both financially and technically, and thus may fail. It is worth considering whether to maintain largely voluntary accessibility requirements as currently is the case, but take measures to incentivise companies and organisations to meet additional requirements.

Conclusion

This chapter investigated the ICT accessibility status quo in China through a policy analysis and a pilot interview study. The chapter suggested possible mechanisms for promoting ICT accessibility in China. The Chinese government has passed laws and regulations in recent years to require information accessibility in both public services and products of IT companies. However, the awareness of accessibility remains low and few governmental organisations or companies have fully implemented practices to ensure ICT accessibility. Myths and misconceptions still exist regarding the needs of people with disabilities and the implementation of accessibility.

This chapter therefore provides two recommendations for advancing the implementation of ICT accessibility in practice. First, IT companies should aim to integrate accessibility into the user experience design processes. The integration of accessibility will not require radical changes to routine practice, but will gain importance as user experience becomes increasingly valued. Second, government and market actors should incentivise compliance with accessibility regulations by requiring accessibility in public and business-to-business procurement.

References

2013 China Statistical Communiqué of Work for People with Disabilities. (2014). Retrieved from www.cdpf.org.cn/sjzx/tjgb/201403/t20140331_357749.shtml.

About CAPA. (n.d.). Retrieved from http://accessibilityunion.org/about.

Blanck, P. (2014a). *eQuality: The struggle for web accessibility by persons with cognitive disabilities.* New York: Cambridge University Press.

Blanck, P. (2014b). The struggle for web eQuality by persons with cognitive disabilities. *Behavioral Sciences & the Law, 32*(1), 4–32. doi:10.1002/bsl.2101.

Brown, A., Jay, C., Chen, A. Q., & Harper, S. (2012). The uptake of Web 2.0 technologies, and its impact on visually disabled users. *Universal Access in the Information Society, 11*(2), 185–199.

BSI. (2010). *BS 8878:2010 Web accessibility – Code of practice*: BSI. http://shop.bsigroup.com/en/ProductDetail/?pid=000000000030180388&rdt=wmt.

Cooper, M. (2007). Accessibility of emerging rich web technologies. In *Proceedings of the 2007 international cross-disciplinary conference on Web accessibility - W4A '07* (p. 93). New York, USA: ACM Press.

Ellis, K., & Kent, M. (2011). *Disability and new media*. New York: Routledge.

Evolution of Internet in China. (2001). Retrieved from www.edu.cn/introduction_1378/20060323/t20060323_4285.shtml.

Forum on China Information Accessibility. (n.d.). Retrieved from www.cfdp.org/jsgc/node_302877.htm.

Giannoumis, G. A. (2014a). Regulating web content: the nexus of legislation and performance standards in the United Kingdom and Norway. *Behavioral Sciences & The Law*, 32(1), 52–75. doi:10.1002/bsl.2103.

Giannoumis, G. A. (2014b). Self-regulation and the legitimacy of voluntary procedural standards. *Administration & Society*, 1–23. doi:10.1177/009539 9714548270.

Giannoumis, G. A. (2014c). The web as a site of intractable governance. In H. Caltenco, P.-O. Hedvall, A. Larsson, K. Rassmus-Gröhn, & B. Rydeman (Eds.), *Universal Design 2014: Three Days of Creativity and Diversity* (pp. 384–393). Lund, Sweden: IOS Press.

Giannoumis, G. A. (2015a). Auditing web accessibility: The role of interest organizations in promoting compliance through certification. *First Monday*, 20(9).

Giannoumis, G. A. (2015b). Transatlantic learning: From Washington to London and beyond. *Inclusion*, 3(2), 92–107.

Giannoumis, G. A. (2015c). Transnational convergence of public procurement policy: a 'bottom-up'analysis of policy networks and the international harmonisation of accessibility standards for information and communication technology. *International Review of Law, Computers & Technology* (ahead-of-print), 1–24.

Gibson, B. (2007). Enabling an accessible web 2.0. In *Proceedings of the 2007 international cross-disciplinary conference on Web accessibility (W4A) - W4A '07* (pp. 1–6). New York, USA: ACM Press.

Goggin, G., & Newell, C. (2003). *Digital disability: The social construction of disability in new media*. Lanham, MD, USA: Rowman & Littlefield.

Introduction to CDPF. (2007). Retrieved from www.cdpf.org.cn/zzjg/jggk/.

ISC Website. (n.d.). Retrieved from www.isc.org.cn/english/.

Jaeger, P. T., Bertot, J. C., & Shilton, K. (2012). Information policy and social media: Framing government—citizen web 2.0 interactions. In *Web 2.0 technologies and democratic governance* (pp. 11–25). New York: Springer.

Jaeger, P. T., & Xie, B. (2009). Developing online community accessibility guidelines for persons with disabilities and older adults. *Journal of Disability Policy Studies*, 20(1), 55–63.

Jia, W., & Wang, X. (2014). Comparative study on accessible design laws and regulations of USA, Japan & China. *Urban Research*, 4, 116–120.

Kelly, B., Sloan, D., Brown, S., Seale, J., Petrie, H., Lauke, P., & Ball, S. (2007). Accessibility 2.0: people, policies and processes. In *W4A '07 Proceedings of the 2007 international cross-disciplinary conference on Web accessibility* (pp. 138–147). New York, USA: ACM Press.

Lisney, E., Li, C., & Liu, S. (2007). The potential of web accessibility in China: a hypothesis on its impact on the global web interface. *Universal Access in Human-Computer Interaction. Applications and Services* (pp. 79–87). Berlin, Heidelberg: Springer.

Magro, M. J. (2012). A review of social media use in e-government. *Administrative Sciences, 2*(2), 148–161.

MIIT of PRC. (n.d.). Retrieved from www.miit.gov.cn/.

Petrie, H., Savva, A., & Power, C. (2015). Towards a unified definition of web accessibility. In *Proceedings of the 12th Web for All Conference on - W4A '15* (pp. 1–13). New York, USA: ACM Press.

Ragnedda, M., & Muschert, G. W. (2013). Introduction. In M. Ragnedda & G. W. Muschert (Eds.), *The digital divide: The internet and social inequality in international perspective* (Vol. 73). New York: Routledge.

Rau, P-L. P., Zhou, L., Sun, N., & Zhong, R. (2016). Evaluation of web accessibility in China: Changes from 2009 to 2013. *Universal Access in the Information Society*, 1–7.

Regulations on building a barrier-free environment. (2012). Retrieved from www.gov.cn/zwgk/2012–07/10/content_2179864.htm.

Rodriguez, J. E. (2011). *Social media use in higher education: Key areas to consider for educators.* Invited presentation at the National Association for Kinesiology in Higher Education Leadership Development Workshop (2014).

Shi, Y. (2006). E-government web site accessibility in Australia and China a longitudinal study. *Social Science Computer Review, 24*(3), 378–385.

Shi, Y. (2007). The accessibility of Chinese local government web sites: An exploratory study. *Government Information Quarterly, 24*(2), 377–403.

Thatcher, J. (2006). *Web accessibility web standards and regulatory compliance.* New York: FriendsofED; Distributed by Springer-Verlag.

United Nations Treaty Collection. (2016). Retrieved from https://treaties.un.org/Pages/ViewDetails.aspx?src=IND&mtdsg_no=IV-15&chapter=4&lang=en.

Visually impaired man sues China Railway Corp over ticketing website. (2016). Retrieved www.ecns.cn/cns-wire/2016/01–26/197125.shtml.

Without speaking Captcha, visually impaired passengers will not be trapped. (2016). Retrieved from http://opinion.people.com.cn/n1/2016/0128/c1003-28092732.html.

Yao, D., Qiu, Y., Huang, H., Du, Z., & Ma, J. (2011). A survey of technology accessibility problems faced by older users in China. *Universal Access in the Information Society, 10*(4), 373–390. doi:10.1007/s10209-011-0222-3.

Yin, R. K. (2013). *Case study research: design and methods.* Thousand Oaks, CA: Sage Publications.

Zhang, J. (2015). On the current situation, existing problems, tactics and countermeasures of information accessibility of China. *Journal of Academic Library and Information Science, 33*(3), 5–22.

11 The Accessibility of Chinese Social Media Applications

A Heuristic Evaluation of the WeChat App

Weiqin Chen, Way Kiat Bong, and Nan Li

Introduction

China has the fastest growth in term of its social media usage worldwide (Lien & Cao, 2014). According to the research report by Kantar Group Limited (Kantar, 2016), China ranks third highest in social media penetration when compared with the USA, UK, France and Brazil. A total of 51 percent of the urban population in China use social media in their daily life, an increase of 17 percent from 2015. This acceleration is happening across all age groups – the report also shows that among the social media users, 30 percent are over 50 years old, while 10 percent are over 60 years old. Among the Chinese social media services, WeChat (Weixin) is the most popular and attracts 75.9 percent of the total internet users, while QQ attracts 50 percent and Weibo 35 percent.

Social media services in China provide platforms for communication and sharing information. For example, people use microblogs (Weibo) to share information about public incidents or disseminate information during natural disasters (Qu, Huang, Zhang, & Zhang, 2011). Chinese cities have used social media to establish city brands and promote city images (Zhou & Wang, 2014). Social media services have also been considered as having the potential to empower elderly and persons with disabilities (Leist, 2013; Shpigelman & Gill, 2014). However, the increasing popularity of social media services has also created new digital barriers, such as poor colour contrast, small font size, lack of clear instruction related to the operations users are currently carrying out and complicated and crowded interfaces. Such barriers make social media services difficult to learn and use, not only for the elderly and people with disabilities, but also for people without disabilities. This causes people to be excluded from using social media services, thus resulting in inequality in sharing and accessing information and in participating in societal activities.

To ensure equality in society it is essential for social media services to be accessible for all, by which we mean that the design of social media should work for people of all ages and abilities in different situations and under various circumstances, such as in a noisy environment, in a dark room or using an older version of operating system. In the past decade, equal rights for people with disabilities has been gaining increasing attention in China, and social media services have become an important platform for increasing awareness and sharing information. However, digital accessibility in China is still a new area. International researchers have carried out studies on the accessibility of non-Chinese social media services, such as Facebook, Twitter, etc; however, at the time of writing, the accessibility of Chinese social media has not been studied.

This paper focuses on one of the most popular Chinese social media services, WeChat, and aims to identify digital barriers in that app for all potential users including the elderly, people with disabilities and people without disabilities. We conducted a heuristic evaluation to study the accessibility of WeChat on different mobile platforms using a set of heuristics adapted from the W3C (World Wide Web Consortium) mobile accessibility considerations (W3C Mobile Accessibility, 2015). Based on the evaluation results, recommendations on improving the accessibility of WeChat are provided. The research presented in this paper is a part of a bigger project conducting systematic evaluations of a carefully selected Chinese social media services on different platforms using a combination of automatic testing, heuristic evaluation and user testing based on relevant principle and guidelines. The goal of the research is to increase awareness of accessibility issues in Chinese social media services and provide recommendations for making these services accessible to all.

This chapter begins by considering the accessibility of social media, including existing and relevant international research. We then provide an overview of the functions and interface of WeChat so that we can later refer to these when presenting the evaluation methods and findings. In the last section, we discuss the findings, reflect on the use of W3C mobile accessibility considerations and present the recommendations for improving the accessibility of WeChat.

Social Media Accessibility

As mentioned above, much research has been carried out regarding the (in)accessibility of a number of different social media platforms. In 2012, Media Access Australia conducted a review to identify accessibility issues in the most popular social media services including Facebook, LinkedIn, Youtube, Twitter, Skype and blogging websites (Media Access Australia, 2012). None of these services were found to be fully accessible. In July 2015, WebAIM conducted a screen reader user survey (WebAIM, 2015). Screen readers are audio interfaces that convert text into synthesised speech so that users can listen to the content. This reported that among the 2,515 respondents, only 1,369 (60.3 percent) considered social media websites as "very accessible" or "somewhat accessible", while 659 (29 percent) considered them as "very inaccessible" or "somewhat inaccessible".

Lee, Hong, An and Lee (2014) investigated the accessibility of four social network services (Facebook, Twitter, Me2day and Yozm) with eight disabled persons focusing on navigation-related tasks. The participants included two blind, two with low vision, two with brain lesions and two with an upper extremity disability. They found that none of the services was fully accessible and the participants experienced substantial difficulties when using these services. Facebook has also been tested by Giraud, Colombi, Russo and Thérouanne (2011) – they discovered accessibility issues that caused blind users to use more time to complete the testing tasks. Based on the discussion with the elderly about the difficulties they faced when using social media services, Arfaa and Wang (2014) reviewed 19 popular social media websites – including social networking, social bookmarking, blogs, photo sharing, video-sharing and wiki sites – for violations against Section 508 compliance and Web Content Accessibility Guidelines (WCAG) 1.0 and 2.0. The results showed that many elderly users had difficulties in interpreting the complex layout of the social networking sites and many of the heavily used social media sites did not adhere to accessibility guidelines. Maneesaeng, Punyabukkana and Suchato (2016) evaluated six popular video call applications on the Android platform – Skype, Line, Tango, HangOut, WeChat and Viber – and found that none of these applications was accessible for blind people.

However, although it can be seen that many social media services have been evaluated, these services are often not available in China. The accessibility of Chinese social media services such as WeChat, QQ and Weibo, is largely ignored. In this research, by focusing on the accessibility of WeChat, we hope to inspire others and put the accessibility issues of Chinese social media on the research agenda.

WeChat

WeChat is a social media product of Tencent. After its release in 2011, it has grown fast and by the end of 2015 it had over 600 million monthly active users from all over the world (Tencent, 2016). One of the reasons WeChat is so popular is because it provides an instant messaging service. Instant messaging is one social media tool that is widely used nowadays due to its convenience and cost-savings (Church & Oliveira, 2013); WeChat also provides a platform where users can play games and make new friends. With the increasing popularity of WeChat, it has also become the focus of research publications in education (Mao, 2014; Zhang, 2014), library studies (Xu, Kang, Song, & Clarke, 2015) and health (Fung et al., 2013). Lien and Cao (2014) have examined users' attitudes and behaviours while using WeChat, while Ke (2015) studied the impact of WeChat on the elderly in urban China.

WeChat has four main tabs (Figure 11.1), which categorise its four main functions – chats, contacts, discover and me.

Figure 11.1 Chats screen with four tabs.

Chats

The chats screen lists all the chat threads. Tapping on the individual chat thread will navigate the user to the corresponding chatting screen (Figure 11.2). Users can send text messages using a virtual keyboard, or send voice messages by tapping and holding the 'hold to talk' button (Figure 11.2b). The audio icon in Figure 11.2a (on top of the emoticons) can be tapped to change to hold to talk in Figure 11.2b, while the keyboard icon in Figures 11.2a and b can be tapped to change back to a virtual keyboard. Tapping the emoticon icon will switch to emoticons. Users can also send photos (selecting photo from gallery and taking a new photo with the camera), short videos (using the 'sight' feature in WeChat), add their location, a name card and favourite items and make voice calls and video calls in WeChat. Tapping the '+' icon (Figure 11.2b) users will be able to make video calls and send other types of messages, such as photos, location, etc.

Contacts

The contacts screen displays a list of contacts that user has added in WeChat. By tapping the 'add contact' icon, the user is directed to the add contact screen where there are several methods in which to add a

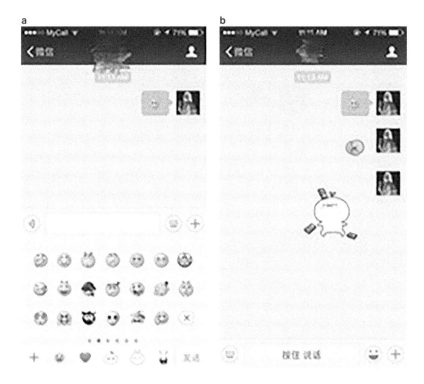

Figure 11.2 Chatting screen, showing (a) emoticons and (b) the 'hold to talk' button.

contact. In order to delete a contact in the Windows and Android mobile operating systems, users have to use 'long press' (press and hold) on the contact and the option to delete the contact will then pop out. In iOS, users must first tap the contact to bring out the profile of this contact (Figure 11.3a), then must tap the '...' icon in order to see the profile setting screen with the option to remove the contact (Figure 11.3b). This is considered to be one of the 'hidden' features in WeChat.

Discover

Discover has five main features – moments, scan QR code, shake, people nearby and games. WeChat version 6.3.8 in iOS 9.2 and WeChat version 6.2.2 in Android 3.2 have all five of them while WeChat version 6.0.6 in Windows phone 8.1 only has four – it does not have games. Moments is a function in WeChat where users can update their statuses, post their own photos or short videos and see what others have posted. In addition to individual updates, users can also share links to interesting websites or videos. By using scan QR code, users can identify other contacts

Figure 11.3 Deleting a contact, showing (a) the profile screen with the '...' in the upper right and (b) the delete button in the profile setting screen.

and then choose to add them into their contact lists. Other people's QR codes need to be scanned within the frame at QR code scanning screen. Shake is a function where users can make new friends with those who are also using shake function. Shake results include other WeChat users who are a long distance away. People nearby displays WeChat users who are only a short distance away. The people nearby results can be filtered based on gender; users can tap on a user to view his or her profile. They can then also choose to send greetings or a report. Finally, users can play games in WeChat, but they need to download them first.

Me

Me is where users manage their personal information and settings in WeChat. They can manage my posts, favourites, sticker gallery, settings, etc. Some versions on some platforms have more functions than others. For example, WeChat version 6.3.8 in iOS 9.2 and version 6.0.6 in Windows 8.1 update 2 have four functions – my posts, favourites, sticker gallery, settings – while WeChat version 6.3.9 in iOS 8.4.1 has other functions such as wallet and coupon. In my posts, users can publish and view their own posts of photos or short videos; the functionalities are similar to moments function in the discover tab. However, in my posts it is only limited to the user's own posts – others' posts will not be shown. While using WeChat, users can choose to save text messages, voice messages, photos, posts in moments, locations, etc. to the favourites folder. They must use long press on a message to prompt the option for saving it into favourites. Users can manage their stickers in sticker gallery where they can choose to download and delete stickers. The last and yet most important functionality in the me tab is settings where users can choose their preferences and manage their personal information. For example, users can choose their preferred text size.

Method

We conducted a heuristic evaluation on WeChat in the period from November to December 2015, covering a selected set of mobile operating systems, device models and WeChat versions (Table 11.1).

There are several 'hidden' features and functions in WeChat which do not show in the interface. Users must know particular gestures or a series of actions in order to be able to use them. For example, in the Android platform, deleting a contact (Figure 11.3) and deleting a message require users to use long press (press and hold) on the contact and message to prompt the option. Because these features are not shown in the interface, they are not covered in our evaluation. Table 11.2 lists all the main functions and features in WeChat and those that were included in the evaluation. They are chats (including all non-hidden features), contacts (including all non-hidden features), moments, scan QR code, shake, people nearby, games, my posts, favourites, sticker gallery and settings. All eleven features were tested for iOS, while 10 features were tested for the Android (missing sticker gallery) and the Windows phones (missing games).

We evaluated WeChat based on the W3C mobile accessibility considerations (W3C Mobile Accessibility, 2015) which describe how WCAG 2.0 and other W3C/WAI (Web Accessibility Initiative) principles, guidelines and success criteria can be applied to mobile applications. The W3C

Table 11.1 Operating System and Versions, Device Model and WeChat Version Evaluated

OS	OS version	Device Model	WeChat Version
Windows	8.1 Update 2	Lumia	6.0.6
Android	3.2	Tablet GT-P7500	6.2.2
iOS	9.2	iPhone 6S	6.3.8

Table 11.2 Functions and Features in WeChat

Main Functions	Details/Features	Appeared on the Interface	Evaluated
Chats	Text message	Yes	Yes
	Voice message	Yes	Yes
	Picture message (photo & camera)	Yes	Yes
	Emoticons/stickers	Yes	Yes
	Short video (sight)	Yes	Yes
	Voice call	Yes	Yes
	Video call	Yes	Yes
	Location	Yes	Yes
	Name card	Yes	Yes
	Favourites	Yes	Yes
	Delete message	No (hidden)	No
	Copy/forward message	No (hidden)	No
Contacts	Add contact	Yes	Yes
	Delete contact	No (hidden)	No
Discover	Moments	Yes	Yes
	Scan QR code	Yes	Yes
	Shake	Yes	Yes
	People nearby	Yes	Yes
	Games	Yes	Yes
Me	My posts	Yes	Yes
	Favourites	Yes	Yes
	Sticker gallery	Yes	Yes
	Settings	Yes	Yes

mobile accessibility considerations dated 26 February 2015 are W3C's first public working draft and aim to provide informative guidance for interpreting and applying WCAG 2.0 to mobile content and applications. The Mobile Accessibility Task Force who created this document have requested feedback on this working draft. At the time we conducted the research, there was no similar Chinese standards nor guidelines that could be used to evaluate WeChat and thus this draft appeared to be the most applicable for our heuristic evaluation. However, while these considerations have been used by developers to guide their development of mobile apps, they have not been used as heuristics to evaluate the accessibility of mobile apps. By using these considerations in our heuristic evaluation, we therefore also aimed to explore the use of these considerations and provide feedback to the Mobile Accessibility Task Force.

Based on the consideration document, we made a list of guidelines and criteria for the heuristic evaluation (Table 11.3). Each individual function and feature in Table 11.2, except for sticker gallery in Android and games in the Windows platform, were evaluated according to the guidelines and success criteria. Notes and screenshots (for non-compliance)

Table 11.3 Mobile Accessibilities Considerations (Heuristics Used in the Evaluation)

Principle/Guidelines	Success Criteria
1. Perceivable	
Small screen size	–
Zoom/magnification	1.4.4 Resize text (level AA)
Contrast	1.4.3 Contrast (minimum) (level AA) which requires a contrast of at least 4.5:1 (or 3:1 for large-scale text) 1.4.6 Contrast (enhanced) (level AAA) which requires a contrast of at least 7:1 (or 4.5:1 for large-scale text)
2. Operable	
Keyboard control for touchscreen devices	2.1.1 Keyboard (level A) 2.1.2 No keyboard trap (level A) 2.4.3 Focus order (level A) 2.4.7 Focus visible (level AA)
Touch target size and spacing	–
Touchscreen gestures	–
Device manipulation gestures	2.1.1 Keyboard (level A)
Placing buttons where they are easy to access	–
3. Understandable	
Changing screen orientation (portrait/ landscape)	–
Consistent layout	3.2.3 Consistent navigation (level AA) 3.2.4 Consistent identification (level AA)
Positioning important page elements before the page scroll	–
Grouping operable elements that perform the same action	2.4.4 Link purpose (in context) (level A) 2.4.9 Link purpose (link only) (level AA)
Provide clear indication that elements are actionable	3.2.3 Consistent navigation (level AA) 3.2.4 Consistent identification (level AA)
Provide instructions for custom touchscreen and device manipulation gestures	3.3.2 Labels or instructions (level A) 3.3.5 Help (level AAA)
4. Robust	
Set the virtual keyboard to the type of data entry required	–
Provide easy methods for data entry	–
Support the characteristic properties of the platform	–

were taken during the evaluation. We gave a score (yes, no or partial) for each guideline/criteria. N/A was given if the criterion was not applicable or related. The same process was repeated for the different platforms and versions (Table 11.1). In addition, for Principle 4: robust – support for the characteristic properties of the platform in the W3C mobile accessibility considerations, we tested WeChat using respective screen reader features in each mobile platform, i.e. TalkBack in Android, VoiceOver in iOS and Narrator in Windows.

Data Analysis and Results

The heuristic evaluation results are summarised in Table 11.4. We added up the scores for all the functions and features in each platform. For example, in the Android version, there is no sticker gallery. The remaining scores for chats (including all non-hidden features), contacts (including all non-hidden features), moments, scan QR code, shake, people nearby, games, my posts, favourites and settings were put together and resulted in six compliance, one non-compliance and three partial compliance for Principle 1: Perceivable – zoom/magnification.

As shown in Table 11.4, there are two considerations which failed in all three different mobile platforms, meaning that none of the functions/ features in WeChat complied with the criteria. Principle 3: understandable – Success criterion 3.3.5: Help (Level AAA) assesses whether and how help information related to the function currently being performed is provided – WeChat failed to provide help information in all the test platforms. For example, in the chatting screen, there was no indication that message had been delivered (refer to chatting screen in Figures 11.2a and b). In addition, none of the functions and features in WeChat provided assistance information; this means that users do not get help inside WeChat when facing difficulties. Principle 4: robust – sets the virtual keyboard to the type of data entry required means to automatically set different keyboards depending on what type of data the user is required to put in. WeChat itself did not provide such automatic adaptation.

There are other important considerations in which WeChat scored very few 'yes' points. For example, for when assessing Principle 1: perceivable – resize text (success criteria level AA) it was found that text messages could not be zoomed in or zoomed out. When double tapping the text message, it popped out as single page text message where the text message was enlarged to a certain font size. WeChat itself has font size options, so it was possible to enlarge the font size. However, in the Android version, it did not comply with the criterion to enlarge up to 200 percent without assistive technology, something that was needed as not much enlargement is offered in the WeChat standard setting.

Colour contrast was also found to be an issue in WeChat. Principle 1: perceivable – contrast (minimum) (success criteria level AA) requires

Table 11.4 Evaluation Results

	Android	iOS	Windows
Principle 1: Perceivable			
Small screen size	9 yes 1 partial	9 yes 2 partial	9 yes 1 no
Zoom/magnification	6 yes 1 no 3 partial	4 yes 2 no 5 partial	1 yes 9 no
1.4.4 Resize text (level AA)	10 no	4 yes 2 no 5 partial	1 yes 9 no
1.4.3 Contrast (minimum) (level AA) which requires a contrast of at least 4.5:1 (or 3:1 for large-scale text)	1 yes 9 no	2 yes 9 no	2 yes 6 no 2 partial
1.4.6 Contrast (enhanced) (level AAA) which requires a contrast of at least 7:1 (or 4.5:1 for large-scale text)	1 yes 9 no	1 yes 10 no	1 yes 7 no 2 partial
Principle 2: Operable			
2.1.1 Keyboard (level A)	10 yes	11 yes	10 yes
2.1.2 No keyboard trap (level A)	10 yes	11 yes	10 yes
2.4.3 Focus order (level A)	10 yes	11 yes	10 yes
2.4.7 Focus visible (level AA)	10 yes	11 yes	10 yes
Touch target size and spacing	10 yes	11 yes	10 yes
Touchscreen gestures	7 yes 3 partial	9 yes 2 partial	9 yes 1 partial
Device manipulation gestures	N/A	N/A	N/A
2.1.1 Keyboard (level A)	N/A	N/A	N/A
Placing buttons where they are easy to access	10 yes	11 yes	9 yes 1 partial
Principle 3: Understandable			
Changing screen orientation (portrait/landscape)	6 yes 3 no 1 partial	11 no	10 no
3.2.3 Consistent navigation (level AA)	10 yes	11 yes	10 yes
3.2.4 Consistent identification (level AA)	10 yes	11 yes	8 yes 2 partial
Positioning important page elements before the page scroll	10 yes	11 yes	10 yes
Grouping operable elements that perform the same action	10 yes	11 yes	10 yes
2.4.4 Link purpose (in context) (level A)	N/A	1 no 10 N/A	N/A
2.4.9 Link purpose (link only) (level AA)	N/A	1 no 10 N/A	N/A
Provide clear indication that elements are actionable	6 yes 2 no 2 partial	7 yes 2 no 2 partial	4 yes 3 no 3 partial
3.2.3 Consistent navigation (level AA)	10 yes	11 yes	9 yes 1 partial
3.2.4 Consistent identification (level AA)	10 yes	11 yes	9 yes 1 partial

	Android	iOS	Windows
Provide instructions for custom touchscreen and device manipulation gestures	N/A	N/A	N/A
3.3.2 Labels or instructions (level A)	2 yes 6 no 2 partial	4 yes 5 no 2 partial	3 yes 5 no 2 partial
3.3.5 Help (level AAA)	10 no	11 no	10 no
Principle 4: Robust			
Set the virtual keyboard to the type of data entry required	10 no	11 no	10 no
Provide easy methods for data entry	10 partial	11 partial	10 partial
Support the characteristic properties of the platform	10 partial	11 partial	10 partial

a contrast of at least 4.5:1 (or 3:1 for large-scale text) and contrast (enhanced) (success criteria level AAA) requires a contrast of at least 7:1 (or 4.5:1 for large-scale text). Referring to the same chatting screen in Figures 11.2a,b and 11.4, we can see that messages were either in black font with a white background or black font with a bright green background. These offered good colour contrast. However, the problem with contrast was where it showed the date and time and other indications – the contrast ratio for these colours was only 1:57:1. The colour contrast in the moments screen was also poor, especially where it showed 'tap to change album cover' (Figure 11.4b).

In addition, not all gestures in WeChat were easy to use (Principle 2: operable – touchscreen gestures). One of them was the 'hold to talk' button (Figure 11.2b) – the need to use long press on this button while recording audio messages could be difficult for users with muscle control problems. Further actions such as deleting a contact, saving message to favourites, copying and deleting a message could also be problematic since they were 'hidden' and users would not know that they needed to use either long press or tap the message/contact and then tap '…' on the next screen to bring out the options.

Another serious issue of WeChat was its compatibility with a screen reader (Principle 4: robust – support the characteristic properties of the platform). When using the voiceover in iOS with WeChat, we experienced much confusion with the names of icons, for instance, the icons for the four tabs (Figure 11.1). When selecting chats, the voiceover read 'selected chats chat 1 of 4'. The word 'chat' should be removed. The same happened with the other three tabs as the voiceover read 'contacts chat 2 of 4', 'discover chat 3 of 4' and 'me chat 4 of 4' respectively.

Besides the confusion with icon names when using the voiceover in iOS, there were also failures when using the screen reader which resulted in users not being able to proceed with further actions. For example,

Figure 11.4 Poor colour contrast screen, showing (a) the time and indications in the chatting screen and (b) the 'tap to change album cover' information in the moments screen.

when we tested WeChat on a Windows phone, narrator was unable to read the tab icon at the top (highlighted in Figure 11.5 with a square). It read 'image' instead of what the tab icon was. It was then impossible to navigate or perform any further actions. When double tapping on an icon, the narrator read 'command not available'. In Android, TalkBack did not read the emoticons, stickers nor send icon in the chatting screen. When double tapping on the text message, TalkBack only read 'clicked'. Screen reader users would have problems sending emoticon and stickers and knowing what was written in the text message.

We added up all the scores in the heuristic evaluation for the three different platforms. As shown in Table 11.5, 'partial' and 'no' together constitute 38.8 percent of the total score. This clearly indicates that WeChat still has room for improvement in term of accessibility. We acknowledge that Tencent have conducted testing and evaluations of WeChat as a part of the software design and development process, some of which might have been heuristic evaluations. However, the number of non-compliances found in our evaluation show that Tencent may have

Figure 11.5 WeChat's chat screen while testing using narrator.

Table 11.5 Summary of the Heuristic Evaluation Scores

Platform	Yes	Partial	No
Android	158	32	60
iOS	172	40	65
Windows	145	35	70
Total	475	107	195

focused only on usability and not accessibility in their evaluations, and they certainly have not followed the W3C mobile accessibility considerations or similar mobile accessibility guidelines.

Recommendations and Conclusion

Through the heuristic evaluation we found a number of accessibility issues in WeChat. Based on the evaluation, we have provided a list of recommendations on the issues with high severity. We acknowledge that

WeChat is under constant improvement and updating and that, since our evaluation, new updates of WeChat have been published for different platforms. Some of the issues may have been fixed in the new updates. The six recommendations are to:

1   Provide information related to the function currently being performed (Principle 3: understandable – help, level AAA). It is important to provide just-in-time help and feedback rather than making users stop the task at hand to look for documentation.
2   Set different keyboards automatically when the user is required to type in different types of data (Principle 4: robust – set the virtual keyboard to the type of data entry required).
3   Make sure text can be enlarged up to 200 percent without assistive technology (Principle 1: perceivable – resize text, level AA).
4   Improve colour contrast. This is related to Principle 1: perceivable – contrast (minimum, level AA) which requires a contrast of at least 4.5:1 (or 3:1 for large-scale text) and contrast (enhanced, level AAA) which requires a contrast of at least 7:1 (or 4.5:1 for large-scale text).
5   Provide explicit and simpler operations. For example, the long press gesture for bringing up options for further actions is difficult for users to figure out and perform (Principle 2: operable – touchscreen gestures). To delete a message in iOS, users need three steps to come to the delete button. These solutions are not particularly intuitive or easy to perform.
6   Make sure WeChat is compatible with screen readers (Principle 4: robust – support the characteristic properties of the platform). We have found some issues related to the compatibility with screen readers. For the third-party screen readers, it is important to make sure that WeChat works together with them.

Through the evaluation we have also explored the use of W3C mobile accessibility considerations as heuristics to evaluate the accessibility of mobile apps and provided some feedback to the Mobile Accessibility Task Force.

W3C mobile accessibility considerations provided us with a set of defined guidelines and criteria as heuristics for evaluating WeChat. Previously we have used the success criteria in WCAG 2.0 as heuristics to evaluate the accessibility of websites (Sanderson, Chen, & Kessle, 2015). We found the considerations helpful in understanding the applicability of WCAG 2.0 to mobile applications. The format of the information was also found helpful for our evaluation and we were able to give score (yes, no or partial) based on the consideration. One issue we have identified is the relationship between the guidelines and the relevant success criteria from WCAG 2.0. For example, in the zoom/magnification under Principle 1: perceivable, we understand that this covers the zoom and magnification feature in OS-level and browser-level, while the related WCAG 2.0 success criteria 1.4.4: resize text (level AA) covers the requirements for resizing text without assistive technology. Therefore, we used them as two separate heuristics in our evaluation. We also found out that some other accessibility issues were not covered by the considerations. First, there are no considerations that are directly related to the understanding of a mobile interface. Principle 1: perceivable focuses only on size, magnification and colour contrast while Principle 3: understandable emphasises positioning of the elements on the interfaces and indications that they are actionable. For instance, the '...' in WeChat could be difficult to understand when there was no extra information (Figure 11.3a). In addition, the considerations do not explicitly cover the issue of 'hidden' functions and features, such as deleting contacts and taking further action of messages, i.e. copying, deleting or forwarding them. These are not visible on the interface and need special gestures or actions to prompt the options.

By conducting this research, we aim to highlight the importance of social media accessibility, increase the awareness of accessibility issues and improve the accessibility in Chinese digital systems and services, as well as contribute to the accessibility principles and guidelines. At the time of writing, we are conducting accessibility evaluation of WeChat with elderly user groups (Yang, 2014) and planning an evaluation of Weibo on mobile devices. We will report the results from these studies in future publications.

References

Arfaa, J., & Wang, Y. (2014). An accessibility evaluation of social media websites for elder adults. In G. Meiselwitz (Eds.), *Social Computing and Social Media* (pp. 12–24). Switzerland: Springer.

Church, K., & Oliveira, R. D. (2013). *What's up with whatsapp? Comparing mobile instant messaging behaviors with traditional SMS*. Paper presented at the 15th International Conference on Human-Computer Interaction with Mobile Devices and Services. Munich, Germany.

Fung, I. C., Fu, K. W., Ying, Y., Schaible, B., Hao, Y., Chan, C. H., & Tse, Z. T. (2013). Chinese social media reaction to the MERS-CoV and avian influenza A (H7N9) outbreaks. *Infectious Diseases of Poverty*, 2(1), 1–12.

Giraud, S., Colombi, T., Russo, A., & Thérouanne, P. (2011). *Accessibility of rich internet applications for blind people: A study to identify the main problems and solutions*. Paper presented at the Proceedings of the 9th ACM SIGCHI Italian Chapter International Conference on Computer-Human Interaction: Facing Complexity. Alghero, Italy.

Kantar. (2016). *Social media impact report*. Retrieved from http://cn-en.kantar.com/media/1190989/kantar_social_media_impact_report_2016.pdf.

Ke, Y. (2015). Ageing on WeChat: The impact of social media on elders in urban China. *Journal of Visual and Media Anthropology*, 1(1), 8–21.

Lee, S. M., Hong, S. G., An, D. H., & Lee, H. M. (2014). Disability users' evaluation of the web accessibility of SNS. *Service Business, 8*(4), 517–540. doi:10.1007/s11628–013–0205-y.

Leist, A. K. (2013). Social media use of older adults. *Gerontology, 59*, 378–384.

Lien, C. H., & Cao, Y. (2014). Examining WeChat users' motivations, trust, attitudes, and positive word-of-mouth: Evidence from China. *Computers in Human Behavior, 41*, 104–111.

Maneesaeng, N., Punyabukkana, P., & Suchato, A. (2016). Accessible video-call application on android for the blind. *Lecture Notes on Software Engineering, 4*(2), 95.

Mao, C. (2014). Friends and relaxation: Key factors of undergraduate students' WeChat using. *Creative Education, 5*, 636–640.

Media Access Australia (2012). *SociAbility: social media for people with a disability.* Retrieved from www.mediaaccess.org.au/sites/default/files/files/MAA2657-%20Report-OnlineVersion.pdf.

Qu, Y., Huang, C., Zhang, P., & Zhang, J. (2011). *Microblogging after a major disaster in China: a case study of the 2010 Yushu earthquake.* ACM 2011 Conference on Computer Supported Cooperative Work (CSCW 2011), Hangzhou, China (pp. 25–34). New York: ACM.

Sanderson, N. C., Chen, W., & Kessel, S. (2015). The accessibility of web-based media services – An evaluation. In M. Antona & C. Stephanidis (Eds.), *Universal Access in Human-Computer Interaction: Access to Today's Technologies* (Vol. 9175, pp. 242–252). Switzerland: Springer.

Shpigelman, C.-N., & Gill, C. J. (2014). Facebook use by persons with disabilities. *Journal of Computer-Mediated Communication, 19*, 610–624.

Tencent. (2016). *Tencent 2015 fourth quarter and annual results.* Retrieved from http://tencent.com/en-us/content/at/2016/attachments/20160317.pdf.

W3C Mobile Accessibility (2015). *Mobile accessibility: How WCAG 2.0 and other W3C/WAI Guidelines apply to mobile.* Retrieved from www.w3.org/TR/mobile-accessibility-mapping/.

WebAIM (2015). Screen reader user survey #6 results. Retrieved from http://webaim.org/projects/screenreadersurvey6/#socialaccess.

Xu, J., Kang, Q., Song, Z., & Clarke, C. P. (2015). Applications of mobile social media: WeChat among academic libraries in China. *The Journal of Academic Librarianship, 41*(1), 21–30.

Yang, F. (2014). *How to use the social capital and social media tools to construct the old-age service system under the shortage of relevant resources: policy and experiences in China.* Paper presented at the Proceedings of the 8th International Conference on Theory and Practice of Electronic Governance, Guimaraes, Portugal.

Zhang, Y. (2014). Mobile education via social media: Case study on WeChat. In Y. Zhang (Eds.), *Handbook of mobile teaching and learning* (pp. 381–402). Berlin, Heidelberg: Springer.

Zhou, L., & Wang, T. (2014). Social media: A new vehicle for city marketing in China. *Cities, 37*, 27–32.

Part IV

Chinese Social Media in Greater China and Overseas

12 From (Anti-mainland) Sinophobia and Shibboleths to Mobilisation on a Taiwanese Message Board

Joshua Cader

This chapter examines the rise in Taiwanese anti-Chinese sentiment, drawing particular connections to language use on the locally-grounded PTT[1] bulletin board system (BBS), specifically its largest board, Gossiping. While the language prevalent on PTT is not limited to this platform, the elite character of the forum and its influence on news coverage – and thus the political process – make it an important window into the crystallising Taiwanese identity.

I start by discussing why Taiwan continues to use a telnet system (a non-hypertext application protocol) as common social media today, when the rest of the world has long since abandoned such systems in favour of the web and mobile apps. I follow with a look into increasing Taiwanese fear of the People's Republic of China (PRC), and discuss the emergence of a new Taiwanese-identifying identity inclusive of the formerly supreme Chinese Civil War-remnant *waishengren*[2] class. The role of language in this transformation is explained, particularly various forms of outsider-policing language play found in elite-identified alternative media such as PTT. The type of 'insiderness' fostered by such forums in general is explained. In the Taiwanese context, however, this insiderness is particularly politically potent, for reasons of language, culture and geography, which may have consequences not only for the future of Taiwan, but also for international security.

Taiwan's Use of a Telnet BBS

BBSs are among the earliest social media – their public availability, beginning in the late 1970s, predates that of the internet by a decade. Initially, use required a point-to-point connection via modem, thus only one user could be accommodated per phone line. The user would leave notes – hence the 'bulletin board' – for others to see. The point-to-point requirement gave BBSs a local character as long-distance calls were expensive. Today, most BBSs are accessed using telnet, itself antiquated, but allowing for many more users simultaneously – over 150,000 in the case of PTT. On PTT, a system limited to initial text-only posts and 80 character comments, there are consistently over 100,000 users online – with user-friendlier and far flashier web-based offerings available, this is a testament to its environmental necessity. Taiwan's mass media are generally seen to be bowing to the economic imperative of the massive Chinese market (Hsu, 2014), thus the need for an independent, non-monetisable, elite-identified BBS – the National Taiwan University (NTU) club-run PTT.

Justified Fears – Viable Outlets

Taiwanese fear of China is not an easily-condemned xenophobia – it inevitably ties into Taiwan's continued existence as a separate community. While in the past much fretting concerned standard dangerous others – such as female marriage migrants who were seen as uneducated and thus undesirable infusions into the body politic – the new fears are based on the potential negation of Taiwanese democracy. The counter-attack is class-based, pointing out that the beneficiaries of cross-strait investment pacts are largely entrepreneurs and big firms investing in mainland production centres. Yet while the government relies on such firms' tax revenue, the welfare of Taiwanese workers as well as national security must also be taken into account. Even without adopting an alter-globalisation mindset, an easy case can be made for strategic hedging and thus locating production in Southeast Asia instead, with costs being similar.[3] While there are understandable motives for said pacts, including the need to find a way around the ASEAN-China Free Trade Area, there is a sinking feeling that those pushing them may be purposely "encasing" Taiwan (Wright, 2014), setting up an eventual choice between unification and economic shambles.

These fears are particularly heightened among the young, not only because the slow slide to unification would culminate on their watch, but because of the ever-increasing cost of housing in Taipei due in part to mainland buyers making winners of those with property and losers of the educated young. While such graduates commonly speak English and could thus seek their fortunes elsewhere, a mass exodus to make way for Chinese money at the high end and workers at the low is not a responsible solution. These 'encasement' fears are no longer inert, having generated the desperation required to storm and occupy the legislature in the spring of 2014 in opposition to the Cross-Strait Service Trade Agreement as part of the Sunflower Movement – an alliance of class-based concerns with Taiwanese nationalism (Rowen, 2015).

Such alliances are not limited to Taiwan, of course. The 'one country two systems' formula under which Hong Kong was transferred to the PRC was intended to apply to Taiwan, thus the 'one China principle' enshrined under the 1992 Consensus adhered to by the Kuomintang (KMT) and the PRC.[4] Hong Kong's similar path yields less of a framework for peaceful unification and more a cautionary tale. Initially, similarly to Taiwan, Hong Kongers saw themselves as superior to their "illegal immigrant" (Hung, 2014) "country cousins" (Jones, 2014), but since the Asian financial crisis of 1997 such comfort in superiority has been less secure. While dominant discourse once concentrated on mainlanders displaying their peasant ways (for example by defecating in the streets), a sense of helpless dependency has set in, with 'parallel traders' and gaudy tourists represented by a menacing locust as in the infamous ad appearing in *Apple Daily* paid for largely by users of popular local forum HK Golden (Hung, 2014). The benefits of mainlander buying power, as in Taiwan, accrue to the entrepreneurial class (Jones, 2014), while adequate housing for the masses remains out of reach. The locust trope can also be understood to indicate a deeper fear – as locusts move on once they eat their fill, so too will Hong Kong be discarded in favour of Shanghai.

While Hong Kongers are exhorted to embrace further economic integration with the mainland by their leaders in a similar manner to former President Ma's appeals to the Taiwanese, and both polities grumble about such policies on social media, the Taiwanese have a crucial advantage – the ability to fire leaders bent on integration. The Taiwanese mood, and that of their technologically-inclined youthful elites on PTT, has a clear outlet in both electoral politics and protest movements that, unlike in Hong Kong, do not need to fear a People's Liberation Army garrison equipped with armoured personnel carriers.

Drawing Together and Pushing Away

While, as is common on message boards, Gossiping users attack many broad categories of people – women and gays, for instance, as well as more idiosyncratic targets such as academically inferior 'humanities people' (*wenzu*)[5] – attacks on mainland Chinese and their language use are particularly interesting.

The cleavage between Taiwanese and Chinese culture in Taiwan was ironically abetted by a policy whereby although Mandarin was pushed as the 'national language', replacing Japanese following WWII, the orthodoxy represented by Mandarin (Liu, 2012) extended to orthodoxy in general, with Taiwan being more 'Chinese' than China itself, especially following the destruction of the Cultural Revolution (Damm, 2011b; Zhong, 2016). Thus Taiwan is, if Chinese, a representative of a China that no longer exists. Sinicisation (in the form of Mandarin usage) and Taiwanisation (in the form of forging a coherent national polity clearly different than the mainland) are thus not at odds. Pressures from without merely give a name to this cleavage. The PRC monopolising China-as-concept in the eyes of the world requires a new identifier (Wu, 2004; Zhong, 2016) so one would not be mistaken for the mainland Chinese who are no longer 'Chinese'.

Waishengren Incorporated

Waishengren or "outside-province-people"[6] quickly managed to alienate the *benshengren* or "this-province-people" when they were sent to rule Taiwan following Japan's surrender after WWII. On 27 February 1947 a riot broke out over the beating of a grey-market peddler. A bystander was shot by police, igniting general disappointment with the KMT. The governor promised reform as a stalling tactic – when reinforcements arrived, thousands were killed[7] and thus began the 'white terror' – 40 years of martial law.

During the martial law period, the government – in name, as it largely remains today[8] but also in form – explicitly claimed to represent all of China, thus justifying temporary *waishengren* dominance as representative of the areas to be retaken. By the time the United States changed its diplomatic recognition of Chinese government from the Republic of China to the PRC in 1979, however, retaking the mainland no longer seemed legitimately possible. Thus began a push for 'indigenization' (*bentuhua*)[9] which no longer required a government-in-exile apparatus – making *waishengren* vestigial colonialists.

Though animosity between *waishengren* and the rest of Taiwanese society remains to an extent – as seen in simmering arguments over their historical role revealed in such forms as the Chinese Wikipedia entry talk page[10] (Damm, 2011a) and the outing of a *waishengren* diplomat as a virulently anti-Taiwanese blogger (Turton, 2009) – this has been alleviated somewhat in the younger generation, and even in the older as they are made aware of their 'Taiwaneseness'. In spite of ethnic affinity, the relaxation of laws on travel to the PRC has made many aware that nostalgia for their ancestral home is misplaced, or at least not tied to a place currently existing (Hillenbrand, 2006; Lin, 2011). Such an effect has been exacerbated in recent years by economic trends. With Taiwanese investment less necessary, a sincere welcome accompanying any sort of investment has been replaced by lists of demands (Lin, 2011) when investment is courted at all (Yu, Yu, & Lin, 2016).

Among the young, such disillusionment fostering a feeling of perhaps being Chinese, but not the "Chinese Chinese" (Lin, 2011), is unnecessary – their inclusion in the Taiwanese polity at large abetted not only by intermarriage but also by the democratisation process whereby professing a local identity became an obvious electoral asset. The former President Ma, certainly not one to abandon mainland ties, upon being elected the mayor of Taipei in 1998 "famously said in Hoklo [Taiwanese]: 'I eat Taiwanese rice, drink Taiwanese water, I am a New Taiwanese'" (Dupré, 2014). The "post-reform generation" (Le Pesant, 2011) – those born into this new democratic reality – have been found to be relatively uninterested in ethnic categorisation and identify primarily as Taiwanese across ethnic categories. Identity has become territorialised based on common life experience including a "shared feeling of being constantly unfairly treated by the international community and being victims of China's repeated humiliations and negation of their existence" (Le Pesant, 2011) due to being shut out of most international organisations.

The Divisive Role of Language on Two Chinese Internets

Language has been another coalescing factor, with Mandarin having become a language of Taiwan – and *the* language among the young and educated – with the majority of the young regarding it as their mother tongue (Liao, 2010). Mandarin usage in Taiwan, however, has taken on what its speakers regard as a "placid" tone, making it a "refined, cultivated, and sophisticated language that categorically differs from the PRC Mandarin" taken as "coarse and aggressive" (Liao, 2010). Structure can also be differentiated, with Taiwanese Mandarin drifting towards features of Southern Chinese dialects, such as commonly placing the verb before the object of a sentence, rather than vice-versa as in the Altaic-influenced Beijing Mandarin (Cheng, 1985). These differences allow for discrimination and the creation of an intra-Taiwanese sphere thereby. Written computer-mediated communication allows for even more rapid shifts, and thus cleavages.

Language use on internet forums will, even assuming intelligibility, tend towards the creation of insider cultures with community standards reinforced textually, sensory cues being absent. Humour and playfulness – in a sea of content – are capital in the attention economy. Funny differs between forums or even subforums, with users invited to leave if they show themselves unable to discern what passes as 'forum dialect' use.

On PTT/Gossiping, exclusion is managed similarly. As a Chinese-language forum, excluding those who cannot read Chinese is easy. Shibboleth forging against unwelcome incursions by mainland Chinese is only somewhat less so, given the divergence in both writing systems and their adaptations for social media use. There is the obvious marker of a different character set, with China using the simplified and Taiwan the traditional. While a mainlander seeking to blend in can simply change his input method allowing him to type traditional characters, this is not foolproof. Some words, for example, the commonly used *zheme* ('such') and *duiyu* ('about'), serve as a shibboleth – the default characters, while technically correct, would not be those chosen by a Taiwanese user.[11] This will commonly yield responses telling the mainland Chinese user to leave – in simplified characters, mocking their failure.

Other than character set, the defining characteristic of mainland Chinese internet text is "stylized initials" (Yang, 2007), specifically those using pinyin romanisation initialisms as representative of Chinese expressions, often rude (Chen, 2014) – such as TMD for *tamade* ('his mother's') – or sexual – with YY for *yiyin* ('thinking/fantasizing sexually') being especially common. Such tactics mitigate offensiveness by not using the native characters, which may be too direct an affront, as well as speed up input and circumvent censorship (Chen, 2014). As Taiwan uses *zhuyin fuhao* syllabics as means of inputting characters this is far less prevalent.[12]

Conversely, Gossiping bears markers of the Taiwanese context described above. Mandarin provides the basic language – Taiwanese adds certain expressions. While Taiwanese shares a character set with Mandarin (having both inherited the writing system of literary Chinese), the full range of colloquial expression in Taiwanese is impossible to render using standard Chinese characters. There was no official effort to make the jump from literary Chinese to a standard Taiwanese due to Taiwan having spent the twentieth century ruled by those with designs at integration with those speaking other languages, whether the more recent *Guoyu* Standard Mandarin or Japanese. While Taiwanese has structural influence on Standard Taiwanese Mandarin, there are also more playful manifestations which given the aforementioned nature of internet forums are especially likely to crop up. Taiwanese BBS users "rely on the morphosyllabic nature of the Chinese writing system and search for characters that represent sounds similar to the language or to the accent they intend to imitate" – one that is uniquely Taiwanese. "The effect is what sounds like the mimicry of an intelligible Mandarin sentence heavily influenced by Taiwanese phonology, while the strings of characters present an anomaly in meaning" (Su, 2009). That is, the characters as read aloud make sense when imagining the use of a Taiwanese accent, but are incomprehensible otherwise for those unfamiliar with Taiwanese Mandarin as their meanings are different – this juxtaposition often being amusing, thus privileging its use and propagating the shibboleth.

The reclaiming of such an accent as a marker of what it means to be Taiwanese in the educated community that frequents a forum intimately connected to the most prestigious university on the island serves to further distinguish Taiwanese society from that of the mainland and the Chinese-speaking world in general. While such a heavy accent used in daily life is stigmatised as a marker of the uneducated (Su, 2005), this is reclaimed on the Taiwanese internet as lovable and sincere, marking out mainland Chinese society as lacking these qualities.

Intraforum Insidership, Taiwanese Insidership

Internet forums have, as explained above, the tendency to create insider cultures when they require particular subcultural understanding. To be a respected member of the tribe, one must continuously acquire and mobilise cultural capital (in line with Bourdieu, 1993). When the forum is anonymous or pseudonymous as in the case of PTT,[13] the relative lack of Facebook-style reputation management increases the "collective, agglutinative character of social space" (Auerbach, 2012). Though some posters aberrantly connect their posting to a real-life identity (though with little verifiability), most maintain a situation wherein the "only defining characteristics of participants are their memberships in these forums. This instantly provides a point of commonality among all participants by which they can define themselves in opposition to all nonparticipants, or some chosen subset of them" (Auerbach, 2012).

When this tendency of forum culture towards a collective identity is married to the marks of distinction provided by a geographically bounded language community (if 'imagined'[14]) as described above, negating the 'global village' concept pushed in the Anglosphere – the internet as place where the world comes together to speak English – the political ramifications both internally and for international relations can be profound, as is seen in Taiwan.

Mobilisation

Students, especially in advanced countries where industrial labour – and thus its strikes – has become less common, are the backbone of social struggle. In Taiwan in particular there is a sense that interfering with or co-opting student struggle would be counterproductive, as students "can get away with action and expression that no other segments of the population could" (Wright, 2014) as their concerns belong to a "pure current of society – the up-and-coming generation, the not-yet soulless and cynical future leaders and elites of the nation whose ideals and hopes remain intact and uncrushed by the contingencies, corruptions, and compromises of the so-called 'real world' that the generations above them are running and ruining" (Wright, 2014). During the Sunflower Movement protests, for example, the KMT and allied media attempted to "paint the occupation [of the legislature] as a DPP plot" (Rowen, 2015), though their role was engineered to be supportive yet passive, with party officials being so careful as to "forbid the display of any DPP signs or logos within the occupation zone" (Rowen, 2015). Such a privileging of studenthood is clearly visible in the makeup of Taiwan's politicians,[15] with all three candidates for president in the 2016 election, for example, holding doctorates from prestigious universities. PTT, embedded in student culture from the time of its creation in a dormitory, and relying on a university network for its continued existence, thus has distinct advantages in its ability to mobilise from that base compared to similar forums in other countries. It is also shielded from interference by lack of economic pressure, being funded by user donations.

Gossiping is particularly suited for real-world mobilisation due to largely being used for *news pasting*, whereby media content (mainstream or otherwise) is copy-pasted to the forum and comments invited. As the media has a habit of obtaining news from Gossiping and covering the user feedback on stories as citizen commentary (Hsieh & Li, 2014), a symbiotic relationship is fostered and the importance of the forum as a deliberative venue is increased (Li et al., 2017). The types of comments generated thereby are commonly quite knowledgeable, with the elite students of NTU and other top universities who formed the core usership during their undergraduate years maintaining the habit after graduation and entry into various professions (Li et al., 2017).

Hong Kong's HK Golden serves a similar function of "circulating local news faster than any other media" (Hung, 2014). While the forum can be caustic as seen in the aforementioned locust ad, it is heartening that this tendency is tempered in the translation to mass movement – the Umbrella Movement's firm commitment to non-violent principles was explicitly designed to generate sympathy from an ambivalent public. This is similar to Taiwan post-democratic transition, but strikingly different to tactics both anticipating and precipitating violent confrontation with police present not only in dictatorships such as Egypt and flawed democracies such as Ukraine, but also in student protests under consolidated democracies, for example in Quebec in 2012.

PTT has been a crucial support for and generator of social movements at least since 2008's Wild Strawberry Movement, which pushed for amendment to the Assembly and Parade Law requiring outdoor assembly to be approved beforehand by government.[16] The trend began with several hundred students in front of the Executive Yuan after a call for a sit-down demonstration on PTT. This was followed in 2013 after some accrued experience by protests demanding justice for an army conscript who died of organ failure while being punished for minor violations of military discipline. Several hundred thousand protesters were mobilised by leveraging the initial network nurtured on Gossiping into a call for action on the more widely-used Facebook. Finally, the anti-China – or at least anti-opaque integration with China – Sunflower Movement erupted in Spring 2014 from a coalition comprising the Gossiping-generated Citizen 1985 group that drove the conscript protest and other civil society groups (Li et al., 2017). Sunflower then spawned a political party (New Power) picking up five seats in the 2016 election – one of those seats won by the sister of the dead army conscript, who removed an 18-year incumbent.

Conclusions and Consequences

While my comments have been tinged by positive assessment of a national community slowly uniting – pushed on by play and language games and rooted in a common way of life – and the interesting role non-commercial social media can play, it is fair to end with a consideration of the consequences. Taiwanese nationalism is seen as dangerous by many analysts and diplomats – particularly those in the United States (Bush, 2016; Wang, 2016) – as, in the extreme case of a declaration of independence with no hedging, a world war may well be triggered. While a survey dating from 2001 notes that "the rapid nativization of ethnic consciousness is only partially reflected in positions on national identity and the independence/unification question, and its influence on concrete policy positions [related to cross-strait economic relations] is even more limited" and that "[p]ut simply, the trend toward

Taiwanization in basic ethnic consciousness has not evolved into a political demand for Taiwan independence" (Rigger, 2006; Wu, 2001), three years later the same researcher's outlook is considerably more alarmist (Wu, 2004). Recent studies confirm demands for independence are eschewed by the vast majority when taking into account a likely PRC attack (Kastner, 2016), though accommodating a slow slide towards unification by economic entanglement is a different matter. If President Tsai fails to get the balance right, the social media-birthed New Power Party will be there as a check. Today, with the China-accommodating KMT in disarray, we should look on with hope and admiration at such organising by the aforementioned 'pure current of society', but with dread at the likelihood the world's superpowers may not tolerate the instability precipitated thereby, or worse – use it as bargaining chip.

Notes

1 PTT is not a proper acronym. The founder's name is Tu, his nickname, Panda, and he thought it needed another T. See "PTT Name" (2016).
2 Those who came to Taiwan with the retreat off the mainland of the Republic of China's army and Nationalist Party or KMT with the loss of the Chinese Civil War and their descendants. While in Taiwan, *waishengren* are now considered one of four 'major ethnic groups', due to relatively recent diversity of origin it is perhaps more helpful to think of the grouping as a class. However, this in turn may be misleading as while the Taiwanese overclass does (and once did to an even greater degree) consist of many *waishengren*, many former KMT soldiers and their descendants live in poverty in situations that may be surprising when one considers only ostensible privilege as in the case of the South African White underclass, for instance.
3 See Lynch (2004) and Fell (2015) for efforts at such hedging under past less PRC-friendly governments than that of the former President Ma (2008–2016). For the renewal of such efforts under the Tsai administration, see "Ex-minister touts southbound policy" (2016).
4 Though denied by the Democratic Progressive Party (DPP), winners of the January 2016 elections.
5 This becomes more understandable considering PTT's history as a project begun, and continuously maintained by, students in the Department of Computer Science at NTU – see Li, Lin and Huang (2017) for an in-depth history.
6 Implying Taiwan is a province of the Republic of China with its claim to all areas once ruled by the Qing dynasty.
7 See "February 28th Incident" (2016) for two contemporary accounts in American newsmedia.
8 E.g. "Republic of China".
9 See Makeham and Hsiau (2005) for a book-length treatment.
10 Where edits to the page are discussed; see "Talk:Waishengren".
11 For example, *zheme* is rendered 這麼 in the traditional character set and 这么 in the simplified. When attempting to blend in, a mainland user may type 這么, which has resulted in the common pejorative 么么人 (*yaoyaoren*) –么么 people. I am indebted to my colleague Lin Yi-Ren for this and related insights.
12 The use of *zhuyin fuhao* characters alone, that is, not as input device, but used for their sound or shape serves as another distinction.

13 Though PTT enforces usernames, one may simply reregister with a different name (and thus identity).
14 Following Anderson (1991), with the national community of largely invisible and thus 'imagined' ritual newspaper readers transmuted into 'real' BBS posters leaving traces: up or down votes and comments. For further on imagined national communities and consequences of media shifts, see Soffer (2013) and Mihelj (2011).
15 See Duh (2016) for an NTU professor complaining of the scholar-politician's ubiquity.
16 This law was later declared to be in violation of the constitution by the Judicial Yuan. See "Constitutional Court Decision 718" (2014).

References

Anderson, B. (1991). *Imagined communities: Reflections on the origin and spread of nationalism*. London: Verso.
Auerbach, D. (2012). *Anonymity as culture: Treatise. Triple Canopy, 15*. Retrieved from www.canopycanopycanopy.com/issues/15/contents/anonymity_as_culture__treatise.
Bourdieu, P. (1993). *Sociology in question*. Thousand Oaks, CA: Sage.
Bush, R. C. (2016). US policy toward Taiwan. *Asian Education and Development Studies, 5*(3), 266–277. doi:10.1108/AEDS-10-2015-0052.
Chen, S. Y. (2014). From OMG to TMD – Internet and Pinyin acronyms in Mandarin Chinese. *Language@Internet, 11*(3). Retrieved from www.languageatinternet.org/articles/2014/chen.
Cheng, R. L. (1985). A comparison of Taiwanese, Taiwan Mandarin, and Peking Mandarin. *Language, 61*(2), 352–377. doi:10.2307/414149.
Constitutional Court Decision 718. (2014). Retrieved from www.judicial.gov.tw/constitutionalcourt/p03_01.asp?expno=718.
Damm, J. (2011a). Taiwan's ethnicities and their representation on the internet. *Journal of Current Chinese Affairs, 40*(1), 99–131.
Damm, J. (2011b). The cross-strait perception of the Taiwanese in cyberspace: The case of Xiamen. *Journal of Cyberculture and Information Society, 21*, 52–85.
Duh, B. (2016, May 3). *Academics wasted in government*. Taipei Times. Retrieved from www.taipeitimes.com/News/editorials/archives/2016/05/03/2003645366.
Dupré, J.-F. (2014). *The politics of linguistic normalization in 21st century Taiwan: Ethnicity, national identity, and the party system*. (Dissertation). The University of Hong Kong. Retrieved from http://hub.hku.hk/handle/10722/209619.
Ex-minister touts southbound policy. (2016, May 18). *Taipei Times*. Retrieved from www.taipeitimes.com/News/taiwan/archives/2016/05/18/2003646534.
February 28th Incident: New York Times and The Nation reports. (2016, May 5). Retrieved from www.taiwandc.org/hst-1947.htm.
Fell, D. (2015). The China impact on Taiwan's elections: Cross-strait economic integration through the lens of election advertising. In G. Schubert (Ed.), *Taiwan and the "China impact": Challenges and opportunities* (pp. 53–69). London: Routledge.

Hillenbrand, M. (2006). The national allegory revisited: Writing private and public in contemporary Taiwan. *Positions: East Asia Cultures Critique, 14*(3), 633–662. doi:10.1215/10679847-2006-016.

Hsieh, Y. P., & Li, M.-H. (2014). Online political participation, civic talk, and media multiplexity: How Taiwanese citizens express political opinions on the Web. *Information, Communication & Society, 17*(1), 26–44. doi:10.1080/1369118X.2013.833278.

Hsu, C.-J. (2014). *The construction of national identity in Taiwan's media, 1896–2012.* Leiden: Brill.

Hung, R. Y. (2014). What melts in the "melting pot" of Hong Kong? *Asiatic, 8*(2), 57–87.

Jones, C. (2014). Lost in China? Mainlandisation and resistance in post-1997 Hong Kong. *Taiwan in Comparative Perspective, 5*, 21–46.

Kastner, S. L. (2016). Is the Taiwan strait still a flash point? Rethinking the prospects for armed conflict between China and Taiwan. *International Security, 40*(3), 54–92. doi:10.1162/ISEC_a_00227.

Le Pesant, T. (2011). Generational change and ethnicity among 1980s-born Taiwanese. *Journal of Current Chinese Affairs, 40*(1), 133–157.

Li, S. L., Lin, Y.-R., & Huang, A. H. (2017). A brief history of the Taiwanese internet: The BBS culture. In G. Goggin & M. McLelland (Eds.), *The Routledge companion to global internet histories*. London: Routledge.

Liao, S. (2010). *Identity, ideology, and language variation: A sociolinguistic study of Mandarin in Central Taiwan.* (Dissertation). University of California, Davis. Retrieved from http://linguistics.ucdavis.edu/pics-and-pdfs/Dissertation Liao.pdf.

Lin, P. (2011). Chinese diaspora "at home": Mainlander Taiwanese in Dongguan and Shanghai. *The China Review, 11*(2), 43–64.

Liu, R.-Y. (2012). Language policy and group identification in Taiwan. *Mind, Brain and Education, 6*(2), 108–116.

Lynch, D. C. (2004). Taiwan's self-conscious nation-building project. *Asian Survey, 44*(4), 513–533. doi:10.1525/as.2004.44.4.513.

Makeham, J., & Hsiau, A. (Eds.). (2005). *Cultural, ethnic, and political nationalism in contemporary Taiwan: Bentuhua.* New York: Palgrave Macmillan.

Mihelj, S. (2011). *Media nations: Communicating belonging and exclusion in the modern world.* Basingstoke, UK: Palgrave Macmillan.

PTT Name (Origin and Significance). (2016, May 5). Retrieved from http://pttpedia.pixnet.net/blog/post/163568837.

Rigger, S. (2006). *Taiwan's rising rationalism: Generations, politics, and "Taiwanese nationalism" (Policy Studies No. 26).* Washington, DC: East-West Center Washington.

Rowen, I. (2015). Inside Taiwan's Sunflower Movement: Twenty-four days in a student-occupied parliament, and the future of the region. *The Journal of Asian Studies, 74*(1), 5–21. doi:10.1017/S0021911814002174.

Soffer, O. (2013). The internet and national solidarity: A theoretical analysis. *Communication Theory, 23*(1), 48–66. doi:10.1111/comt.12001.

Su, H.-Y. (2005). *Language styling and switching in speech and online contexts: Identity and language ideologies in Taiwan.* (Dissertation). The University of Texas at Austin. Retrieved from http://lib.utexas.edu/etd/d/2005/sud41040/sud41040.pdf.

Su, H.-Y. (2009). Reconstructing Taiwanese and Taiwan Guoyu on the Taiwan-based internet: Playfulness, stylization, and politeness. *Journal of Asian Pacific Communication, 19*(2), 313–335. doi:10.1075/japc.19.2.08su.

Talk:Waishengren. Wikipedia. Retrieved from https://zh.wikipedia.org/wiki/Talk:外省人.

Turton, M. (2009, March 16). Kuo Kuan-ying=Fan Lan-chin? Retrieved from http://michaelturton.blogspot.com/2009/03/kuo-kuan-ying-fan-lan-chin.html.

Wang, V. W. (2016). Prospects for U.S.-Taiwan relations. *Orbis, 60*(4), 575–591. doi:10.1016/j.orbis.2016.08.004.

Wright, D. C. (2014). Chasing sunflowers: Personal firsthand observations of the student occupation of the legislative Yuan and popular protests in Taiwan, 18 March–10 April 2014. *Journal of Military and Strategic Studies, 15*(4), 134–200.

Wu, Y.-S. (2001). China and Taiwan consciousness in cross-strait relations. *China Affairs, 4*, 71–89.

Wu, Y.-S. (2004). Taiwanese nationalism and its implications: Testing the worst-case scenario. *Asian Survey, 44*(4), 614–625. doi:10.1525/as.2004.44.4.614.

Yang, C. (2007). Chinese internet language: A sociolinguistic analysis of adaptations of the Chinese writing system. *Language@Internet, 4*(2). Retrieved from www.languageatinternet.org/articles/2007/1142.

Yu, Y-W., Yu, K.-C., & Lin, T.-C. (2016). Political economy of cross-strait relations: Is Beijing's patronage policy on Taiwanese business sustainable? *Journal of Contemporary China, 25*(99), 372–388. doi:10.1080/10670564.2015.1104871.

Zhong, Y. (2016). Explaining national identity shift in Taiwan. *Journal of Contemporary China, 25*(99), 336–352. doi:10.1080/10670564.2015.1104866.

13 Chinese Internet Companies go Global

Online Traffic, Framing and Open Issues

Gianluigi Negro

The importance of the Chinese internet industry is becoming more and more apparent worldwide. To address this reality, the Chinese Communist Party's State Information Strategy (2006–2020) has played a crucial part in this by enhancing the internet's role in promoting national economic informatization while at the same time adjusting the economic structure and transforming the patterns of economic growth. In more general terms, the development of the Chinese internet industry has been inserted into a comprehensive 'soft power' (*ruanshili*) government strategy that is aimed at increasing the ability to produce outcomes through persuasion and attraction rather than coercion and payment (Nye, 2012).

Of course, the media has also played and continues to play a crucial role in this plan. The soft power strategy does not include only the international industry, indeed traditional media, television in particular also played an important role. Wanning Sun has highlighted the importance of the Chinese media's "communication capacity" (*chuaabo nengli)* and the relevance of Chinese television (Sun, 2009). Referring to the words of the former chief of the Communist Party of China, Li Changchun, the main goal of Chinese television was (and is still) "strengthening [Chinese] foreign language channels, expanding partnership with foreign television organizations [...], so that our images and voice can reach thousands of homes in all parts of the world" (Sun, 2009).

Despite the great efforts made by the Chinese government over the last few years, this soft power strategy regarding promotion of traditional media has not yet achieved success. Indeed, most of the academic literature to date focuses on the role played by television, the movie industry and press agencies. Nye contested the lack of direct involvement of the Chinese civil society in specific fields like literature and cinema (2012). Hu and Ji (2012) stressed the importance of traditional media, mentioning the huge investment addressed to the internationalization of the press agency *Xinhua*, the expansion of *China Central Television* (CCTV) in foreign markets and the growth of English language newspapers such as the *People's Daily* and the *Global Times*. Moreover, Hu and Ji (2012) argued that the role of Chinese culture risks becoming de-contextualised because of "the deepening integration of globalized marketing operations regulated by WTO related agreements" that deprived policymakers of their role and were now subordinated to the role of "trade rules" (Kalsey, 2007). Last but not least, Sun and other scholars like Lupano (2012) lamented a "crisis of credibility" despite an increasing Chinese emphasis on technology innovation and development in the field of technical and infrastructural terms (2010). For this reason the Chinese government started to apply original strategies also in the Internet industry.

The goal of this chapter is to analyze the role of Chinese news media, internet companies in particular, in order to explore their role in the going out strategy (*zouchuqu zhanlue*) and their impact on the soft power strategy. This article will present the general characteristics of the three most important Chinese internet companies – Baidu, Alibaba and Tencent, also known as BAT. Baidu leads in the field of search engines, Alibaba is the leading e-commerce company and Tencent is famous for its online and mobile phones' value added services. Their economic success has been particularly significant within China's domestic borders. Nevertheless, starting from the first years of the 2000s, the three companies started to implement dedicated strategies in order to expand their business activities outside of China's borders.

In order to evaluate the effectiveness of BAT, this paper will provide two analyses. The first one will focus on the domestic and international. Second, the fact that Chinese internet companies are not inclined to provide disaggregate data on their international users will be considered, as well as a content analysis focused on the media coverage of some of the most prominent newspapers at the international level since BAT were established.

The State of the Art

From a domestic point of view, the impressive development of the Chinese internet has been analyzed in depth both in terms of infrastructure (Esarey & Qiang, 2008; Hughes & Wacker, 2003; Tai, 2006; Yang, 2009; Yu, 2017, Zhou, 2006) as well as its political and social implications (Abbott, 2001; DeLisle, Goldstein & Yang, 2016) ; Kluver & Yang, 2005; MacKinnon, 2010; Yang, 2003, 2015). Nevertheless, it is possible to argue that most of the academic literature focused on the characteristics and management of internet usage (see Goldsmith & Wu 2006; OpenNet Initiative, 2009). Less attention has been paid to viewing the Chinese internet as a business and its implications on the global market from a political economy perspective (Arsène, 2012; Liu, 2012; Wu, 2009).

On a national level, the Chinese internet industry constitutes a very important pillar for the country's 'going out strategy' (*zouchuqu zhanlue*).

This trend was also confirmed during President Xi Jinping's visit to Brazil in July 2014 and the contemporary launch of Baidu Brazil. A more convincing example was provided by the official visit of President Xi Jinping in Seattle in September 2015, 1 week before the official meeting at the White House hosted by President Obama. The event in Seattle was important also for the presence of Lu Wei, senior executive official in charge of internet policy in China at the USA–China internet Industry forum, and was another event co-organised by the NGO Internet Society of China and Microsoft that included the presence of other USA internet corporations like Facebook, Apple and IBM. Moreover, during the same visit, the think tank the Paulson Institute hosted another round-table with 15 executives from China and 15 from the United States. The majority of the represented companies came from the tech sector, and the event started with a policy speech delivered by President Xi. During the meeting, Chinese official media highlighted the importance of more Chinese internet companies competing internationally, as they have the ability to make the world's cyber environment more balanced. They argued that "breaking the information monopoly and building a fairer and safer cyberspace have become the need and consensus of many countries, bringing new opportunities for Chinese internet service providers" (Fu, 2014). Xi Jinping was also the first Chinese president to attend the World Economic Forum in Davos on January 2017, his entourage included two of the most important Chinese businessmen: Ma Yun (Jack Ma), founder of e-commerce platform Alibaba and president of web services Baidu. In his speech, President Xi clearly stated "China will vigorously foster an external environment of opening-up for common development" (Xi, 2017).

On a global level, Chinese internet companies are undergoing a round of overseas stock market listings, and internet companies in China have represented a strong pole of growth in recent years. For example, in December 2007 Baidu was the first Chinese company to be included in the NASDAQ 100 index. Thereafter, many other Chinese internet companies (ranging from video-sharing to social networking sites) have been listed on the USA stock exchange. The most recent initial public offering (IPO) of the three companies was filed by the e-commerce company Alibaba in September 2014, and it overtook Facebook's 2012 debut as the largest tech IPO in the USA (Lawer, 2014). Further evidence confirming the important role of the internet industry in China comes from a report published by Boston Consulting Group in 2012, which stated that China is the world's third most lucrative country in terms of the internet economy, with internet contributions representing almost 5.5 percent of the Chinese GDP ($5.9 trillion). This is behind Great Britain (8.1 percent) and South Korea (7.2 percent) but ahead of the European Union (3.9 percent), Japan (4.9 percent) and the USA (4.9 percent). Despite its present role as a developing country, the impact of China's internet industry on GDP is highly impressive as confirmed by the developing market average index (3.6 percent) and the developed market (4.3 percent) (Dean, 2012).

This trend was already taken into account by the time Telecommunication Minister Wu Jichuan stated in June 1994 that "China's telecommunications construction can leap over some development stages and technical levels which Western countries had gone through and directly adopt highly efficient new technology and equipment" (Dai, 2003). In 2000, Premier Zhu Rongji once again reiterated in the Fifth Plenum of the CCP Central Committee, "Leapfrogging in productivity development may be achieved... by melding informatization and industrialization, the two processes reinforce each other and progress simultaneously" (Dai, 2003).

Chinese Internet Going Global: What Does It Mean?

Even though the Chinese internet population is comprised of 731 million users – that is 53.2 percent of the Chinese population (CNNIC, 2017) – most Chinese internet market niches are considered saturated (Ng, 2014). Moreover, the necessity of investing in foreign markets is also supported and promoted by the government's going out strategy, which aims to support Chinese corporations in investing outside Chinese borders. This policy took its first steps at the end of the '90s and is distinguished by the following five guidelines (Central People's Government of the People's Republic of China, 2006):

- Increase Chinese direct foreign investment linked to the country's systemic reform.
- Pursue product diversification beginning with the country's most representative industries.
- Improve the capacity to effectively control risks.
- Expand foreign financial funding in order to create and promote a system based on services.
- Support the brand recognition of Chinese companies in foreign markets.

This phase of the Chinese internet attempting to access foreign markets came after the internationalization stage of Chinese hardware and telecommunication producers such as Lenovo, TCL, Haier, Huawei and ZTE. Lu Tang and Hongmei Li (2011) provided a very interesting case study on this concern, analyzing the experience of Huawei in Africa and highlighting the importance of policy makers and business leaders working together strategically. It also explored how companies like Huawei could support Chinese public diplomacy by promoting "a global worldview and sharing management practices". Like their predecessors in the hardware sector, such as Huawei and ZTE, Chinese internet companies began to establish cooperation programmes with foreign corporations at the international level and to invest in overseas operations.

BAT

BAT began their activities overseas by setting up offices during the early years of the 2000s. Though the headquarters of all three companies are based in China, several offices were opened outside mainland China. Alibaba opened an office in Hong Kong, three in Taiwan, one in India, one in the UK and one in the USA. Baidu has seven offices in several different countries outside of China, including Japan, the USA, Thailand, Brazil, Egypt and Indonesia. Tencent offices outside of mainland China were set up in Malaysia, Korea, Taiwan, Hong Kong, Japan, India and the USA.[1] Another shared characteristic is that all three completed their IPOs – two of them on NASDAQ (Alibaba in 2014; Baidu in 2006) and one in Hong Kong (Tencent). On 19 September 2014, Alibaba landed a record-breaking $21.8 billion in an IPO in New York. The case of Alibaba is even more impressive, as it started business in 1999 with a mere $60,000 and its present value is now $231.4 billion, larger than that of Amazon and eBay combined.

BAT Online Traffic

Despite these attempts to explore foreign markets, BAT still has to face some limitations and issues. The first one is related to its online traffic (for a comprehensive view, see Table 13.1).

According to the statistics collected by the author on Alexa, a web service that provides commercial web traffic data and analytics at the

Table 13.1 BAT Traffic in China and its Secondary Markets (data provided by Alexa)

Site	Rank in China	% of Visitors in China	Secondary Markets	Rank	% of Visitors Overseas
Alibaba	3	94.7	Taiwan	25	1.1
			Hong Kong	6	1.0
			USA	345	0.8
			South Korea	28	0.7
Baidu	1	95.5	USA	95	1.3
			South Korea	23	0.6
			Taiwan	24	0.6
			Hong Kong	7	0.5
Tencent	2	96.1	USA	257	1.0
			Taiwan	40	0.6
			South Korea	45	0.6

time this chapter was written, Baidu ranked first in the Chinese market, but its performances were not very positive in its main secondary markets – the USA (covering the 95th national rank), South Korea (23rd), Taiwan (24th) and Hong Kong (7th). In these countries, the percentage of viewers was lower than 2 percent. Baidu's traffic was also low in countries where it officially launched its services – Brazil, 121st; Singapore, 28th and India and Vietnam were not even in the first 250 positions. Alibaba's situation looked very similar. Indeed, Taobao, the most representative website of the Chinese e-commerce platform, holds the third position in terms of visitors in China (97 percent). Its secondary markets are Taiwan, Hong Kong, the USA and South Korea. In this case, the percentage of visitors in all the secondary markets was under 1.5 percent. In the case of Tencent, the online traffic of QQ, which covered the second position in China but was underperforming in its secondary markets, was analyzed. Their positions were: the USA, 257th position; Taiwan, 40th and South Korea, 45th. Also, in this case, the percentage of visitors outside Chinese borders was below 1 percent.

BAT in Western Newspapers

Although two of the BAT companies are listed on NASDAQ, their annual reports do not provide an accurate overview on its users based outside China. For this reason, a content analysis was conducted based on the database Factiva using Baidu, Alibaba and Tencent as keywords and selecting the most representative newspapers in the most important markets in which BAT launched its international promotional activities. The selected newspapers are *The Guardian* for the UK, *The New York Times* for the USA, *Le Monde* for France, *El País* for Spain, *O'Globo* for Brazil and *Il Corriere della Sera* for Italy. The timeframe of the analysis started in the year the company was established in China (see Tables 13.2–13.4).

The dataset of Baidu is composed of 564 articles. *The New York Times* had the largest coverage with 262 published articles followed by *The Guardian* with 197 and *El País* with 58. The sections of these articles

Table 13.2 Baidu in Western Newspapers (1 Jan 2002–31 Dec 2013): Dataset 564

Most Mentioned Sources		Most Mentioned Subjects	
The New York Times	262	Censorship	110
The Guardian	197	Corporate/industrial news	55
El País	58	Columns	34
Corriere della Sera	47	Internet/online	34

Sources: The Guardian, The New York Times, Le Monde, Il Corriere della Sera, El País, O'Glob.

Table 13.3 Alibaba in Western Newspapers (1 Jan 1998–31 Dec 2013): Dataset 694

Most Mentioned Sources		Most Mentioned Subjects	
The New York Times	473	Acquisitions	134
The Guardian	109	Columns	88
Il Corriere della Sera	66	Corporate/ industrial news	87
El País	46	Blogs	66

Sources: The Guardian, The New York Times, Le Monde, Il Corriere della Sera, El País, O'Globo.

Table 13.4 Tencent in Western Newspapers (1 Jan 1996–31 Jan 2013): Dataset 254

Most Mentioned Sources		Most Mentioned Subjects	
The New York Times	184	Internet/online	24
The Guardian	40	Social media	16
Il Corriere della Sera	16	Industrial goods	15
El País	14	Networking	14

Sources: The Guardian, The New York Times, Le Monde, Il Corriere della Sera, El País, O'Globo.

were mainly focused on censorship (110) and industrial news (55). Baidu newspaper coverage had fallen over the years. The dataset of Alibaba is the biggest compared to the other two websites and is made of 694 articles. Also, in this case, *The New York Times* was the most productive with 473 articles followed by *The Guardian* with 109 and the Italian *Il Corriere della Sera* with 66. The articles mainly referred to acquisitions, mergers and shareholdings (134), columns (88) and corporate industrial news (87). Another finding is that the coverage has been growing over the years. Tencent had the smallest coverage with 254 articles published, 184 in *The New York Times*, 40 in *The Guardian* and 16 in *El País*. Two interesting findings are that the newspaper coverage has been growing over the years and that the topics are related to internet/online (24), social media (16) and industrial goods (15).

Moving to Europe

Although a series of investments and promotion activities have been implemented in the USA and Latin America, Alibaba and Baidu did not consider the European market as the primary market for their going out strategy. Indeed, Baidu made one of its rare public appearances in Europe only in June 2013 in Paris. Although that event was basically informative, it was a chance to present Baidu services and Chamclickm,

Baidu's intermediary and representative, in Europe. In other words, the event was addressed to European companies interested in leveraging Baidu's services to reach Chinese consumers and not to get into the European market. Alibaba's strategy is different. In October 2015 it confirmed the opening of three offices in three new European countries (Italy, France and Germany) in order to increase its growth. Among the reasons that could be offered to explain Alibaba's strategic choice to expand into foreign markets is the slowing of the Chinese domestic economy. According to Alibaba chairman Ma Yun, "China should shift from exporting to importing" (Bloomberg, 2015).

The Case of WeChat

Tencent differs both from Baidu and Alibaba because it is the only company that actively and concretely invested in the European market, launching its mobile application WeChat (*Weixin*). Moreover, as shown by the content analysis presented in this chapter, most of the Western newspaper coverage is not related to negative topics of censorship and political issues. For this reason, its experience in Italy, one of the most representative countries in Tencent's international ambitions, is the focus.

WeChat is a multi-platform mobile application with instant text, voice and video messaging. WeChat's popularity is based on the fact that it can be used on most of the mobile platforms worldwide, such as Android, iPhone, Blackberry, Windows phones and Symbian. Its functions include texting, asynchronous one-to-one or one-to-many voice broadcasting and file-, photo- and video-sharing. Other more original features differentiate WeChat from its competitors, including the 'shake' feature, which localizes new users all around the world who would like to interact in that moment with other new users. 'People nearby' is another feature aimed at finding new users located nearby who would like to get in touch with other users – this service is provided by a GPS integrated in the smartphones. 'Drift bottle' is another new feature – a text or voice message is broadcast and sent to unknown users who want to start a conversation with new users.

Another point that can explain the success of WeChat is its social-oriented structure. Indeed, it incorporates options that allow new users to subscribe to the service. One of the most popular is to connect to a Facebook account, which is a particularly original option considering that Facebook is blocked in China. An alternative to Facebook is the Tencent QQ account, the most popular social network in China as confirmed by its 798.2 million subscribed users and its peak of 176.4 million users online simultaneously (PR Newswire, 2013).

The promotional activities of WeChat are not limited to China. In April 2012 Tencent released the English version of its most representative mobile application in order to promote the brand internationally. Another decision was made to translate the application into several languages. Presently, WeChat can be used in Chinese (simplified and traditional characters), English, Indonesian, Spanish, Portuguese, Turkish, Malaysian, Japanese, Korean, Polish, Italian, Thai, Vietnamese, Hindi and Russian. It is possible to argue that that strategy has been successful because at the time of writing of this chapter WeChat had 697 million subscribers with 70 million of these located outside of China (Tencent Q2 financial report, 2015a). This is particularly important for Tencent because it tried to strengthen the credibility of the company as a whole around the world compared to other main Chinese internet services such as Baidu. It is important to highlight that Baidu has tried to challenge Google in the international search engine market. In 2007 it launched Baidu Japan, and in 2011 it entered into a partnership with Orange, a major French mobile telecommunication company in order to create a new browser for the Arab and African markets. In the same year, Baidu also started its 'knowledge market' (*baidu zhidao*) service in Egypt, and the web directory Hao123 was translated into Thai for the Thai market. Nevertheless, none of the above-mentioned investments have been successful so far.

WeChat in Italy

Aside from the above-mentioned features, it is important to note that WeChat was also promoted in the traditional media, television in particular. This was an original choice that differentiates WeChat from other Chinese and Western social networks, which did not promote their product on traditional media. One of the most successful experiences WeChat had in Europe was in Italy. The Italian market represented a strategic choice for the Chinese company because, from a historic perspective, Italy had been one of the earlier adopter European countries in the field of mobile telecommunication (Balbi, 2008; Goggin, 2010) and 3G standards (Balbi & Magaudda, 2014). Moreover, at the time this was written, Italy had more than 40 million smartphones for a population of 60.7 million inhabitants (Pew Research, 2016).

The promotion of WeChat in Italy started in July 2013. At that time, the most popular Italian television channels began to broadcast a spot in which the famous football (soccer) player Lionel Messi provided a celebrity endorsement for WeChat. Messi is not only the celebrity endorser but his role is also important for another marketing strategy – all of Messi's fans can follow his updates and see all the texts, messages and videos shared by the player on his profile (La Stampa, 2013; Millward, 2013b). This promotional activity may sound new to the European and American markets, but it has been a fairly common strategy in China since 2005, when the blog was branded the "Chinese internet phenomenon" (MacKinnon, 2008) of the year. Unfortunately, the mentioned report did not specify how many WeChat users were based outside mainland

China. The last data provided by the company in this regard at the time this article was written is dated August 2015 (Tencent, 2015b).

The WeChat promotional media campaign lies in traditional media. Indeed, the promotion of internet companies and mobile applications has never been so supported by Italian newspapers and television channels. The results of the WeChat promotional campaign in Italy consists of a series of forms of cooperation signed with Italian companies. At the time this book was written, WeChat already supported several Italian companies in opening their official accounts. The Italian market of cooperation was divided into 10 fields – B2B, celebrities, community, e-commerce, events, luxury, media, retail, sports and tourism.[2] It is worth mentioning that some markets should not be considered a coincidence. Indeed, soccer is not only the most popular sport in Italy but it also has an important value on Italian GDP, being the tenth national industry with a value of 13 billion Euros (Reportcalcio, 2015). For this reason, the choice to support famous teams like AS Roma and Juventus is strategic. Similar considerations should be addressed in the field of media, like in the case of the mass media companies *CondéNast* and *Corriere della Sera*, the most read and distributed Italian newspaper, or in the field of luxury thanks to the engagement of companies like *Vogue Italia* and *Yoox.com*.

WeChat was officially launched in Italy in September 2013. According to Mr. Ghizzoni, country manager of WeChat in Italy, "The Italian market represents the entrance door for the whole European market" (Pennisi, 2014). In the long run, WeChat will try to increase its user base in order to become more attractive to online advertisers, to purchase services and games and to support more online transactions. This last point seems to be crucial. In September 2012 the Chinese company signed a partnership agreement with Tenpay, the online payment system provided by Tencent, which is one of the three Chinese firms with the highest revenue (the other two companies are Baidu and Alibaba). Tenpay supports the e-commerce function on WeChat using QR codes, two-dimensional barcodes that can be translated into information related to the item using a smartphone. It is also important to note that WeChat first used the QR code to find new users – each user is assigned a QR code after subscription – while its economic purpose only arrived afterwards.[3] Of course, all of the online transactions would take place within the WeChat framework (Hu, 2013). Tencent stated that it banked over $46 million from bank transfer fees from WeChatpay, specifying that the majority came from China (Russell, 2016).

One last point is addressed to creativity. While WeChat and WhatsApp are in competition with each other, a notable upgrade to the WhatsApp service was the August 2013 introduction of the function of recording and broadcasting voice messages. This option was actually inspired by its Chinese competitor's function (Olson, 2013).

From a Systemic Point of View

WeChat's attempt to approach foreign markets is important because it represents a watershed in the going out process of Chinese internet companies. WeChat's experiences lead to four considerations. First, although the official going out strategy was officially launched in 2006, internet companies started to follow this programme later than other hardware companies, such as Huawei or ZTE. At that time, there was a lack of interest in overseas markets because the Chinese domestic market was big enough to ensure growth in terms of revenues. In other words, the domestic market was considered safer than foreign ones. Tencent is the first Chinese internet company that tried to target foreign markets accurately. A second relevant consideration is the lack of expertise of Chinese companies when it comes to accessing foreign markets. The BAT companies are aware of the costs and risks they have to face to adapt their services in order to be successful in new markets. They learned from the failure of eBay and Amazon in China that access into foreign markets is expensive, time consuming and difficult to approach properly. One of the main challenges is to find appropriate personnel. The third issue explains the delay of the implementation of the going out strategy by Chinese internet companies, which could be explained by various political issues. One example is provided by Baidu. They do not allow Vietnamese users to use Vietnamese expressions referring to contested territory in the South China Sea. This choice has led to political consequences that forbid discussion of all "sensitive" content on its pages (Logan, 2015, see also Ruan, Knockel, Ng, & Nishihata, 2016). A similar case involving WeChat showed maps that the Vietnamese consider under Vietnam's sovereignty under Chinese domination. In both cases, the decision resulted from the government's requests. Under these circumstances, Chinese companies decided to avoid other potential risks. The fourth reason is related to the Chineseness brand (see Chow, 1998; Wang, 1991). Stereotypes and negative Western media coverage of Chinese issues like censorship on Chinese traditional and new media slow down or even compromise the creation of a positive image of Chinese internet companies abroad. WeChat can be considered an exception because as one internet analyst stated, "If you didn't know WeChat was from China, you wouldn't be aware of that fact" (Week in China, 2013). On the other hand, WeChat's international presence is also unsuccessful despite its massive international media promotion. In fact, according to stats provided by AppAnnie's collected data and the official Android Application store, Google Play, WeChat does not appear in the first positions of several national rankings, not even in Brazil and India, which are countries in which Tencent promoted its mobile application. At the time this chapter was written, the main WeChat competitors are WhatsApp, Facebook and Facebook Messenger (Millward, 2016).

Going Global: Some Clarifications?

The fast growth of mobile phone and internet users in China has surely contributed to this greater economy of scale. As more Chinese internet companies embarked on their journey overseas, the long-standing concern over information control presents a challenge for their success. One example is from January 2013, when the international version of WeChat was discovered to be blocking messages that contained certain sensitive words. Tencent responded by stating that it was a "technical glitch" (Millward, 2013a) and unintentional. Such incidents show that as Chinese internet companies expand overseas and offer their services to a greater market, issues like freedom of expression and information control can no longer be seen as domestic problems. There are wider implications regarding the profitability of the business when censorship takes place by these publicly listed companies on content flowing on the globally connected internet, thereby rendering it secretive. Moreover, Chinese internet companies have to face international competition in several markets that already have a long-term presence of USA competitors, such as Google in the case of Baidu and WhatsApp, Facebook, and Facebook Messenger in the case of WeChat.

Conclusion

This chapter explored some of the most important attempts implemented by the three most representative Chinese internet companies in exploring markets outside Chinese borders. It confirms that the Chinese government largely adopted an instrumental view of the internet and intends to harness the economic potential of the internet for national economic development. Particular attention has been addressed to the case of WeChat, especially in Italy.

At the present stage, BAT still has to face several issues, such as freedom of expression, information control and censorship. How these battles will be fought remains to be seen. As things are changing rapidly, more attention should be paid to Chinese internet companies, especially issues of control, regulation and subsidies as well as their social and political implications on both a domestic and global level. A second issue that should be taken into account for future studies lies in the overlapping analysis between Chinese public diplomacy and practices of Chinese business sectors. Although the mainstream narrative is still based on the clichéd 'development with Chinese characteristics', promoting a general overlapping between public and private interests, the necessity for companies like Tencent is mainly addressed to increase their economies of scale and scope. This situation could lead to unexpected divergences and contrasts with the Chinese government.

Notes

1 Information provided by a source contacted by the author who prefers to keep the anonymity.
2 This information was retrieved from an interview between the author of the present contribution and a manager of WeChat who decided to remain anonymous.
3 There are several ways to subscribe to WeChat. One of them is to use the QR code; other ways are through a mobile number (also outside Chinese borders), email address, QQ account or nickname.

References

Abbott, J. P. (2001). Democracy@internet.asia? The challenges to the emancipatory potential of the net: Lessons from China and Malaysia. *Third World Quarterly, 22*(1), 99–114.

Arsène, S. (2012). *The impact of China on global internet governance in an era of privatized control.* Chinese Internet Research Conference. Los Angeles, May.

Balbi, G. (2008). Dappertutto telefonini. Per una storia sociale della telefonia mobile in Italia. *Intersezioni, 28*(3), 465–490.

Balbi, G., & Magaudda, P. (2014). *Storia dei media digitali: rivoluzioni e continuità.* Rome: GLF Editori Laterza.

Bloomberg. (2015, October 13). *Alibaba to open offices in Europe as U.S. expansion continues.* Bloomberg. Retrieved from www.bloomberg.com/news/articles/2015-10-13/alibaba-to-open-offices-in-europe-as-u-s-expansion-continues.

Central People's Government of the People's Republic of China (2006, March 15) To better implement the "going out" strategy (*Genghao Di Shishi "Zouchuqu" Zhanlue*). Retrieved from www.gov.cn/node_11140/2006–03/15/content_227686.htm.

Chow, R. (1998). Introduction: On Chineseness as a theoretical problem. *Boundary, 2,* 1–24.

CNNIC (*Zhongguo hulianwangluo xinxi zhongxin*). (2017). 39th Statistical Report on the State of the Chinese Internet's Development (*Di 39 Ci Zhongguo Hulianwangluo Fazhan Zhuangkuang Tongji Baogao*), Beijing, 2017 Retrieved from www.cnnic.net.cn/hlwfzyj/hlwxzbg/hlwtjbg/201701/P020170123364672657408.pdf.

Dai, X. (2003). ICTs in China's development strategy. In C. Hughes & G. Wacker (Eds.), *China and the internet: Politics of the digital leap forward* (pp. 8–29). London: Routledge.

Dean, D. (2012). *The Internet economy and the G-20: The $4.2 trillion growth opportunity.* Boston Consulting Group, Boston. Retrieved from www.bcg.com/documents/file100409.pdf.

DeLisle, J., Goldstein, A., & Yang, G. (Eds.) (2016). *The internet, social media, and a changing China,* Philadelphia: University of Pennsylvania Press.

Esarey, A., & Qiang, X. (2008). Political expression in the Chinese blogosphere: Below the radar. *Asian Survey, 48*(5), 752–772.

Fu, P. (2014, July 21). *China voice: More internet companies should go abroad.* Xinhua. Retrieved from http://news.xinhuanet.com/english/china/2014–07/21/c_133500011.htm.

Goggin, G. (2010). *Global mobile media*. London: Routledge.

Goldsmith, J. L., & Wu, T. (2006). *Who controls the internet? Illusions of a borderless world* (Vol. 89). New York: Oxford University Press.

Hu, W. (2013, June 18). Tencent on the hunt for online revenue with WeChat service. *China Daily USA*. Retrieved from http://usa.chinadaily.com.cn/epaper/2013-06/18/content_16634081.htm.

Hu, Z., & Ji, D. (2012). Ambiguities in communicating with the world: the "Going-out" policy of China's media and its multilayered contexts. *Chinese Journal of Communication, 5*(1), 32–37.

Hughes, C. R., & Wacker, G. (2003). Introduction: China's digital leap forward. *China and the Internet: Politics of the Digital Leap Forward (London and New York: Routledge, 2003)*, 1-7

Kelsey, J. (2007). Globalization of cultural policy-making and the hazards of legal seduction. In G. Murdock & J. Wasko (Eds.), Media in the age of marketization (pp. 151–187). Creskill, NJ: Hampton Press.

Kluver, R., & Yang, C. (2005). The internet in China: A meta-review of research. *The Information Society, 21*(4), 301–308.

La Stampa (2013, July 18). *Messi e WeChat, sfida aperta a WhatsApp*. Retrieved from www.lastampa.it/2013/07/18/tecnologia/messi-e-WeChat-sfida-aperta-a-whastapp-yTH2mkemXLh4dKcTPQiQKP/pagina.html.

Lawer, R. (2014, September 19). *Alibaba IPO makes it worth $231 billion, more than Amazon and eBay combined*. Engadget.com. Retrieved from www.engadget.com/2014/09/19/alibaba-ipo-is-probably-the-biggest-ever/.

Liu, Y. (2012). The rise of China and global internet governance. *China Media Research, 8*(2), 46-56.

Logan, S. (2015). Baidu, Vietnam, and the bordered world of Chinese internet companies. *Center for Global Communications Studies*. Retrieved from www.global.asc.upenn.edu/baidu-vietnam-and-the-bordered-world-of-chinese-internet-companies/.

Lupano, E. (2012). *Ho servito il popolo cinese: media e potere nella Cina di oggi*. Milano: F. Brioschi.

MacKinnon, R. (2008). Flatter world and thicker walls? Blogs, censorship and civic discourse in China. *Public Choice, 134*(1–2), 31–46.

MacKinnon, R. (2010). Networked authoritarianism in China and beyond: Implications for global internet freedom. Paper presented at *Liberation technology in authoritarian regimes*. 11-12 Palo Alto, CA: Stanford University.

Millward, S. (2013, January 11). Tencent responds in case of apparent WeChat censorship, *Tech in Asia*. Retrieved from www.techinasia.com/tencent-responds-wechat-censoring-sensitive-words.

Millward, S. (2013, August 15). Boosted by Messi's endorsement, WeChat scores 100 million users outside of China. *Tech in Asia*. Retrieved from www.techinasia.com/tencent-WeChat-100-million-overseas-users/.

Millward, S. (2016, May 25). We Chat global expansion has been a disaster. *Tech in Asia*. Retrieved from www.techinasia.com/WeChat-global-expansion-fail.

Ng, J. (2014). Going global. *World Policy Journal*. Retrieved from www.worldpolicy.org/journal/fall2014/going-global.

Nye, J. (2012, January 17). Why China is weak on soft power. *International Herald Tribune*. Retrieved from http://belfercenter.hks.harvard.edu/publication/21682/why_china_is_weak_on_soft_power.html.

Olson, P. (2013, August 6). WhatsApp launches voice messaging, hits 300M monthly active users. *Forbes.* Retrieved from www.forbes.com/sites/parmyolson/2013/08/06/whatsapp-launches-voice-messaging-hits-300m-monthly-active-users/.

OpenNet Initiative. (2009). *Internet filtering in China* (1st ed.). OpenNet Initiative. Retrieved from https://opennet.net/research/profiles/china.

Pennisi, M. (2014, February 21). Come fa i soldi WeChat. *Wired Italia.* Retrieved from www.wired.it/internet/social-network/2014/02/21/guadagni-WeChat-cina-italia/.

PEW Research (2016, February 22). Smartphone ownership and internet usage continues to climb in emerging economies. *Pew Research Center.* Retrieved from www.pewglobal.org/2016/02/22/smartphone-ownership-and-internet-usage-continues-to-climb-in-emerging-economies/.

PR Newswire. (2013, March 20). *Tencent announces 2012 fourth quarter and annual results.* Retrieved from www.prnewswire.com/news-releases/tencent-announces-2012-fourth-quarter-and-annual-results-199130711.html.

Reportcalcio, (2015), *Figc,* Retrieved from www.figc.it/other/ReportCalcio_2015.pdf.

Ruan, L., Knockel, J., Ng, J, Nishihata, M. (2016, November 30), *One App, Two Systems: How WeChat uses one censorship policy in China and another internationally,* CitizenLab. Retrieved from https://citizenlab.org/2016/11/wechat-china-censorship-one-app-two-systems/.

Russell, J. (2016, May 17). *Messaging app WeChat is becoming a mobile payment giant in China.* Retrieved from https://techcrunch.com/2016/03/17/messaging-app-WeChat-is-becoming-a-mobile-payment-giant-in-china/.

Sun, W. (2009). Mission impossible? Soft power, communication capacity, and the globalization of Chinese media. *International Journal of Communication, 4,* 19.

Tai, Z. (2006). *The internet in China: Cyberspace and civil society.* New York: Routledge.

Tang, L., & Li, H. (2011). Chinese corporate diplomacy: Huawei's CSR discourse in Africa. In J. Wang (Ed.). *Soft power in China: Public Diplomacy through communication* (pp. 95–115). New York: Palgrave Macmillan.

Tencent. (2015a). *2015 Interim Report.* Retrieved from www.tencent.com/en-us/content/ir/rp/2015/attachments/201501.pdf.

Tencent. (2015b). *Annual Report.* Retrieved from www.tencent.com/en-us/content/ir/rp/2015/attachments/201502.pdf.

Xi, J (2017, 17 January) President Xi's speech at Davos in full, *World Economic Forum.* Retrieved from www.weforum.org/agenda/2017/01/full-text-of-xi-jinping-keynote-at-the-world-economic-forum.

Yang, G. (2003). The internet and civil society in China: A preliminary assessment. *Journal of Contemporary China,* 12(36), 453–475.

Yang, G. (2009). *The power of the internet in China: Citizen activism online* (1st ed.). New York: Columbia University Press.

Yang, G. (2015). *China's contested internet.* Copenhagen, Nias Press.

Yu, H. (2017) Networking China. *The digital transformation of the Chinese economy,* Urbana, Illinois; University of Illinois Press.

Wang, G. (1991). *The Chineseness of China: Selected essays.* Oxford: Oxford University Press.

Week in China. (2013). *Going global. Tencent's WeChat could break Silicon Valley's grip*. Retrieved form www.weekinchina.com/msingle/?mpage=16967.

Wu, G. (2009). In the name of good governance: E-government, internet pornography, and political censorship in China. In X. Zhang & Y. Zheng (Eds.). *China's information and communications technology revolution: Social changes and state responses* (pp. 68–85), New York: Routledge.

Zhou, Y. (2006). *Historicizing online politics: Telegraphy, the internet, and political participation in China*. Palo Alto, CA: Stanford University Press.

14 The Global Expansion of China-based Social Media Platforms and Its Dynamics in the Australian Context

Jiajie Lu

Introduction

In recent years, the China-based social media platforms have become a widely adopted communication measure of the Chinese diaspora in Australia. This chapter will explore the adoption of major China-based social media platforms such as QQ and WeChat amongst the Chinese diaspora in Australia and its dynamics. Conventionally, the success of China-based social media platforms is explained as a consequence of the censorship and isolation of the internet in mainland China (Zhang & Pentina, 2012). However, the global expansion of China-based social media platforms in Australia, a country without internet censorship and blockage, offers a chance to review this argument from a critical perspective. If the internet users in mainland China are subject to internet censorship and isolation to adopt China-based social media platforms, why do they still use these platforms after their overseas migration? Does the technological censorship entirely isolate mainland Chinese internet users? What are the dynamics for the global expansion of China-based social media platforms?

In order to answer these questions, this chapter firstly analyses Chinese government's internet censorship measures and their limitations. The analysis has found that access blockage and content censoring cannot entirely isolate mainland Chinese internet users from foreign social media platforms nor silence their dissident expressions. In other words, the initial adoption of China-based social media should not be simply seen as a consequence of the censorship and isolation of the internet in mainland China. Cultural and social factors should be included. Secondly, through conducting semi-structured interviews with 30 first-generation Chinese diasporic members in Brisbane and Melbourne, this research has found that the cultural and social factors account more for social media platform adoption than accessibility. Despite the unrestricted accessibility to Facebook, WhatsApp, Twitter and other globally popularly social media platforms in Australia, China-based social media platforms are still a favoured option of Chinese diaspora because they are more convenient for maintaining and re-establishing social connections amongst Chinese people regardless their localities, accessing survival information in Australia and developing transnational connections between Australia and China for both personal and professional purposes.

Two Phases of the Global Expansion of China-Based Social Media Platforms

According to the data collected by interviews, most of the respondents in this research either adopted China-based social media platforms before they migrated to Australia, or got to know these platforms in Australia through their Chinese friends' recommendations. Based on this understanding, the global expansion of China-based social media platforms can be divided into two phases – the first phase refers to the adoption of these platforms in China, and the second phase is concerned with their continued use after the emigration of these Chinese users overseas.

The first phase can be traced back to users' initial adoption of these platforms in China. The question in this phase concerns the competition between China-based social media platforms and their international competitors – while some global social media platforms such as Facebook, Twitter and WhatsApp are predominant players in most of the major countries worldwide, China, with 668 million internet users (China Internet Network Information Centre, 2015), the largest group in the world (Taneja & Wu, 2014), is a market largely dominated by domestic platforms such as QQ, Weibo and WeChat. The success of these China-based social media platforms is often attributed to the well-known government control and censorship upon the internet that restricts access for foreign competitors to the Chinese domestic market (Zhang & Pentina, 2012). However, in other counties where there is no such access blockage, local users have also been seen to favour domestic social media platforms, for example the dominance of Line in Japan and Kakao Talk in South Korea. Like WeChat in China, they are influential instant messaging applications in their own domestic market. Furthermore, these social media platforms have gone global, and enjoy high popularity among specific ethnicities and now compete with their international counterparts in a worldwide market (Clark, 2014). Therefore, attributing the success of China-based social media platforms solely to access restriction and censorship on international competitors is not a convincing argument. Further, in contrast to the mainstream knowledge believing the internet use in mainland China is strictly censored, the Chinese government's censorship on the internet has many limitations and is overestimated to a certain extent. Detailed articulations will be presented in the next section.

The second phase of the global expansion of China-based social media platforms concerns their diffusion due to the migration of people from China. The question in this phase is why these diasporic Chinese insist on using China-based social media platforms after their transnational migration. This question will be answered in the results section.

The Internet Censorship of Chinese Government

The mainstream view argues that the prosperity of China-based social media is fostered by the access restriction to foreign platforms such as Facebook and Twitter in mainland China (Zhang & Pentina, 2012). This argument actually has two connotations. First, the internet users in mainland China are isolated from foreign social media platforms so they have no choice but to use domestic substitutes. Second, the mainland Chinese internet users are passively subject to censorship and would abandon China-based social media platforms once they go abroad. In regard to these connotations, this section attempts to articulate that mainland Chinese users' preference for China-based social media platforms is not a direct consequence of the censorship applied by the Chinese government. The Chinese government's internet censorship has many technological limitations (e.g. failing to censor homophones and homographs), which are often used by Chinese users to bypass its restrictions.

Like other types of media, the internet is tightly controlled and regulated by the government in China. Generally, the Chinese government's censorship can be categorised into two types –access blockage (mainly applied on foreign-based media institutions) and content censoring (widely exerted on domestic websites) (Taneja & Wu, 2014).

Access Blockage

The feasibility of access blockage is based on the specific condition of the internet's infrastructure in China. To a certain extent, China's internet environment is more like a big local area network rather than an internet interconnecting network. All internet service providers in China are required to go through the official international gateways and comply with government control and regulation to access the Web (Liang & Lu, 2010). The censorship applied on the official gateways can block overseas websites which distribute inappropriate content (e.g. pornography).

The Chinese government has used the GFW (the Great Firewall) as the predominant method for access restriction and is constantly updating the system (Liang & Lu, 2010). However, the efficiency of the GFW is often overestimated to some extent. First, the GFW is a delayed censorship measure. It was launched in 2006, 12 years after China's first fully functioning linkage to the Web which was established in 1994 (Taneja & Wu, 2014). Moreover, the GFW can only block websites after their exposure. Many of the now-blocked websites were once accessible – such as Twitter and Wikipedia – until they had attracted massive public attention or conveyed banned content.

Most importantly, the blockage applied by the GFW can be easily bypassed via convenient and affordable techniques. On the website administrator side, changing IP address and using backup addresses are common methods – such methods are often adopted by pornographic websites. The website administrators frequently change the IP address of their websites to avoid blockage – users can get the most recently accessible IP addresses in an auto-reply email by sending a blank email to the specific email addresses. On the user side, free online proxies and low-cost VPN (virtual private network) services are common and legal actions to bypass the GFW.

What recently happened on the Facebook page of Tsai Ing-wen, a Taiwanese politician with Taiwan independence inclination, is typical evidence to show the limitations of the GFW. In January 2016, less than 24 hours after Tsai Ing-wen and her Democratic Progressive Party won an election in Taiwan, more than 70,000 posts criticising Taiwanese independence had been posted by mainland Chinese internet users (Leng, 2016). Contradicting the conventional argument that mainland Chinese internet users are totally isolated from Facebook, this event is telling us that Facebook is accessible in mainland China if the users really want to use it.

Content Censoring

In addition to access blockage, the Chinese government also exerts content censoring on the internet which primarily relies on keyword filtering. Keyword filtering is an automated process that prevents users from distributing texts including forbidden words and phrases. This method is efficient in monitoring mass content. However, it can be easily circumvented by using simple homophones or homographs. For instance, the word 独裁 (dictatorship) is sensitive, if not totally forbidden, in some online forums in mainland China. The posts including this word are highly likely to be filtered. Therefore, some users employ its homophone 毒菜 (poisonous vegetable) to avoid automated content censoring. In the case of homograph, given 自由 (freedom) is banned in the online game World of Warcraft within mainland China, players use 目田 (this phase verbatim means "eye field" but it is not literally meaningful but just looks like 自由) instead to cheat the automated filtering programme (King, Pan, & Roberts, 2013).

Although some scholars have already discovered that the use of homophones and homographs can breach censorship, some other tactics are still overlooked, and there are at least two other methods to bypass the automated content censoring. Firstly, since Chinese characters are in the form of pictograph, users can split one character into two or more characters which form the one they want to display. For instance, the word 法轮功 (the banned organisation Falun Gong) is not allowed to be posted by ordinary internet users. Nevertheless, users can break 轮 into 车 and 仑 to bypass automated content censoring. They also can do the same trick to break 功 into 工 and 力. In the Chinese language context, audiences can easily understand 法车仑工力 refers to 法轮功 even though the three-character forbidden phrase is transformed into a five-character phrase, which is allowed to pass censoring.

Moreover, the automated content censoring becomes even more inefficient if internet users have a tacit understanding towards a forbidden keyword and its substitute. For example, 周永康 (Zhou Yongkang, the name of a former Chinese Communist Party senior leader) was once forbidden in Chinese online forums and search engines several years ago. During the days when this name was banned, users used 康师傅 (literally means Master Kang) instead, which is the name of a popular instant noodle brand in China so the Chinese government were unable to effectively censor it.

The analysis above has illustrated the complexity of the internet media landscape in China. As noted before, the access blockage on some international social media platforms is, practically, possible to breach. In summary, the China-based social media market is not entirely capsulated from international companies and, although censorship on social media does exist, it can be circumvented by various convenient and affordable methods.

The choice of adoption of social media platforms therefore relies more heavily upon users' existing social networks and their cultural traditions. These social and cultural factors are more influential on the social media platform adoption of overseas Chinese because of their physical displacement. The Chinese diaspora in host countries is facing two urgent issues – integrating themselves into the mainstream society in host countries, while still maintaining their cultural and social connections with their places of origin. The first one is a survival issue, while the second one is related to identity construction. Both of them are key questions in the era of globalisation as well as the dynamics behind the global expansion of China-based social media platforms.

The Global Expansion of China-based Social Media Platforms

Many people are now living in a highly globalised society "which is fundamentally characterised by objects in motion: idea and ideologies, people and goods, images and messages, technologies and techniques" (Appadurai, 2001, p. 5). The flows of people and information are blurring the boundaries between nations. This transnational migration and the complementary diffusion of technologies are two salient characteristics of contemporary society. For example, along with the increasing population outflow from China to other countries, China-based social media platforms are experiencing a simultaneous global expansion. Through analysing the distribution of geotagged Weibo posts, Liu and Wang (2015) have identified several regions with heavy Weibo usage outside mainland China – Southeast England, the east and west coasts of the United States, Thailand and Singapore are the hotspots.

Australia has also become one of the most favourable destination countries of Chinese emigrants. Mainland China is now the third largest source of immigrants to Australia – a population of 481,000 makes the Chinese diaspora the largest Asian ethnic group in Australia (Australian Bureau of Statistics, 2016). Accordingly, China-based social media platforms have been spread across Australia as well. According to the data released by Oz Entertainment, Weibo's Australian business partner, there are about 500,000 Weibo users in Australia, most of whom are from mainland China (Jiang, 2013). Besides these users, celebrities such as Kevin Rudd (former Prime Minister of Australia), Stephen Hawking (English physicist) and Narendra Modi (Prime Minister of India) are also overseas users of Weibo. Since the Chinese diaspora is the third largest ethnic group in Australia, many Australian politicians have also employed Weibo as an important channel to communicate with voters (Jiang, 2013).

WeChat is another popular China-based social media platform in recent years. Users can use WeChat to send texts, pictures and audios, as well as have free audio and video calls. Moreover, the Moments and Official Accounts functions of WeChat make it a powerful platform for publishing personal or public information. By the end of 2015, the number of monthly active users of WeChat was 697 million (Tencent, 2016) globally.

In addition to individual users, institutions such as student associations, enterprises and interest groups are also using China-based social media platforms to promote their services. Facilitated by the transaction function of WeChat, some diasporic Chinese in Australia are using WeChat as a business platform to procure Australian products for their clients in China as WeChat can satisfy all their needs – displaying products, communicating with clients and receiving payments.

Yet, living in host countries with brand new cultural and social environments and without access blockage, the diasporic Chinese should have many motivations to also embrace some international social media platforms such as Facebook and Twitter. However, as mentioned above, WeChat is significantly more popular than any other social media platforms among overseas Chinese communities, especially mainland Chinese. The need to establish and maintain social connections with other Chinese people, either within or outside of China, is an important motivation for adopting China-based social media platforms. Therefore, the perspective of social connection is a viable approach to investigate the global expansion of China-based social media platforms as a supplement to the approach of technology and policy.

Methodology

In order to explore the dynamics behind the global expansion of China-based social media platforms, 30 semi-structured interviews were conducted in Brisbane and Melbourne between August 2015 and April 2016. The respondents were recruited by convenient sampling and snowball sampling methods. They had to be over 18 years old and born either in mainland China, Hong Kong, Taiwan or Macau. Respondents had been settled in Australia between 1.5 and 31 years. Their age ranged between 21 and 57. Their China-based social media platform usage status is listed in Table 14.1.

This research selected three China-based social media platforms – WeChat, Weibo and QQ – as supported by their penetration rates. According to the official data released by China Internet Network Information Centre (2016), QQ and WeChat are the top two instant messaging applications among Chinese users, with a penetration rate at 90.3 and 81.6 percent respectively. Meanwhile, Weibo is the most adopted social media platform as the source of current affairs and interest related information in China.

Interviews adopted a semi-structured approach. Questions covered three aspects of respondents' experiences and opinions: their migration

Table 14.1 The China-based social media platforms usage status of respondents

		Sum of Respondents*	Active Users**			Inactive Users
			WeChat	Weibo	QQ	
Age	21–30	7	2	1	0	5
	31–40	20	12	2	1	8
	41 or above	3	1	0	0	2
Gender	Male	9	3	1	0	6
	Female	21	12	2	1	9
Place of origin	Mainland China	14	13	2	1	1
	Hong Kong	8	2	1	0	6
	Taiwan	7	0	0	0	7
	Macau	1	0	0	0	1
Years in Australia	1–10	17	9	2	0	8
	11–20	9	5	1	1	4
	21 or above	4	1	0	0	3
Residency status	Australian citizen	16	8	1	1	8
	Permanent	5	4	1	0	1
	Temporary	9	3	1	0	6

* Since some respondents are active users of more than one platform, so the sum of active users and inactive users may exceed the sum of respondents.
** Respondents who state or imply they frequently use the mentioned platforms in the interviews are identified as active users in this research.

experiences, their usage of China-based social media platforms and their motivations for adopting China-based social media platforms.

Results

Since more than half of the respondents claimed they used China-based social media platforms 'frequently' or 'occasionally', a better way to identify the users was to determine who was not accessing these platforms. Through a typology analysis on the respondents, their place of origin and age were two significant factors affecting China-based social media platform adoption among the Chinese diaspora. The latter factor is often interrelated with their social patterns.

As demonstrated by Table 14.1 above, 13 out of 14 respondents from mainland China claimed to be frequent users of WeChat. However, there were just two out of seven respondents from Hong Kong who frequently used WeChat, one of whom was born in mainland China and migrated to Hong Kong after university education. It should also be noted that none of the Chinese immigrants from Taiwan were frequent users of the China-based social media platforms mentioned above, although some of them had connections with mainland Chinese friends in Australia. In most cases, they just occasionally used WeChat for specific reasons:

> I knew about WeChat quite a long time ago. But I had not used it until I became the landlady of a mainland Chinese student. She preferred to contact me via WeChat so I started to use it. However, I do not use it much
>
> Mini, 37 years old, from Taiwan

> I only use WeChat when I have business trip in (mainland) China because Line and Facebook are blocked there. Therefore, I use WeChat to keep my family informed about my whereabouts
>
> Sherry, 39 years old, from Taiwan

In addition to the place of origin, age was another factor affecting social media platform adoption. Some senior respondents migrated to Australia long before the advent of social media, so their social patterns do not rely heavily on China-based social media platforms. For example, Horgan is a 57 year old male from Hong Kong. He was born in Beijing and migrated to Hong Kong with his parents during his childhood in the 1960s. Horgan was the only respondent who did not use any social media platforms at all, not even the China-based ones. He was dispatched to Australia by his employer in 1983. A few years later, his employer went bankrupt, but Horgan decided to settle down in Australia. Living overseas for more than 30 years, with his main family members in China having already passed away, Horgan had a distant feeling about China and did not have the urge to use China-based social media to maintain connections with acquaintances in China. Nor did Horgan have many social connections in Australia. He used to run a restaurant but he closed it several years previously because he needed more time to raise his son alone. Horgan centred his life on his 14-year old son, and did not need to use social media:

> I use phone call to communicate with my son when we are dispersed. But I am often with him. We live together. When he needs to travel abroad for (tennis) competitions, I will go with and take care of him
>
> Horgan, 53 years old, Hong Kong/Beijing

Xavier was another case of a non-frequent user of China-based social media platforms. He came to Australia to pursue his doctoral degree of engineering in 2003 when he was 35 years old. Soon after he graduated, Xavier settled down in Australia and arranged the immigration application for his wife and son. As a well-educated engineer, Xavier had good knowledge about information communication technologies and a successful career in industry. However, he refused to use any social media platforms and saw them as a burden:

> I think social media are very time-consuming. I always try my best to keep away from them. When I was doing my PhD, I had witnessed one of my schoolmates failed in finishing his degree because he spent too much time chatting on QQ. I don't understand why the young people always keep their heads down and stare at their mobile phones, even when they are crossing the road. I prefer many other communication methods to social media. I can use the landline phone in my office and email for business communication. I can have unlimited calling within Australia with my mobile plan. I can also use phone call and email to contact my parents and siblings in China
>
> Xavier, 48 years old, from mainland China

Despite the rationality Xavier insisted, he had been subject to the pressure from his relatives and siblings recently to adopt QQ and WeChat. Although Xavier emphasised that he just occasionally used these social media platforms and rarely posted content, his change actually reflects an important motivation for adopting China-based social media platforms among the Chinese diaspora – to maintain connections with peers in the age of social media. This is the first dynamic of the global expansion of China-based social media platforms discussed in this chapter. The other two are how the respondents access survival information in the host country and how they develop connections between China and Australia.

Dynamic One: Maintain and Re-establish Social Connections

In the modern context, diaspora is often regarded as a group of displaced people who are physically away from their places of origin but still maintaining sentimental, social and material connections with their homelands (Sheffer, 1986, p. 3). Transnational migration often implies a loss of social connections, particularly among the people with few information communication technologies. Nevertheless, people are highly mobile in contemporary society, which is a significant characteristic of globalisation. Social relations are often lifted from localities and must therefore be examined in a global context (Giddens, 1991). As to the Chinese diaspora, how to maintain existing social connections and re-establish lost social connections is an inevitable problem along with their migration, especially in the age of late modernity (Giddens, 1991) and liquid modernity (Bauman, 2012).

China-based social media platforms have brought forward both a lure and urge simultaneously to this problem. On one hand, compared to their predecessors, the diasporic Chinese today can use WeChat to maintain their connections with peers in China in a more economical and convenient way. As noted by the respondents who migrated to Australia before the mid-2000s, the most common method to contact their family in China at that time was using international calling cards. Despite the relatively low cost of this service, making international phone calls was a financial burden to Chinese students at that time:

> I only had international phone calls with my parents, because the cost was too high. After I bought my computer later, I almost gave up making international phone calls and switched to QQ as my primary way to contact my parents
>
> Hilary, 35 years old, from mainland China

Besides the low cost, social media technologies have another advantage of enabling various forms of communications. Users can send texts, graphs, voices or even videos through social media platforms. To some extent, China-based social media platforms have therefore largely replaced international phone calls as the most-adopted method of the diasporic Chinese to contact their family and friends in China:

> Now we all use WeChat, it is very easy to initiate a chat just by sending a text. In the age when we did not have WeChat, we needed phone calls to contact each other. But now our communications are more convenient and flexible because of WeChat. We can maintain instant and ubiquitous communications. In this case, the usage of phone calls is decreasing; we would probably use video chat instead
>
> Edward, 34 years old, from mainland China

On the other hand, overseas Chinese have few options but to adapt to their contacts' preference for social media platforms if they want to maintain their connections with peers in China in the current media landscape. This research discovered that nine out of 14 respondents from mainland China had dropped QQ – some of them had switched to WeChat to maintain existing social connections:

> I used to use QQ to maintain my social connections. But I have gradually abandoned it because most of my contacts in QQ have switched to WeChat
>
> Ursula, 37 years old, from mainland China

In addition to maintaining existing social connections, re-establishing lost connections was another motivation of the Chinese diaspora to adopt China-based social media platforms:

> I had lost my QQ account soon after I migrated to Australia. The service provider identified it was stolen. I lost almost all my contacts in QQ. Later, I registered a WeChat account linked to my mobile number so I regained the connections with some of my high school classmates and former colleagues. And then I was introduced to some group chats and re-established more lost connections
>
> Coral, 38 years old, from mainland China

In summary, the global expansion of China-based social media platforms is firstly fostered by the social connections between the diasporic Chinese and their contacts in China. These platforms have provided a more convenient method to have multimedia communications. Compared to WhatsApp, Line and other competitors, WeChat offers more functions, such as Moments (a wall to share texts, photos or webpages with all contacts), Red Packet (a sort of lucky money game), Transfer (real-time money transferring) and so forth. Moreover, using China-based social media platforms is a prevalent way to maintain and develop social networks among Chinese communities, both overseas and domestically, in the current media landscape. Even those who are not chasers of new technologies would adopt these platforms under the pressure from their family and other social networks. In this sense, China-based social media platforms are not only new technologies, but also a precondition of social and media practice (Couldry, 2012) among Chinese users regardless their localities.

Dynamic Two: Access Survival Information in the Host Country

Settling in enclaves with ethnic fellows is a common phenomenon among the Chinese diaspora because it is a good way to access survival information in host countries such as an affordable residence, job opportunities, community service and so forth (Zhou, 1992; Zhou & Logan, 1989, 1991). However, along with the growth in population, some of the diasporic Chinese have moved out of conventional Chinatowns and accommodated in scattered areas. Because of this reduced physical communication with the ethnic Chinese communities, digitally mediated communication has therefore become a popular way for the diasporic Chinese to access survival information. This is the second dynamic of the global expansion of China-based social media platforms.

Ursula was a typical case of this motivation. She worked as a professional accountant and taught Chinese part-time. Since her adoption of WeChat, she had used it for job hunting many times successfully:

> I use the function of People Nearby in WeChat a lot. I often receive friend request from Australian men who are interested in Chinese language because I have posted my CV in my WeChat Moments. I have become friends with some of them and given Chinese tutorials. One of my friends, we can call him Mark here, was outsourcing the accountancy of his company at that time. When he got to know I have a master degree in accounting, he hired me to replace his external accountant
>
> Ursula, 37 years old, from mainland China

Dynamic Three: Develop Connections between China and Australia

Apart from individual usage, many institutions such as the associations of Chinese international students and property agencies have also started to use WeChat and Weibo to promote their services or business. This trend reflects the third dynamic of the expansion of China-based social media platforms in Australia, that of developing connections. As reported by the respondents, the overseas users of China-based social media platforms included not only the diasporic Chinese but also Australian users. William was originally from Guangzhou, mainland China. He migrated to Australia with his father in 1997 when he was 13 years old. He initially got to know about WeChat from his Australian born Chinese friends:

> I don't really remember when I started to use WeChat. But I am sure it was introduced by my Australian born Chinese friends. Just like Facebook and Twitter may sound novel to Chinese users, some Australian users consider WeChat, a China-based social media platform, as an exotic and interesting one. They had known about it from their friends from China and adopted it
>
> William, 31 years old, from mainland China

Besides those who have a Chinese cultural background, some Australian people also adopt China-based social media platforms as a method to maintain the connections with their business partners in China. Cheryl was working in the international marketing department of a university in Australia. She had several Australian scholars in her WeChat. When she was asked whether she introduced WeChat to them, her answer revealed a new finding about how China-based social media platforms expand:

> Many of them just adopt WeChat by themselves. Some of them have Chinese friends or business in China, so they have already had the networks in WeChat. Just a very few of them got to know WeChat via me
>
> Cheryl, 32 years old, from mainland China

However, Cheryl's case does not necessarily mean the Chinese diaspora is irrelevant to the global expansion of China-based social media platforms. Actually, it plays the role as a catalyst in some cases. As noted before, WeChat has become a platform for transnational procurement between Chinese consumers and Australian suppliers. Jill was a practitioner in this industry. She was a shareholder of a store which procured Australian products for their clients in China and ran an official account for her store in WeChat to communicate with her clients. Moreover, her Australian suppliers also adopted WeChat as the primary method for business contact with her:

> More and more of my suppliers, who are local Australian people, start to use WeChat for our communications. They all say it is a convenient way for communication. We have gradually switched from phone call to WeChat because we can send texts and voices via WeChat which don't require instant replies. Both of us can have enough time for further consideration about our business without awkward silence on the phone
>
> Jill, 23 years old, from mainland China

In summary, the global expansion of China-based social media platforms is largely driven by cultural and social factors. The need for maintaining and re-establishing connections with their family and friends is a strong motivation for overseas Chinese to adopt China-based social media platforms. Additionally, these platforms are also important channels for them to obtain survival information and build careers in host countries.

Conclusion and Discussion

This research intended to explore the global expansion of China-based social media platforms from a cultural and social perspective. Social media are not just a form of technologies which is naturally adopted by users around the world in a homogeneous way. Instead, as Couldry (2012) argues, people are not just consumers of media content or users of media technologies, they are also practising their social behaviours in the condition that is shaped by media. In the age of globalisation and digital media, social media platforms have become a significant domain in which people practise their social relations in a mediated way, especially in the case of diaspora. Based on this understanding, this research argued the investigation on China-based social media should go beyond the concern on technological aspect and include cultural and social factors.

Instead of separating the Chinese and international context, this research tried to outline a complete diffusion path of China-based social media platforms. This path starts from the media environment in China and ends with the social media usage pattern of the Chinese diaspora in Australia. Through analysing the limitations of the Chinese government's censorship on the internet, this research argued that the access restriction on international social media platforms is not the crux causing users' adoption of China-based social media platforms because they are not entirely technologically capsulated. For further articulation, this research investigated a sample of diasporic Chinese who had lived both in China and overseas. The first generation of Chinese diaspora is an ideal sample for investigating China-based social media platform adoption because they have experienced internet censorship in China as well as the free access to any platforms in host countries. This unique experience puts them in a unique position for observations and comparisons between two contexts. According to the respondents, they still favour China-based social media platforms even though they are currently living overseas because of their importance in socialising and maintaining connections with their peers in China. In contrast to the concern on WeChat's proclivity to narrow and fragment users into atomised and locally oriented groups (Harwit, forthcoming), this empirical research has found that China-based social media platforms including WeChat actually make the social networks of diasporic Chinese more transnational and comprehensive. Additionally, these platforms are also indispensable channels for them to maintain necessary connections in their current lives with regards to both connecting and 'surviving' in their host countries.

References

Appadurai, A. (2001). Grassroots globalization and the research imagination. In A. Appadurai (Ed.), *Globalization*. Durham: Duke University Press.
Australian Bureau of Statistics. (2016). *3412.0 - Migration, Australia, 2014–15*. Retrieved from www.abs.gov.au/AUSSTATS/abs@.nsf/Latestproducts/3412.0Main%20Features32014–15?opendocument&tabname=Summary&prodno=3412.0&issue=2014–15&num=&view=.
Bauman, Z. (2012). *Liquid modernity*. Cambridge: Polity.

China Internet Network Information Centre. (2015). *The 36th survey report on Internet development in China*. Retrieved from www.cnnic.net.cn/hlwfzyj/hlwxzbg/hlwtjbg/201507/P020150723549500667087.pdf.

China Internet Network Information Centre. (2016). *Chinese social media users behaviour study report 2015 (2015年中国社交应用用户行为研究报告)*. Retrieved from www.cnnic.net.cn/hlwfzyj/hlwxzbg/sqbg/201604/P020160408334860042447.pdf.

Clark, D. (2014). *WhatsApp in Asia? WeChat, Line embrace ads, games and gimmicks*. Retrieved 2015-10-02, from www.forbes.com/sites/duncanclark/2014/03/26/whatsapp-in-asia-wechat-line-embrace-ads-games-and-gimmicks/.

Couldry, N. (2012). *Media, society, world: Social theory and digital media practice*. Cambridge: Polity Press.

Giddens, A. (1991). *Modernity and self-identity: Self and society in the late modern age*. UK, Cambridge: Polity Press.

Harwit, E. (forthcoming). WeChat: Social and political development of China's dominant messaging app. *Chinese Journal of Communication*.

Jiang, Y. (2013). The use of Weibo to connect Chinese communities in Australia by Australian politicians. *Asia Pacific Public Relations Journal, 14*(1 & 2), 69–84.

King, G., Pan, J., & Roberts, M. E. (2013). How censorship in China allows government criticism but silences collective expression. *American Political Science Review, 107*(02), 326–343.

Leng, S. (2016, 2016–01–21). Taiwan president-elect Tsai Ing-wen's Facebook page bombarded with comments attacking any move by island towards independence, *South China Morning Post*. Retrieved from www.scmp.com/news/china/policies-politics/article/1903627/taiwan-president-elect-tsai-ing-wens-facebook-page.

Liang, B., & Lu, H. (2010). Internet development, censorship, and cyber crimes in China. *Journal of Contemporary Criminal Justice, 26*(1), 103–120.

Liu, X., & Wang, J. (2015). Featured graphic: The geography of Weibo. *Environment and Planning A, 47*(6), 1231–1234.

Sheffer, G. (1986). A new field of study: Modern diasporas in international politics. In G. Sheffer (Ed.), *Modern diasporas in international politics* (pp. 1–15). London: Croom Helm.

Taneja, H., & Wu, A. X. (2014). Does the Great Firewall really isolate the Chinese? Integrating access blockage with cultural factors to explain Web user behavior. *The Information Society: An International Journal, 30*(5), 297–309.

Tencent. (2016). *Tencent Announces 2015 Fourth Quarter and Annual Results*. Retrieved from www.tencent.com/en-us/content/ir/news/2016/attachments/20160317.pdf.

Zhang, L., & Pentina, I. (2012). Motivations and usage patterns of Weibo. *Cyberpsychology, Behavior, and Social Networking, 15*(6), 312–317.

Zhou, M. (1992). *Chinatown: The socioeconomic potential of an urban enclave*. Philadelphia: Temple University Press.

Zhou, M., & Logan, J. R. (1989). Returns on human capital in ethic enclaves: New York City's Chinatown. *American Sociological Review, 54*(5), 809–820.

Zhou, M., & Logan, J. R. (1991). In and out of Chinatown: Residential mobility and segregation of New York City's Chinese. *Social Forces, 70*(2), 387–407.

Part V

Chinese Social Media Critique

15 Re-imagining Guangzhou on Sina Weibo

Geo-identity and Chinese Social Media

Wilfred Yang Wang

Despite the rich insights provided by current research on Chinese social media, studies tend to conceptualise China's cyberspace as placeless, where the political implication and cultural imagination are geographically indifferent. Going against this conventional wisdom, in this chapter I contend that Chinese social media displays distinct geographic features. In light of the notion of "online groundedness" (Rogers, 2009), I draw on the data and examples from the southern Chinese city of Guangzhou to envisage those practices and representations of Sina Weibo (microblog) in reproducing Guangzhouers' sense of place (*difang*) and locality. This chapter offers valuable contributions towards understanding the role of social media in people's everyday lives in China.

In this chapter, I offer a reflexive critique into Chinese social media research by re-engaging with the notion of geography. In doing so, I refer to examples and data from the southern Chinese city of Guangzhou to examine the formation of local identity on the microblog Sina Weibo. As one of the most popular social media platforms since its launch in 2009, Weibo has become a key site to facilitate public opinion formation and citizenry engagement in China (Huang & Sun, 2014; Poell, de Kloet & Zeng, 2014). Despite these insights, studies tend to conceptualise China's Weibo as placeless, where the political implication and social significance of Weibo are being treated as geographically indifferent. However, Chinese geographers have long observed that local place is "intrinsic to the Chinese formation of social space and... ways of being in society" (M. Wang, 1995, p. 33). In other words, any enquiries into China must consider and reflect upon those geographic elements in shaping people's everyday lives and identities. Henceforth, my approach here resembles Richard Rogers's (2009) notion of 'online groundedness' – that internet research should 'ground' the findings and treat the internet as a site of study to understand the societal and cultural changes within a specific context.

In this chapter, Guangzhou is chosen to be that "specific context" for a number of reasons. First, Guangzhou is the capital city of Guangdong, the first province to launch China's economic reform (Vogel, 1989). Second, as a result of being the regional centre, Guangzhou has experienced the transformations and contradictions of the restructuring process (Cheung, 2002). Third, in relation to the economic development, Guangzhou has one of the highest internet penetration rates and the highest 'socio-informational index' amongst all the provincial capital cities in China (Chen, 2015), an index that measures the process of social integration of the information and communication technologies. In other words, Guangzhou is, at least infrastructural-wise, an 'information society' (Chen, 2015). This provides an excellent backdrop to envisage the social and cultural significances of social media within a Chinese context. Lastly, Guangzhou has developed rather localised cultural identities and social values because of its cultural and geographic proximity with Hong Kong (Fung & Ma, 2002). As a result of the cross-border economic ties, Guangzhou's media had also had more administrative autonomy compared to its inter-provincial counterparts. For example, even though the State Administrations of Radio, Film and Television (SARFT) has made it mandatory that only Mandarin is permitted to be used on all broadcasting media in China (Liu, 2004), Cantonese has been the primary broadcasting language on Guangzhou's television and radio. These geo-specifics of Guangzhou provide crucial references to contrast and compare with the rest of China in learning about the diverse social imaginations and cultural representations in a digital era.

To follow the above scholarship and contextual backdrops, this chapter is organised in a way to redeem the relevancy and importance of Chinese geography rather than taking the notion of geo-identity for granted. The chapter refers to the scholarly interventions of Chinese media studies and internet research to emphasise the intellectual origin of this chapter, offering a 'grounding' of the data. The chapter bridges these scholarly critiques with the broader notion of internet geography – an emerging field of research in response to the advent of locative mobile technology – to call for greater emphasis on locative contexts and historicity. These ideas are then considered alongside the relevant historical and cultural perspectives of spatiality and politics in China, bringing the conceptual in dialogue with the contextual to formulate this geo-identity approach by examining the examples and data from Guangzhou.

Grounding Chinese Social Media

Studying the Chinese internet can act as a productive line of enquiry that explores the processes of the structural transformations and power relations in Chinese society (see for example Qiu, 2009). More importantly, China's authoritarian political structure also greatly expands the conceptual and methodological buildings of new media research which has traditionally been developed against the western democratic context (see Yang, 2009; Yu, 2009). These conceptual advancements have provided rich insights into research regarding the development of

Weibo in recent years. Scholars generally identify Weibo's dualities in both enacting and suppressing popular politics in China. On the one hand, Weibo empowers ordinary Chinese to challenge the state authorities (Sukosed & Fu, 2013). On the other hand, Weibo facilitates more sophisticated mechanisms of online control as the Chinese government uses online censorship to 'reduce the probability of collective action' being organised (King, Pan & Roberts, 2013, p. 339).

Despite these insightful accounts, the field of Chinese internet research has, over time, received considerable criticisms for its conceptual and analytic approaches. In a recent review of digital research in Asia, Schneider (2015) notes that both 'the digital' and 'Asia' have been highly 'political' in the academic enquiries. This resembles with Hjorth, Wilken and Gu's (2012, p. 45) argument that Chinese internet studies have over-emphasised the political aspects of the technology yet some of the seemingly 'less political' sides have been relatively 'overlooked'. This kind of critique is in fact not new to Chinese media research in general. Hong, (2011, p. 87) for example, writes that 'scholarship on Chinese journalism is characterised by intense discussion around democracy'. As a result, the literature on Chinese media from 1990 onwards has anchored within the dualistic assessment from the optimistic to the pessimistic about the current state and future outlook of the country's media and the process of democratisation (Yu, 2011). Some of these conceptual issues and dilemmas have also been inherited in research regarding social media. As Yang (2014) states, the current enquiry into the Chinese internet has been largely framed within the 'dichotomous analytical categories' of the state versus netizen, politics versus entertainment and authoritarianism versus democracy. Accordingly, the research limitation at present is related to the 'focus on technology at the expense of meaning and people' (Yang, 2014, p. 36). Yang's argument echoes with Nip's (2011) findings which suggest that the 'American empiricist communication' has replaced the 'humanistic approach' in media/journalism studies of the media studies in and of China since the 1980s. As a result, technology access has become the centre of enquiry in the field of Chinese internet studies, overlooking those cultural and societal conditions in which technology operates (Lindtner, 2014).

In responding to the above criticism, some scholars have attempted to re-think the Chinese Internet through a cultural historical lens. In examining the political economy of the Chinese online video streaming industry, Li (2016) treats those vernacular online streaming activities as part of Chinese people's cultural expressions and social lives instead of merely being the act of (political) activism and consumerism. While this is an innovative approach to re-assess the overall political economy of the Chinese Internet, I would like to go further by being more specific with the notion of 'culture' and 'history' from a cultural geography's lens. At here, I find Wanning Sun and Jenny Chio's edited volume of *Mapping*

Chinese Media: Region, Province Locality (2012) useful. In referring to the uneven pace of economic development of the economic reforms, Sun and Chio (2012, p. 3) point out that 'inequality, often measured in purely economic terms, is also intrinsically social-spatial'. Consequently, they contend that 'there are now many "Chinas" within the national entity' (p. 3) of the People's Republic of China (PRC) as inter-regional disparities contribute to various forms of social imagination and cultural expression through China's broadcast and print media. It seems like geography and its related notions of place and locality are therefore crucial in rethinking Chinese media studies. Henceforth, if geography were important to the enquiry of Chinese broadcast and print media, would it be as relevant to social media studies?

The omission of geography as an integral part of new media studies as outlined above is, however, hardly surprising. Since the early 1990s there has been a sense of loss of 'physicality and locality' in the common perception of cyberspace (Crang & Graham, 2007, p. 190) and the internet has been perceived as the 'amorphous, spaceless, and placeless cloud' (Graham, 2014, p. 99). However, this interpretation of the internet is changing with the advent of locative media and scholars have started to note distinct geographic characteristics of cyberspace (Graham, 2014). As Graham, Zook and Boulton (2012) suggest, geographic information is coded and digitally stored, represented and disseminated through the online networks. The online representation of geography redefines our way of life and everyday doings (de Waal, 2014). As a result, there is a renewed interest in 'shifting the focus away from placeless flows and back to geography' (Nitins & Collis, 2013, p. 69) in the field of new media research. "Internet geography" emerges as field of study that aims to explore the spatial organisation of human society through digital content and platforms. For example, in commenting on Miller and Slater's works on internet usage in Trinidad and Tobago (2002), which challenges the idea that the internet disregards the relevancy of physical location, Rogers (2009, p. 6) believes there is room for generalisation, 'if Trinis were using the Internet to stage Trini culture, the expectation is that other cultures are doing the same'. This process of place-making and geographic imagination provides a vital foundation for rethinking how the knowledge of social media in China should be formulated. In doing so, we must first re-engage with the relevant context and significance of Chinese geography from an historical and cultural perspective.

China's Spatial Politics: An Historical and Cultural Perspective

The notion of place (*difang*) is historically significant in shaping the diverse and rich humanistic culture, political system and economic orientation in China. Place is not merely a point on the map, instead it provides us with a sense of direction, a sense of being and existence in the greater world (Casey, 1993). Geographers have emphasised the procedural and experiential characteristics of place in constructing human histories, memories and hence our sense of community and self (Agnew, 2011; Kahn, 1996). This is why Ma (2003, p. 9) defines place as the spatial structure, the formation of political and economic processes that are both articulated by individuals and institutions. Hence, seizing control of place is effectively an attempt to control the material resources and symbolic meanings of lives and culture (Castells, 2009). Castells, however, would also be quick to remind us that the expansion of the dominant power will not proceed without meeting resistance from below because most people in the world still live in physical places (2009).

As folk ritual and local ways of life continue to define people's sense of self and being, place as a spatial unit continues to reconfigure social networks and power relations in the greater world. In discussing contemporary urban politics, Sassen (2011, p. 574) argues that the city is no longer just a space for enacting ritualised routines as stated in the classic European notion but also as a space of action, 'where new forms of the social and the political can be *made* (Sassen's *italic*)'. While I am with Sassen in recognising the city as a form of place which has become the primary site to organise popular politics and citizenry, I do not see the need to distance political actions from ritualised routines. Unlike Sassen, I argue that the formation of place relies heavily on those online and social practices in constituting people's sense of self and belonging.

An example of this idea of politics emerged from place and everyday lives can be seen in the following example. In July 2010, angered by a proposal to increase the proportion of Mandarin language broadcasting and to eliminate local Cantonese broadcasting components on Guangzhou's mainstream television and radio news programmes, thousands of people in Guangzhou marched on the streets – in two separate rallies as a response to Weibo petitions – to protest against what they believed was the central government's attempt to 'eliminate local Cantonese culture' (Ramzy, 2010). During the protest, Guangzhouers made use of local Cantonese to bypass the Internet censoring system because Cantonese has a different syntactical structure and expression from Mandarin, which is the language Chinese censorship is based on. Further, typing and reading in Cantonese also allowed Guangzhouers to access Hong Kong's media coverages of the protests, which contained banned protest-related information, such as the time, location and slogan of the protest back in Guangzhou. Therefore, despite the interventions from the local authorities and the online censorship, the protest was organised, mobilized and executed. Since the protest has received considerable regional supports from Hong Kong, Macau and even overseas Cantonese communities (Ramzy, 2010), the government was pressured to withdraw the proposal but to instead, issue a statement in support of preserving the Cantonese culture and language.

This example showcases Guangzhou as both the space of action and the space of ritualised routines – and Weibo has played a central role in mediating these transitions. For example, Guangzhou Weibo users defied the Chinese government's will of promoting Mandarin by typing Cantonese in their Weibo communication. This was both personal and political as Cantonese was both the ritualised routine and the action of resistance. Further, Guangzhou Weibo users made use of the visualisation functions of Weibo to upload old photos, political satires in Cantonese and Cantonese pop music to maximise the digital presence of their culture, ritual, language and, most importantly, themselves as distinct geo-cultural subjects who are independent from the discursive national identity imposed by the Chinese Communist Party. This pro-Cantonese protest illustrates that the source of contention was less about the unequal access to material goods and economic resources but more about the issue of cultural representation.

Guangzhouers' pro-Cantonese protest serves as a crucial reminder of the geographic dimension of Chinese politics. Conquering local powers has always been a top priority for Chinese emperors throughout China's dynastic era. As a result, China has one of the world's oldest and most enduring systems of territorial hierarchy – this has been the case since the Han Dynasty (206 BC–AD 220) when hierarchies were arranged vertically to ensure imperial decrees and central policy guidelines were disseminated throughout the district, the county and the township (Oakes & Schein, 2006; J. Wang, 2005). The political system is supported by orthodox Confucianism, which perceives 'local' as being a site that requires reform and cultivation, and the state as having 'an official position of paternal guidance through moral leadership to revitalise the local' (Oakes & Schein, 2006, p. 3). The civilization of a local place is therefore 'the product of the state's cultivation, rather than a natural quality of the local itself' (Oakes & Schein, 2006, p. 3).

This ruling philosophy was adopted by the CCP when it came to power in 1949. During the Maoist era, the government set up the *hukou* (permanent household registration) system to prevent the influx of rural population into urban cities in an effort to maintain its overall societal controls (Cartier, 2001). The separation between rural and urban spheres, however, created a new spatial hierarchy in which the opportunities to access social welfare, schooling and job security change depending on a persons location (Cartier, 2001). Consequently, there is always a spatial dimension attached to the notion of citizenship and political subject in China (Rankin, 1993). The political spatiality was further reinforced during the decades of economic reforms – the processes of decentralisation and regionalisation have been the basic logic for China's economic development due to the CCP's concern over the uncertainties of economic reform (Goodman, 1994). Since Guangdong's cities (including Guangzhou) are not important locations in China's existing administrative system, 'but were strategically linked to historic trading economies or Chinese overseas communities, or both' (Cartier, 2001, p. 4), Guangdong was chosen to be a test-bed for the economic reforms.

The historical accounts above provide a crucial backdrop to rethink Chinese social media. A closer look at the Chinese internet will identify the obvious geographic features that drive the development of the technology. Internet service providers in China have been constantly reminding people of their respective senses of locality. For example, Baidu, China's largest search engine, offers filters to regionalise online traffic for a certain news and events through its online traffic service, Baidu Index (http://index.baidu.com/). Discussion forums, such as the Strong Nation Forum (*Qiangguo Luntan*) launched by *People's Daily*, offer a 'Regional Forum' section (http://bbs1.people.com.cn/board/15.html) that specifically focuses on local issues and events. This connection to locality is also apparent in a comparative study by Harp, Bachmann and Guo (2012) which found that, compared to their American and Latin American counterparts, Chinese internet users are concerned with city or town issues most, instead of national issues. This is supported by the argument that the internet in China is mainly used to address those concerns that relate to the users' immediate locative environment (Qiu, 2009). In connecting the historical and the digital through the lens of spatiality, it therefore appears that there is a need to reconsider the analytic scope of the enquiry into social media in China.

Guangzhou: A City as the Unit of Analysis

The difference between using China (the nation) as the unit of analysis and using a city (such as Guangzhou) lies in choices of emphasis. The main object of dialogue of a city as the unit of analysis is local- and place-centric, but it is also trans-border and regional. It also recognises that the elements of the nation state have become internal to this place-based identity in local cities, hence there is always a desire to examine the issue in a relational language – that is, cities are the nation state and the nation is the cities. Further, in shifting towards the city as a local place, it complicates the imagination of technological homogenisation to embrace diverse and competing digitally embodied representational practices, namely that our view of social media and China includes pluralistic horizons. Finally, its core theoretical agenda is to transform Chinese subjectivities into a digital era. Rethinking Chinese social media through this decentralised and place-centric approach can begin to formulate conceptual and methodological accounts of reflection. I have indeed made use of such notion to formulate such approaches elsewhere (Wang, 2015) to examine the 'online' data in relation to the specific context of Guangzhou. Such a grounded approach allowed me to collect those online posts specifically speaking to Guangzhouers' folk culture, lived experience and social imagination in relation to the broader transformation of the nation.

This "groundedness" of Weibo is well illustrated through another incident in Guangzhou. In September 2012 the territorial dispute between China and Japan over the *Diaoyu* Islands (the *Senkaku* Islands in Japanese) intensified and triggered nationwide anti-Japan protests in China. Since Guangzhou was one of the main protest sites, thousands of people from other parts of China travelled there to launch their campaign against Japan. However, the protest turned violent as protesters damaged private and business properties in the city (Wu, 2012). In responding to these disruptions, Guangzhou's Weibo users launched an online campaign to boycott the anti-Japan protest to protect Guangzhou from chaos and disruptions. The phrase '*Diaoyu* Islands are China's, but Guangzhou is ours!' was the campaign slogan. Going against the conventional wisdom that the Chinese internet has become the brewing ground of popular nationalism (Yang, 2009), Guangzhou's experience tells a more complicated story by contesting the otherwise indisputable prestigious status of the nation state in China.

Weibo has played a critical role in mediating Guangzhouers' experience throughout the anti-Japan demonstrations. First, Weibo acted as the venue to express Guangzhouers' critical response to the expression of nationalism. The circulations of photos and videos showing protesters damaging cars, shop fronts and throwing rocks into buildings in Guangzhou questioned the legitimacy of irrational nationalism, which was endorsed by the government at the early phase. Weibo also facilitated the campaign to boycott the anti-Japan demonstrations – this featured several prominent local figures in Guangzhou. These opinion leaders – including local media commentators, celebrities and public figures – made use of their large "fan base" (followers) on Weibo to urge the people of Guangzhou to defy the expression of irrational nationalism and to report (through taking photos on phone cameras) those who committed violent acts in Guangzhou, as a measure to protect Guangzhou, their home (*jiayuan*). Guangzhouers' resistance and defiance then triggered an online debate about the meaning of nationalism in China – as Guangzhou Weibo users urge, the expression of nationalism should not be made on the expense of local interest and security. Finally, Weibo then elevated the people of Guangzhou's concerns regarding addressing the broader power imbalance between the nation and place. This case is important as it shows that Weibo can reconfigure the asymmetric spatial power between local and centre by enabling local values to critically reflect upon the notion of nationhood.

In reflecting upon the case of this anti-Japan demonstration in 2012, geo-identity is the notion I use to refer to the reproduction of the sense of self and belonging in relation to people's collective *experience* in living in the specific geographical context. The term is a stream of the broader concept of cultural identity but it differs with cultural identity in the sense that its premise is location specific. For example, Cantonese cultural identity is shared by people living in Guangzhou and some of its surrounding cities (like Shenzhen, Foshan and Zhuhai), as well as Hong Kong, Macau and even by some Chinese diaspora who are living outside of these immediate geographic locations. Hence, the term 'cultural identity' can be too elusive and is in danger of overlooking the significance of specific geo-contexts.

To expand this idea further, the notion of geo-identity as a framework works on several premises. First, its physical specification quantifies the grounded social imagination and cultural expression. Cartier (2001) defines a place identity as the 'geographic imagination' created by people who live in a particular place. However, as illustrated by Chinese history, place is always the site of contention and power contestation because the attempt to control place is essentially the practice to control the material and symbolic resources for people to conduct their everyday lives. Henceforth, the geographic imagination of place is often resistant in nature as the reproduction and representation of locality serve as the critical response to counter the expansion of institutional power from the state. Therefore, geo-identity is the building block of society and culture because the geographic imagination defines the formation of collectivity through shared practices, discourse and values in constituting a sense of belonging for its members. Finally, Weibo and other social media can act as a socio-cultural intermediary that reconfigures the power relations and interplays between the centre and locals and institutions and individuals. Importantly, geo-identity as a framework allows enquiries into Weibo to examine the changing spatial structure and power relations in China. A geo-identity approach is then a decentralised approach that rejects the notion of a monolithic conceptualisation of China, which enables a pluralistic line of enquiry to rethink the practices, discourses and cultural transformation of Chinese social media.

Concluding Remarks

This chapter has attempted to develop a geo-identity framework through carefully reviewing some of the recent critiques into Chinese internet studies. In doing so, I have attempted to redeem the relevancy and significance of Chinese geographies by re-engaging with the country's social and political history. The interaction between communication technology and cultural geography opens up new windows to understand the progress of social change during the course of economic and technological developments. While this chapter is about Weibo and Guangzhou, in the longer-term I hope it can open up multi-disciplinary dialogues between social media theories, political communication, cultural geography and critical analysis, to evaluate China's social media. As new communication technologies reconfigure the relationship between space and place, they also reconfigure people's daily experience and social practices, which ultimately redefine people's sense of self and belonging.

References

Agnew, J. (2011). Space and place. In J. Agnew & D. N. Livingstone (Eds.), *The SAGE handbook of geographical knowledge* (pp. 316–330). London, UK: Sage.
Cartier, C. (2001). *Globalizing South China*. Hoboken, NJ: Wiley-Blackwell.
Casey, E. S. (1993). *Getting back into place: Toward a renewed understanding of the place-world*. Bloomington: Indiana University Press.
Castells, M. (2009). *The power of identity: The information age: Economy, society and culture Volume II*. Hoboken, NJ: Wiley-Blackwell.
Chen, Q. (2015, July 29). Guangdong cities rank top six of ICT penetration rate in the country (cities in the nation Dianhua Diannao Wangluo Pujilv Quanguo Qian Liuming Jun Zai Guangdong). *Yangcheng Evening News*. Retrieved from www.ycwb.com/ePaper/ycwb/html/2015–07/29/content_756230.htm?div=-1.
Cheung, P. (2002). Guangdong under reform: social and political trends and challenges. In J. Fitzgerald (Ed.), *Rethinking China's provinces* (pp. 125–152). New York: Routledge,
Crang, M., & Graham, S. (2007). Sentient cities: Ambient intelligence and the politics of urban space. *Information, Communication & Society, 10*(6), 789–817.
de Waal, M. (2014). *The city as interface – how new media are changing the city*. Netherlands: NAI Uitgevers/Publishers Stichting.
Fung, A., & Ma, E. (2002). Satellite modernity: Four modes of televisual imagination in the disjunctive socio-mediascape of Guangzhou. In S. H. Donald, Y. Hong, & M. Keane (Eds.), *Media in China: Consumption, content and crisis* (pp. 67–79). London, UK: RoutledgeCurzon.
Goodman, D. S. (1994). The politics of regionalism: economic development, conflict and negotiation. In D. S. Goodman & G. Segal (Eds.), *China deconstructs politics, trade and regionalism* (pp. 1–20). London, UK & New York: Routledge.
Graham, M. (2014). Internet geographies: Data shadows and digital divisions of Labour. In M. Graham & W. H. Dutton (Eds.), *Society & the internet: How networks of information and communication are changing our lives* (pp. 99–116). Oxford, UK: Oxford University Press.
Graham, M., Zook, M., & Boulton, A. (2012). Augmented reality in urban places: Contested content and the duplicity of code. *Transactions of the Institute of British Geographers, 38*(3), 464–479.
Harp, D., Bachmann, I., & Guo, L. (2012). The whole online world is watching: Profiling social networking sites and activists in China, Latin America and the United States. *International Journal of Communication, 6*, 298–321.
Hjorth, L., Wilken, R., & Gu, K. (2012). Ambient intimacy: A case study of the iPhone, presence and location-based social media in Shanghai, China. In L. Hjorth, J. Burgess, & I. Richardson (Eds.), *Studying mobile media: Cultural*

technologies, mobile communication and the iPhone (pp. 43–62). New York: Routledge.

Hong, J. (2011). Mapping "Chinese media studies": A diagnostic survey. *Media International Australia, Incorporating Culture & Policy, 138*, 88–97.

Huang, R., & Sun, X. (2014). Weibo network, information diffusion and implications for collective action in China. *Information, Communication & Society, 17*(01), 86–104.

Kahn, M. (1996). Your place and mine: Sharing emotional landscapes in Wamira, Papua New Guinea. In S. Feld & K. H. Basso (Eds.), *Senses of place* (pp. 167–196). Santa Fe, NM: School of American Research Press.

King, G., Pan, J., & Roberts, M. (2013). How censorship in China allows government criticism but silences collective expression. *American Political Science Review, 107*(2), 326–343.

Li, L. N. (2016). Rethinking the Chinese internet social history, cultural forms, and industrial formation. *Television & New Media*, 1–17.

Lindtner, S. (2014). Hackerspaces and the Internet of things in china: How makers are reinventing industrial production, innovation, and the self. *China Information, 28*(2), 145–167.

Liu, H. (2004). Code of professional ethics of radio and television hosts of China (Zhongguo guangbo dianshi boyinyue zhuchiren zhiye daode zhunze). *People's Daily*. Retrieved from www.chinasarft.gov.cn/articles/2005/02/07/20070920151122290946.html.

Ma, L. J. (2003). Space, place and transnationalism in the Chinese diaspora. In L. J. Ma & C. Cartier (Eds.), *The Chinese diaspora space, place, mobility, and identity* (pp. 1–50). Oxford: Roman & Littlefield Publishers, Inc.

Miller, D., & Slater, D. (2002). The internet: An ethnographic approach. *Economic Geography, 78*(1), 100.

Nip, J. (2011). A meta-review of Chinese media studies, 1998–2008. *Media International Australia, 138*, 112–127.

Nitins, T., & Collis, C. (2013). Grounding the internet: Categorising the geographies of locative media. *Media International Australia, 146*, 69–78.

Oakes, T., & Schein, L. (2006). Translocal China: An introduction. In T. Oakes & L. Schein (Eds.), *Translocal China: Linkages, identities and the reimagining of space* (pp. 1–35). Hoboken, NJ: Taylor and Francis.

Poell, T. B., de Kloet, J., & Zeng, G. (2014). Will the real Weibo please stand up? Chinese online contention and actor-network theory. *Chinese Journal of Communication, 7*(1), 1–18.

Qiu, J. L. (2009). *Working-class network society: Communication technology and the information have-less in urban China.* Cambridge. MA: MIT Press.

Ramzy, A. (2010, August 2). *Protesters stand firm on Cantonese tights.* Time World. Retrieved from www.time.com/time/world/article/0,8599,2008060,00.html.

Rankin, M. B. (1993). Some observations on a Chinese public sphere. *Modern China, 19*(2), 158–182.

Rogers, R. (2009). *The end of the virtual digital methods.* Amsterdam: Vossiuspers UvA.

Sassen, S. (2011). The global street: Making the political. *Globalizations, 8*(5), 573–579.

Schneider, F. (2015). Searching for "digital Asia" in its networks: Where the spatial turn meets the digital turn. *Asiascape: Digital Asia*, 2(1–2), 57–92.

Sukosed, M., & Fu, K.-W. (2013). How Chinese netizens discuss environmental conflicts? Framing and functions on Sina Weibo. *Department of Media and Communication Seminar* (pp. 1–19). Hong Kong: Department of Media and Communication, City University of Hong Kong.

Sun, W., & Chio, J. (2012). Introduction. In W. Sun & J. Chio (Eds.), *Mapping media in China region, province, locality* (pp. 3–12). Oxon & New York: Routledge.

Vogel, E.F. (1989) *One step ahead in china: Guangdong under reform.* Cambridge, MA: Harvard University Press.

Wang, M. (1995). Place, administration, and territorial cults in late imperial china: A case study from south Fujian. *Late Imperial China*, 16(1), 33–78.

Wang, J. (2005). Introduction: the politics and production of scales in China How does geography matter to studies of local, popular culture? In J. Wang (Ed.), *Locating China: Space, place and popular culture* (pp. 1–30). Hoboken, NJ: Taylor and Francis.

Wang, W. Y. (2015). Remaking Guangzhou: Geo-identity and place-making on Sina Weibo. *Media International Australia, Incorporating Culture & Policy*, 156, 29–38.

Wu, Z. (2012). *Beijing faces protests dilemma.* Asia Times. Retrieved from http://atimes.com/atimes/China/NI19Ad02.html.

Yang, G. (2009). *Power of the internet in China: Citizen activism online.* New York: Columbia University Press.

Yang, G. (2014). Political contestation in Chinese digital spaces: Deepening the critical inquiry. *China Information*, 28(2), 135–144.

Yu, H. (2009). *Media and cultural transformation in China.* New York: Routledge.

Yu, H. (2011). Doing Chinese media studies: A reflection on the field's history and methodology. *Media International Australia*, 138, 66–79.

16 The Decline of Sina Weibo

A Technological, Political and Market Analysis

Jonathan Benney and Jian Xu

Sina Weibo,[1] the Chinese-operated microblog service, has received a great deal of attention over the past decade (see Tai, Liang & Liu, Chapter 5; Wang, Chapter 15 in this volume). For some years, media and academic analysis suggested that China was experiencing a "microblogging revolution" in which Weibo would continue to grow and would have a significant effect on Chinese society (Sullivan, 2012). The nature of this effect was debated, but was normally linked to greater public engagement with contentious issues (Benney, 2011). Even broader analyses suggested that microblogging could create a "counter-hegemonic" presence (Tong & Lei, 2012). However, Weibo is now clearly in decline. The rate of growth of regular users, new signups and individual users is either slowing or negative. Contrary to the suggestion that the use of Weibo would lead to greater social openness, the most obvious recent development has been a greater presence from government (Esarey, 2015).

In parallel with this decline, the use of mobile instant messaging services (MIM), such as Weixin, has increased. Weixin, known in English as WeChat, literally translates as 'micro-message' in English – its best-known global counterparts are LINE and WhatsApp. It is a popular MIM service and was first released by Tencent in January 2011. It provides hold-to-talk voice messaging, text messaging, photo and video sharing, online payment, games and many other services. The Kantar China Social Media Impact Report 2016 shows that WeChat was the most frequently used social media in China from 2013 to 2015, with an increasing number of users every year. QQ (originally a computer-based instant messaging service, also operated by Tencent, which now incorporates features of social media and is available on phones) and Weibo, ranking second and third respectively, have both dramatically lost users in the same period (Shi, 2016). By contrast, from the first quarter of 2013 to the fourth quarter of 2015, the number of monthly active WeChat users in China and overseas increased from 194.4 million to 697 million. By the third quarter of 2016, there were 846 million WeChat users (Statista.com, 2016).

The reasons for Weibo's decline are varied, but they share one common factor – the desire of the People's Republic of China (PRC) party–state to restrict and manipulate online flows of information. Consequently, understanding the decline of Weibo allows us to understand both the content of Chinese internet policy and the strategies which are used to implement this policy.

Our chapter therefore considers both why the use of Weibo has declined and why the use of Weixin has increased. We analyse this phenomenon through three frameworks – technological factors, political factors and market factors. Ultimately, though, we argue that it is the convergence of these factors, linked to the PRC's current policies and to changes in Chinese society, that have led to this decline. However, we also note that the adaptability of Weibo and the flexibility of the market means that it is impossible to rule out its resurgence – or, in parallel, the decline of WeChat.

Context and Analytical Framework

Individual internet services, such as Weibo and Weixin, are best considered as "gangly network[s] of tendrils and tangles" (Deluca, Brunner, & Sun, 2016). While their underlying programming creates a specific interface for users, the interfaces themselves are used in many different contexts and ways. As a result, the most effective analysis of these services is multidisciplinary. In viewing Weibo and its rivals from a technological, political and market perspective, we analyse them as technical services, as immersive 'user experiences', as conduits for information and as competitors in a rapidly changing commercial market.

The shift in market share from Weibo to Weixin is an example of the 'network' or 'bandwagon effect' where increased numbers of users of the service increases the usefulness of the service to its users, as well as encouraging new users to join or move from other services. This process of transfer has been characterised as a "virtual migration" (Chang, Liu, & Chen, 2014). Like any migration, it involves 'push' and 'pull' factors. Perceived problems with Weibo must consequently be counterbalanced against the attractions of its rivals. However, a virtual migration is less permanent than a physical migration. Users "criss-cross" between platforms and applications (Deluca et al., 2016), so their frequency and style of use must be measured as well as their sheer numbers.

In terms of conceptual analysis of these transitions, social networking services (SNSs) and Web 2.0 are well theorised and there are now countless empirical studies on almost every aspect of them. However, MIM services are less well understood. As a rule, discussion of MIM has not made the progression from computer science analysis to social science analysis. Nonetheless, MIM has moved from outside the terrain of Web 2.0 to being part of it. Most MIM services began as computer-based instant messaging programmes (such as QQ) or as SMS replacements (like WhatsApp), but have gradually adopted many features of Web 2.0

services. Compared to its rivals, Weixin has adopted many of the qualities of a SNS; this is similar to the way in which Weibo began as a clone of Twitter but then introduced many new features.

Consequently, our approach in this chapter is to read the 'virtual migration' from Weibo to Weixin under three main themes – technological factors, political factors and market factors. We focus most strongly on political factors, as they have played the most significant role, but it is impossible to study the effect of politics on new media without considering the nature of the medium itself and the market in which it functions. Furthermore, the 'convergence' of MIM services with Web 2.0 functions means that we can use techniques of Web 2.0 analysis to assess how Weixin works in practice. Using these headings enables us to juxtapose theoretical with empirical analysis, to analyse both push and pull factors, and to consider this 'migration' in its broader context.

Technological Factors

The market for online services (such as smartphone apps or web-based services) is characterised by rapid change. Some users remain loyal to their preferred SNS or messaging service, even when most of their friends and colleagues have moved onto a newer or more popular one. Some SNSs, such as Facebook, have achieved such a large share of the market that they have become virtually ubiquitous (at least in places, unlike China, where Facebook is not censored). But this is not common – most smartphone apps or SNSs only have a finite lifespan before their number of users becomes negligible. This competition for market share has therefore led the providers of online services to refine themselves constantly. In addition, the fact that these services often offer extremely similar services has meant that even minor technological differences can have a major effect on market share.

Coupled with this is an important transition in the method of access to online services in China – the shift to smartphones and apps rather than the use of web-based services (Wallis, 2013; Wei, 2014). This can be regarded as a pull factor, drawing users to MIM. Once it became apparent that a substantial market for MIM had developed, competing MIM providers began a race for customers and market share. The main strategy adopted by MIM providers has been convergence, that is, each MIM service has added new features one by one, and many of these features have led to MIM services becoming more and more like SNSs. Some MIM services such as LINE, WhatsApp and Weixin have therefore moved from simple SMS replacements to services comparable to Facebook and indeed Weibo. Further, since the most important factor in the choice of MIM provider is whether one's peers are also using the service, different MIM services have become popular in particular geographic areas. Weixin was able to win a "race" against its competitors in China (Lien & Cao, 2014), largely through positive word of mouth, ultimately achieving an extremely high market share within mainland China and some other neighbouring countries.

What technological factors led to this, and how do they interact with the migration away from Weibo? An examination of the user interface[2] of Weixin and Weibo provides some answers to this question. Previous research has indicated that the Weibo interface has become increasingly complex and that it has become increasingly oriented towards the distribution of information by commercial and government organisations (Benney, 2014; Esarey, 2015). Having originally been designed for computers, Weibo requires more effort to sign up and use. Furthermore, since Weibo has had many extra features added to it over its lifespan, including for example an elaborate user ranking system derived from role-playing games (Benney, 2014), it has become increasingly difficult for users to become comfortable with all its features, particularly on smartphones.

As a result, the comparative complexity of the Weibo interface may detract from the user experience and deter inexperienced users. Also, the aesthetic reorientation of the user experience to achieve state or commercial aims, as well as the increased government presence and the growth of 'opinion guidance management' (as discussed below), tend to marginalise the personal intentions of the user and prioritise the aims of commercial entities and the party–state. These changes can be regarded as push factors. The hypothesis that users prefer the Weixin interface to Weibo's is supported by Gan and Wang's (2014) empirical research.

Whereas Weibo functions on the basic assumption that most users will broadcast their posts publicly, MIM applications grew from person-to-person communication. Weixin allows users to share personal 'moments' (posts, links and so on) in a way that is similar to the Weibo feed but is perceived as more intimate (Chen, Bentley, Holz, & Xu, 2015). While Weixin users can use the app to find and interact with people whom they do not know, by default their communication is broadcast only to a select group of people. A smaller circle of users means that the censorship apparatus affects users less. Like any online service in China, Weixin is subject to state monitoring, but its censorship is largely based on the censoring of "sensitive words" which can be subverted fairly easily by users (Li, 2011). In contrast, Weibo is subject to extremely thorough processes of censorship and state control (Benney, 2014; King, Pan, & Roberts, 2016). Further, because Weixin is perceived as a more private environment, users are more willing to discuss personal issues, knowing that fewer people will be able to view them. Users who originally used Weibo as a kind of diary, recording their daily activities and thoughts, would consequently be relatively likely to shift to Weixin's 'moments' timeline. Also, as a means of chatting and sharing information, Weixin's group communication function is proving more popular than the Weibo timeline.

Overall, we can conclude that the convergent nature of the Weixin interface (which now incorporates person-to-person communication, group communication and public communication), its relative simplicity and ease of use, and the peer effect of its growing popularity are pull factors – the complexity of Weibo and its relative ease of censorship are push factors.

Political Factors

Since Xi Jinping began his presidency in November 2012, the Chinese government has tightened its ideological control and intensified indoctrination of the public (Eades, 2016). To increase the effectiveness of Xi's "ideological campaign", the government has increased its control and censorship of mass media (Wong, 2016). The internet, particularly social media, which are widely seen as a new battlefield for public opinion and a new platform for 'thought work', has been tightened under Xi's leadership with new policies, regulations and strategies. Consequently, the internet has become a tool for surveillance as well as for public expression. Under the banner of making China a "strong internet power", the party–state has centralised control over the internet and information technology in general, developing an organisational model which is characterised by the seniority of its leaders and its similarity to the organisational model of the state's propaganda apparatus (Creemers, 2017). The decline of Weibo is closely linked to this expanding state oversight of the internet. The close links between the Sina Corporation and the party-state, which we discuss further below, have facilitated this transition.

Real-Name Registration

In December 2012, the Standing Committee of the National People's Congress (NPC) issued the Decision on Strengthening Network Information Protection (thereafter 'Decision') (China Copyright and Media, 2012). The new rules require internet users to provide information about their real identity to internet service providers (ISPs) when they sign service agreements for internet access, fixed telephones and mobile phones. The Decision also requires ISPs to work more closely with the government's internet regulations and censorship, including keeping a record of illegal information and reporting it to relevant authorities, and providing necessary technical support to the government. While the Decision appears superficially to protect the information security of citizens and the nation, in action, the requirement of using a real name to access the internet has, to some extent, curbed netizens' freedom of speech online, particularly on Weibo.

Since Weibo was launched in 2009, it has become a popular platform for ordinary people to "publicize and express their discontent" and pose "a new challenge to the state regime of information control" (Sullivan, 2014). A number of controversial events, involving official malfeasance, corruption or human rights violations, have been first exposed by ordinary people on Weibo. Public interest and debate around these issues quickly developed the use of microblogs to post, repost and comment. This process had the potential to set the agenda for the mainstream media and place pressure on the government to respond (see Bondes & Schucher, 2014; Tong & Zuo, 2014). Weibo-enabled civic activism and bottom-up agenda setting has demonstrated the promise of microblogging in facilitating the political participation of ordinary people and strengthening China's civil society and public sphere (Lu & Qiu, 2013; Sullivan, 2014).

In response to this trend, the party-state has gradually increased controls on microblogging. Beijing first officially announced real-name registration for Weibo accounts in December 2011, a precursor to the Decision. Weibo users were required to use real names to register, but could still use pseudonyms for posting. Subsequently, major cities, including Shanghai, Shenzhen, Guangzhou and Tianjin, required new Weibo users to register under their real names (Gu, 2011). At this stage, Hao Jinsong, a human rights lawyer based in Beijing, argued that Weibo real-name registration would limit free expression online. He commented,

> ... in China, it is risky to criticize the government, so many people prefer to be anonymous online. If they need to use real names to criticize the government or social problems, they may choose to be silent and don't want to take the risk.
>
> (quoted from Gao, 2011)

Further, an online survey conducted by ifeng.com on Weibo real-name registration revealed that 54 percent of netizens would not want to use Weibo any more if real-name registration were required (Liu, 2011).

Xi's rise to power, the Decision of December 2012, and the announcement made by the Cyberspace Administration of China to comprehensively enforce real-name registration in February 2015 (see Li & Jaffe, 2015), have all made real-name registration a national hot-button issue. Although the implementation of real-name registration is easier said than done due to the extremely large number of netizens, as well as resistance from ISPs and internet users, the government's attempt to boost real-name registration in recent years has clearly signalled that the government intends to tighten the online speech environment. This has increased concerns about the ability of netizens to speak freely online and has become one the most important reasons for the decline in active users of Weibo.

*Opinion Guidance – the Anti-rumour Campaign
and the Fifty-Cent Party*

A more specific means of internet governance is the nation-wide 'anti-rumour campaign' initiated by the Ministry of Public Security immediately after the National Propaganda and Ideology Work Conference on 19 August 2013. In this conference, Xi ordered the propaganda apparatus to seize the battleground of new media and make online public opinion the top priority of the party's publicity platform (China Digital Times, 2013). This anti-rumour campaign allegedly aims to eliminate unverified online information that may mislead the public and public opinion. In action, it turned out to be a crackdown on online dissidents and critiques in the name of 'rumour-mongering', with a particular target being Weibo.

On 23 August 2013, Beijing police detained Xue Manzi, a Chinese–American venture capitalist and a public opinion leader on Weibo. With over 12 million followers, he was one of the best-known online critics of the party–state (Spegele, 2013). He later appeared on the state media – China Central Television (CCTV) – having been detained on an accusation of soliciting prostitutes. He made a confession stating that it was irresponsible for him to write critical posts and warned the national audiences that freedom of speech cannot override the law (The Straits Times, 2013). The party's public humiliation of Xue Manzi implicitly warned other verified accounts with millions of followers – known as 'Big Vs' on Weibo – to discipline their online speech. The campaign targeted ordinary users as well as opinion leaders. On 9 September, the Supreme People's Court and Supreme People's Procuratorate issued a judicial interpretation stating that if defamatory posts were viewed more than 5,000 times or reposted more than 500 times, the posters would be charged with defamation (Xinhuanet.com, 2013). A few days later, Yang Hu, a 16-year-old student from Gansu Province, became the first to fall foul of the new rule. He was accused of spreading rumours, inciting mass demonstrations and seriously obstructing social order. He was detained for a week because of his widely reposted messages on Weibo challenging the local police's explanation of a recent murder case (Kaiman, 2013).

In China, the government covers crises and scandals in a limited fashion, releasing negative information selectively. The information gap between what the government offers and what the public want to know is sometimes large, which causes unofficial information (consistently framed as 'rumours' by the state) to spread. Rumours usually emerge when people attempt to "construct a meaningful interpretation" of an ambiguous situation by "pooling their intellectual resources" (Shibutani, 1966, p. 17). Hu Yong, a leading PRC internet scholar, argues that rumours are not necessarily bad or malicious – they are sometimes just "inaccurate" rather than "manufactured" and can force the authorities to speak the truth. He further argues that the best way to reduce rumours is to increase credibility of the official information and open up the conversation between the government and the public (see Bandurski, 2013). The 'anti-rumour' campaign, in other words, is essentially a government strategy to control the framing of information.

Attacks on so-called 'rumours' must also be juxtaposed with the 'fabrication' of social media posts by the state – a manifestation of what is termed 'opinion guidance management'. Recent statistical analysis (King et al., 2016) demonstrates that the 'fifty-cent party' – individuals paid by the state to write posts on particular topics, generally supporting the party–state and causes it approves of – together with individuals formally employed by the government, make around 488 million social media posts each year. Weibo is the most important forum for these posts. The overall aim of this strategy is to stifle public engagement on controversial issues and to limit the potential for collective action. This of course demonstrates the failure of Weibo to live up to its potential as a tool for political debate and mobilisation; however, more relevantly in this case, the person-to-person or person-to-group focus on Weixin means that it is far less likely that 'fabricated' posts will reach the user. Weixin's main focus is on private social networking and interpersonal communication, which means that it is less likely that they will engage with people whom they do not know personally. Weixin users have reported that they prefer it to Weibo because of the absence of "rubbish information" (Gan & Wang, 2014).

Collectively, these factors have had a chilling effect on communication of everyday netizens on Weibo. The push factor – excessive government manipulation of information on Weibo – can be juxtaposed with a pull factor – the improved privacy and higher information quality – of Weixin.

Government on Weibo

Separately from the coercive measures described above, the government has also ventured into social media. Central and local governments have incorporated microblogs into everyday administrative operations as innovative forms of 'social management'. In October 2012, Weibo had 60,064 official accounts (Sina Official Weibo Report, 2012), but by December 2015 the number dramatically increased to 152,390, including 114,706 accounts run by government agencies and 37,684 operated by government officials (Zhu, 2016). The rise of this official use of Weibo is linked to the 'mass line' education campaign launched by Xi in late 2012. This campaign called on party officials to prioritize the interests of the people and persist in representing them and working on their behalf. Weibo is taken as an important platform to practise the online 'mass line', as it nominally provides an opportunity for government officials to interact closely with the public.

At the Cybersecurity and Informatization Work Conference on 19 April 2016, Xi stated:

> … wherever the masses are, there our leading cadres must go as well. All levels' Party and government bodies, as well as leading cadres, must learn how to march the mass line through the network, regularly go online to look around, understand what the masses think and want, collect good ideas and good suggestions, and vigorously respond to netizens' concerns, relieve their doubts and dispel their worries.
>
> (China Copyright and Media, 2016)

Research about official Weibo accounts argues that the official use of Weibo has demonstrated the party's adaptive capacity and resilience in governance in the digital age (Schlæger & Jiang, 2014). However, official microblogging has a limited ability to change the state–society relationship or strengthen political stability, because official micro-bloggers usually fail to engage in meaningful dialogue with the public (Esarey, 2015). However, in the aftermath of crises and emergencies, Jiang and Shao (2013) found that official accounts could quickly set the agenda for the mainstream media and have demonstrated the ability to marginalise information sent from unofficial accounts. This is largely caused by the synergistic effect caused by the government enhancing the release of official information on one hand, and tightening control of unofficial information on the other. Overall, the expansion of official accounts has weakened the diversity and attractiveness of information on Weibo and exacerbated the loss of ordinary users.

Market Factors

In addition to the political measures implemented through policies, regulations and campaigns, the increasingly fierce competition that Weibo encounters in China's competitive social media market is another crucial factor in its decline.

Like any product, social media platforms have a life cycle. The loyalty of users to specific social media platforms is inconsistent. For example, RenRen, the Chinese version of Facebook, grew quickly in 2009 and 2010, but then dramatically declined when it was faced with competition from new social media platforms (Millward, 2014). The entry of Weixin into the market had a similar effect on Weibo – the number of Weibo users dropped to 280.8 million in 2013 from 308.6 million in 2012; about 37.4 percent of these users had moved to Weixin (CNNIC, 2014). The increased importance of group communication has also led to Weixin, which was a pioneer in the field, developing a "vendor lock-in" effect (Kang, Wang, Sun, Gao, & Chen, 2014).

Changes in the market for new online devices also affect online services. Smartphones were at first too expensive for the majority of Chinese users (Wallis, 2013), but by the end of 2015, there were 913 million smartphone users in China, about 68 percent of the estimated 1.3 billion mobile phone users (Perez, 2015). There are a number of reasons for this. Firstly, being designed for smartphones, Weixin provides a better user experience for smartphone users than Weibo. Secondly, Tencent, which owns Weixin, operates QQ, China's most popular online messaging software service. The 800 million QQ subscribers can easily register a Weixin account with their QQ accounts and invite their QQ contacts to open Weixin accounts. As a result, Weixin inherently has better user resources than Weibo. Thirdly, Weixin has a relatively closed structure, with the majority of users' connections being with real-life acquaintances, contrasting with the looser Weibo networks, which are based on common interests. Therefore, Weixin users tend to be much more active, and check the app much more frequently than they check Weibo. Finally, Weixin is now available in more than 20 language versions, covering more than 200 countries and territories (South China Morning Post, 2015). Its global expansion strategy has made it more well-known outside China and more competitive in the global social media market, whereas Weibo has concentrated almost exclusively on the Chinese market.

While we argue above that interface factors and political factors have a strong effect on users' choice of online service, it is also clear that the market is constantly in flux. This is demonstrated by the recent shifts in Weibo's orientation. Through 2016, Weibo incorporated and promoted several new features, in particular live video streaming; this has led to a new upswing in users and demonstrates the determination of the Weibo platform to survive (see Koetse, 2016; Ma, 2016).

However, the introduction of these features only serves to re-emphasise that the putative revival of Weibo does not mean that its function as a forum for public discussion of contentious issues is strengthening once again. Rather, the changes reinforce the conclusions of previous research, that Weibo is framing itself as focused on entertainment and celebrity rather than on interpersonal communication or discussion. This, coupled with the closeness of the Sina Corporation to the Chinese government (Benney, 2014) suggests that political and economic factors are the strongest driving factors behind changes to Weibo, at least in the short-term. That is, Weibo has become a forum through which state-approved celebrities can promote the consumption of state-approved products, and this is largely because this is the only politically safe and economically productive strategy that the Sina Corporation can currently take.

Conclusion

The shift to MIM can only be satisfactorily explained through the simultaneous co-existence and interaction of the factors above. That is to say, existing theories for the movements of users between online services, like the network effect and virtual migration, are insufficient on their own for explaining the transition to Weixin, largely because of the influence of the Chinese party–state.

This indicates two key trends. First, it demonstrates the pervasiveness of the PRC party–state in public communication, and the way in which the party–state manipulates online content in broad ways across broad sectors. The distinctive development of Weibo, largely developed in the PRC, can be contrasted with the more internationalised development of Weixin, which has developed more slowly and in step with its competitors. On the other hand, the pressure of the market can mitigate against these trends.

The growth of Weixin also demonstrates a dearth of engagement by Chinese netizens in the public sphere. Zhang and Nyíri (2014) speak of "insurgent public spaces" in which resistance takes place, but the retreat from Weibo and the embrace of Weixin increasingly leads us to question how "public" these spaces are. Weixin, with its semi-public method of communication, seems to be being preferred by users. In large part this has been orchestrated by the party–state, which has driven Weibo users away with its heavy-handed manipulation. However, it may also speak to the preferences of Chinese netizens. In general terms, Chinese society is often interpreted as collective in nature, but there are tendencies towards the increasing stratification and fragmentation of Chinese society, as well as an increasing emphasis on the individual (Yan, 2009). The inter-personal and inter-group nature of Weixin, which allows the individual to express themselves in the confines of small groups, often familial groups, may reflect Chinese society more effectively than the 'public broadcast' nature of Weibo.

Ultimately, however, the 'decline' of Weibo in our chapter is a dynamic process, and that means that there is hope for its resurgence and reorientation. The period which this chapter concentrates on, 2013 to 2015, clearly demonstrates the decline of Weibo's political function (for which it was so famous internationally). This is not to say that Weibo is dying and can never revive; nor does it mean that WeChat will always be dominant. The market trends demonstrate both the value of the Weibo brand and the capriciousness of Chinese Internet users; these clashing factors mean that it is unlikely that one platform will ever monopolise social media completely. Further still, despite its distinctly different interface, WeChat is still subject to the "chilling effect" of strict government supervision and censorship (Chen, 2016), and consequently its users, both in and out of China, may respond in the same way they did when this happened to Weibo.

This phasic study of Sina Weibo has demonstrated the rapidly changing ecology of Chinese social media; while it shows that technological usability is crucial to users' choice of platform, it demonstrates that political and market factors have an even stronger effect on the development of social media.

Notes

1 *Weibo* is a generic term used in China for those internet services which allow users to make short posts of 140 Chinese characters – it is equivalent to the English 'microblog'. The Sina Corporation owns the domain name weibo. com, and its microblog service is the most popular in China. However, there are other microblog providers, of which Tencent and Netease Weibo, which closed down in 2015 (Liang, 2014; ecns.cn, 2014), are the best known. Our chapter will concentrate largely on Sina Weibo, which we abbreviate as Weibo, although the arguments it makes and the data it presents can also be applied to other Chinese-language microblog services.
2 In analysing the Weixin user interface, we are using the "interface aesthetics" paradigm (Andersen & Pold, 2010; Arns, 2010) and which has previously been applied to the gradual changes in Weibo (Benney, 2014).

References

Andersen, C., & Pold, S. (Eds.). (2010). *Interface criticism: Aesthetics beyond buttons.* Aarhus, Denmark: Aarhus University Press.

Arns, I. (2010). Transparent world: Minoritarian tactics in the age of transparency. In C. Andersen & S. Pold (Eds.), *Interface criticism: aesthetics beyond buttons* (pp. 253–276). Aarhus, Denmark: Aarhus University Press.

Bandurski, D. (2013). *Are rumors really so bad?* Retrieved from http://cmp.hku. hk/2013/08/27/33907/.

Benney, J. (2011). Twitter and legal activism in China. *Communication, Politics & Culture, 44*(1), 5–20.

Benney, J. (2014). The aesthetics of Chinese microblogging: State and market control of Weibo. *Asiascape: Digital Asia, 1*(3), 169–200.

Bondes, M., & Schucher, G. (2014). Derailed emotions: The transformation of claims and targets during the Wenzhou online incident. *Information, Communication & Society, 17*(1), 45–65.

Chang, I., Liu, C., & Chen, K. (2014). The push, pull and mooring effects in virtual migration for social networking sites. *Information Systems Journal, 24,* 323–346.

Chen, L. Y. (2016). WeChat censoring messages even outside China, study says. Retrieved from www.bloomberg.com/news/articles/2016–12–01/ wechat-censoring-user-messages-even-outside-china-study-says.

Chen, Y., Bentley, F., Holz, C., & Xu, C. (2015). *Sharing (and discussing) the moment: The conversations that occur around shared mobile media.* Presented at MobileHCI '15, Copenhagen, Denmark, 25–28 August 2015. doi:10.1145/2785830.2785868.

China Copyright and Media. (2012). *National people's congress standing committee decision concerning strengthening network information protection.* Retrieved from https://chinacopyrightandmedia.wordpress.com/2012/12/28/ national-peoples-congress-standing-committee-decision-concerning-strengthening-network-information-protection/.

China Copyright and Media. (2016). *Speech at the work conference for cybersecurity and informatization.* Retrieved from https://chinacopyrightandmedia. wordpress.com/2016/04/19/speech-at-the-work-conference-for-cybersecurity-and-informatization/.

China Digital Times. (2013). 网传习近平8•19讲话全文：言论方面要敢抓敢管敢于亮剑. *(Full text of Xi Jinping's speech of 19 August on the Internet: we must have the courage to assume responsibility for, manage, and attack online opinions).* Retrieved from http://chinadigitaltimes.net/chinese/2013/11/网传习近平8•19讲话全文：言论方面要敢抓敢管敢/.

CNNIC. (2014). 第33次中国互联网络发展状况统计报告 *(33rd Statistical Report on the Development of the Chinese Internet).* Retrieved from www.cnnic.net.cn/hlwfzyj/hlwxzbg/hlwtjbg/201401/P020140116395418429515.pdf.

Creemers, R. (2017). Cyber China: Upgrading propaganda, public opinion work and social management for the twenty-first century. *Journal of Contemporary China, 26,* 85–100.

Deluca, K., Brunner, E., & Sun, Y. (2016). Weibo, WeChat, and the transformative events of environmental activism on China's wild public screens. *International Journal of Communication, 10,* 321–339.

Eades, M.C. (2016). *Chinese nightmare: Education and thought control in Xi Jinping's China.* Retrieved from http://foreignpolicyblogs.com/2016/04/05/education-and-thought-control-in-xi-jinpings-china/.

ecns.cn. (2014). *NetEase to close Weibo operations, surrender to Sina.* Retrieved from www.ecns.cn/cns-wire/2014/11–05/141574.shtml.

Esarey, A. (2015). Winning hearts and minds? Cadres as microbloggers in China. *Journal of Current Chinese Affairs, 44*(2), 69–103.

Gan, C., & Wang, W. (2014). Weibo or Weixin? Gratifications for using different social media. In H. Li, M. Mäntymäki, & X. Zhang (Eds.), *Digital services and information intelligence* (pp. 14–22). Heidelberg, Germany: Springer.

Gao, S. (2011). 微博实名制：为什么？凭什么？ *(The Weibo real name policy: Why and on what basis?).* Retrieved from www.rfa.org/mandarin/yataibaodao/m1226-hc-12272011101450.html.

Gu, J. (2011). *Major Chinese cities to require real-name Weibo registration.* Retrieved from www.2point6billion.com/news/2011/12/27/major-chinese-cities-to-require-real-name-weibo-registration-10612.html.

Jiang, Z., & Shao, L. (2013). 从理论到数据：新浪微博衰落的学术证明 *(From theory to data: academic evidence for the decline of Sina Weibo).* Retrieved from www.guancha.cn/jiang-zhi-gao-and-shao-li/2013_12_01_189528.shtml.

Kaiman, J. (2013). Chinese police chief suspended after online storm over teenager's detention. Retrieved from www.theguardian.com/world/2013/sep/24/chinese-police-chief-suspended-yang-hui-detention.

Kang, M., Wang, T., Sun, S., Gao, Y., & Chen, L. (2014). *Exploring the role of switching costs in explaining micro-group adherence from the socio-technical perspective.* Proceedings of the Pacific Asia Conference on Information Systems. Retrieved from www.pacis-net.org/file/2014/2060.pdf.

King, G., Pan, J. & Roberts, M. E. (2016). *How the Chinese government fabricates social media posts for strategic distraction, not engaged argument.* Retrieved from http://gking.harvard.edu/files/gking/files/50c.pdf.

Koetse, M. (2016). *Weibo's revival: Sina Weibo is China's Twitter, YouTube & InstaGram.* Retrieved from www.whatsonweibo.com/weibos-revival-sina-weibo-chinas-twitteryoutubeinstagram/.

Li, H. (2011). Parody and resistance on the Chinese internet. In D. K. Herold & P. Marolt (Eds.), *Online society in China: Creating, celebrating, and instrumentalising the online carnival* (pp. 71–88). Oxford, UK: Routledge.

Li, B., & Jaffe, S. (2015). *China requires providers to enforce real-name registration and ban on "harmful" usernames.* Retrieved from www.dataprotectionreport.com/2015/02/china-requires-real-name-registration-and-bans-harmful-usernames/.

Liang, F. (2014). *Tencent to reduce Weibo operations.* Retrieved from www.globaltimes.cn/content/872276.shtml.

Lien, C. H., & Cao, Y. (2014). Examining WeChat users' motivations, trust, attitudes, and positive word-of-mouth: Evidence from China. *Computers in Human Behavior, 41,* 104–111.

Liu, Y. (2011). 北京出台微博实名制规定传递什么信号? *(What signals does the introduction of a real-name Weibo system in Beijing transmit?).* Retrieved from www.dw.com/zh/北京出台微博实名制规定传递什么信号/a-15609700.

Lu, J., & Qiu, Y. (2013). Microblogging and social change in China. *Asian Perspective, 37*(3), 305–331.

Ma, A. (2016). *Weibo increases stake in video-streaming service Yixia.* Retrieved from http://english.caixin.com/2016–11–21/101009763.html.

Millward, S. (2014). *Renren, once hailed as China's Facebook, is dead in the water as active user numbers drop.* Retrieved from www.techinasia.com/china-facebook-social-network-renren-losing-users-fast.

Perez, B. (2015). *China has more smartphone users than US, Brazil, and Indonesia combined.* Retrieved from www.businessinsider.com/china-has-more-smartphone-users-than-us-brazil-and-indonesia-combined-2015–7?IR=T.

Schlæger, J., & Jiang, M. (2014). Official microblogging and social management by local governments in China. *China Information, 28*(2), 189–213.

Shi, S. (2016). 谁能主宰中国社交媒体? *(Who can dominate Chinese social media?).* Retrieved from www.ftchinese.com/story/001065985?full=y.

Shibutani, T. (1966). *Improvised news: A sociological study of rumor.* Place: Ardent Media.

Sina Official Weibo Report. (2012). 2012新浪政务微博报告 *(Sina report on official microblogging).* Retrieved from http://news.sina.com.cn/z/2012sinazwwbbg/.

South China Morning Post. (2015). *Tencent scraps WeChat global expansion plans despite strong profits.* Retrieved from www.scmp.com/lifestyle/article/1741792/tencent-scraps-wechat-global-expansion-plans-despite-strong-profits.

Spegele, B. (2013). *Chinese police detain online commentator: Xue Manzi has more than 12 million Weibo followers.* Retrieved from www.wsj.com/articles/SB10001424127887324906304579034473911600230.

Statista.com. (2016). *Number of monthly active WeChat users from 2nd quarter 2010 to 3rd quarter 2016 (in millions).* Retrieved from www.statista.com/statistics/255778/number-of-active-wechat-messenger-accounts/.

Sullivan, J. (2012). A tale of two microblogs in China. *Media, Culture & Society, 34*(6), 773–783.

Sullivan, J. (2014). China's Weibo: Is faster different? *New Media & Society, 16*(1), 24–37.

The Straits Times. (2013). *China airs confession by detained blogger Charles Xue.* Retrieved from www.straitstimes.com/asia/china-airs-confession-by-detained-blogger-charles-xue.

Tong, Y., & Lei, S. (2012). War of position and microblogging in China. *Journal of Contemporary China, 22*(80), 292–311.

Tong, J., & Zuo, L. (2014). Weibo communication and government legitimacy in China: A computer-assisted analysis of Weibo messages on two 'mass incidents'. *Information, Communication & Society, 17*(1), 66–85.

Wallis, C. (2013). *Technomobility in China: Young migrant women and mobile phones.* New York: NYU Press.

Wei, R. (2014). Texting, tweeting, and talking: Effects of smartphone use on engagement in civic discourse in China. *Mobile Media & Communication, 2*(1), 3–19.

Wong, E. (2016). *Xi Jinping's news alert: Chinese media must serve the Party.* Retrieved from www.nytimes.com/2016/02/23/world/asia/china-media-policy-xi-jinping.html?_r=1.

Xinhuanet.com. (2013). *Severe penalties for defamatory retweets in China.* Retrieved from http://news.xinhuanet.com/english/china/2013–09/09/c_ 132705863.htm.

Yan, Y. (2009). *The individualization of Chinese society.* Oxford, UK: Berg.

Zhang, J., & Nyíri, P. (2014). 'Walled' activism: Transnational social movements and the politics of Chinese cyber-public space. *International Development Planning Review, 36*(1), 111–131.

Zhu, H. (2016). 2015政务微博报告解读及趋势研判. *(An assessment of trends in government microblogging in 2015).* Retrieved from www.cpd.com.cn/ n15737398/n26490099/c31812105/content.html.

List of Contributors

Jonathan Benney is a lecturer in Chinese studies in the School of Languages, Literatures, Cultures and Linguistics at Monash University. He studies contentious politics and political communication in modern China. He is the author of *Defending Rights in Contemporary China* (Routledge, 2013).

Way Kiat Bong is currently a PhD candidate at Oslo and Akershus University College of Applied Sciences (HiOA), Oslo, Norway. He received his Master's Degree in Universal Design of Information and Communication Technologies at HiOA in June 2015.

Joshua Cader is a PhD candidate in the Graduate School of Interdisciplinary Information Studies at the University of Tokyo. His research interests include message coherence in contentious politics, street protest tactics and anger on social media.

Weiqin Chen is a full professor in human computer interaction and universal design of ICT at the Department of Computer Science in Oslo and Akershus University College of Applied Science (HiOA), Norway. Her current research interests include universal design of learning management systems (LMS), MOOC accessibility and novel interaction techniques.

Naziat Choudhury is a PhD candidate in the Department of Communications and Media Studies, School of Media, Film and Journalism, Monash University, Australia. Her current areas of interest include social and cultural aspects of social media and internet use.

Yao Ding is a PhD candidate in the Department of Industrial and Systems Engineering with a specialisation in human factors at the University of Wisconsin-Madison. He is interested in universal design and ICT accessibility. More specifically, his dissertation explores ways to help individual consumers in selecting assistive technology (AT) for computer access and to assist professionals in keeping up with the ever-changing AT. His work contributes to the design and development of a decision support tool for AT selection that will be used in clinical practice and by individual consumers.

Katie Ellis is an associate professor and convenor of the Critical Disability Studies Research Network in the Internet Studies Department at Curtin University. She is also a member of both Curtin University's Digital China Lab and the Fudan University and Curtin University joint initiative Culture+8. Her research focuses on social inclusion in the context of digital and networked media. Her co-authored paper with Mike Kent, Jian Xu and He Zhang – *Using social media to advance the social rights of people with disability in China: The Beijing One Plus One Disabled Persons' Cultural Development Centre* (in Ellis & Kent, Routledge, 2017) – was the first published paper to address the topic of disability and Chinese language social media.

G. Anthony Giannoumis is currently an assistant professor of universal design at the Department of Computer Science at Oslo and Akershus University College and an international research fellow at the Burton Blatt Institute at Syracuse University. His research focuses on technology law and policy. He is currently researching the implementation of policies aimed at ensuring equal access to technology. His research interests include universal design, international governance, social regulation and standardisation, and he has also conducted research on assistive technology and intellectual property. Anthony has previously acted as a researcher with DISCIT making persons with disabilities full citizens and as a legal and ethical advisor for Cloud4All – Cloud platforms lead to open and universal access for people with disabilities and for all. He was awarded a Marie Curie Fellowship in 2011 as part of DREAM (Disability Rights Expanding Accessible Markets) and has been a visiting researcher and guest lecturer throughout Europe, North America, Asia and Africa.

David Holmes is a senior lecturer in communications and media at the School of Media, Film and Journalism, Monash University, Australia. He is the author of *Communication Theory: Media, Technology and Society* (Sage, 2005).

Dianlin Huang received his PhDs from Macquarie University and Communication University of China (CUC) under a cotutelle agreement. He is a now a lecturer at the Institute of Communication Studies at CUC. His research interests include Chinese media and public contention, media and representation of citizenship in China and popular culture and labour rights, with a particular focus on marginal groups such as rural-to-urban migrant workers.

Lianrui Jia is a PhD student at York University, Canada. Her research areas are the political economy of the Chinese internet industry, media regulation and policy.

Mike Kent is head of department and a senior lecturer at the Internet Studies Department at Curtin University. Mike's research focus is on people with disabilities and their use of, and access to, information technology and the internet. His edited collection, with Katie Ellis, *Disability and Social Media: Global Perspectives* is available through Routledge in 2017 and his book, also with Katie Ellis, *Disability and New Media* was published in 2011. His other area of research interest is in higher education and particularly online education, as well as online social networking platforms. His edited collection with Tama Leaver, *An Education in Facebook? Higher Education and the World's Largest Social Network* was released in 2014 through Routledge, and his collection with Rebecca Bennett, *MOOCs and Higher Education: What went right, what went wrong and where to next?* is also available through Routledge in 2017.

Nan Li is currently a Master's student in Universal Design of Information and Communication Technologies at Oslo and Akershus University College of Applied Sciences (HiOA), Oslo, Norway.

Jing Liang is a lecturer in the School of Advertising and Communication at Henan Polytechnic University in China. Her research focuses on new media and advertisement.

Xiaolong Liu is an associate professor in the Department of Humanities and Social Sciences at Guangdong Pharmaceutical University, China. His research focuses on the social and political effects of social media in China.

Jiajie Lu is PhD candidate of media and communication at QUT. His research interest sits in the area of media and social change. He is currently working on a project about Chinese diaspora's identity formation in the digital media landscape.

Gianluigi Negro is a postdoctoral researcher at the Università della Svizzera Italiana (USI), in the Faculty of Communication Sciences and assistant editor at the China Media Observatory, USI. Dr. Negro's researches focus on the internet in China and its impact on Chinese civil society.

Zixue Tai is an associate professor in the College of Communication and Information at the University of Kentucky. His research interests pertain to a multitude of issues in the new media landscape of China and he is the author of *The Internet in China: Cyberspace and Civil Society* (Routledge, hardback in 2006; paperback released in 2013). His publications can also be found in *International Communication Gazette, Journalism & Mass Communication Quarterly, New Media & Society, Journal of Communication, Sociology of Health & Illness* and *Psychology & Marketing*.

Xiaoli Tian is an assistant professor in the Department of Sociology, The University of Hong Kong. She received her PhD in sociology from the University of Chicago. Her research focuses on traditional Chinese medicine in contemporary China, as well as new media in the Chinese context, including a project on Facebook use in Hong Kong and another one on digital production (especially online literature) in mainland China.

Yang Wang is a PhD student in Department of Communications and New Media, National University of Singapore. She received her master's degree in mass communication from Peking University in China. Her research interests mostly focus on the social impact of new media, including ICT's domestication in transnational households, public participation in digital media environment, social media use and identity.

Wilfred Yang Wang received his PhD in media and communication studies from QUT. His research interests include digital geography, migrants and digital media, (digital) queer migrant culture and online deliberations.

Jian Xu is a research fellow in media in the School of Communication & Creative Arts, Deakin University. He was a 2015 Endeavour Postdoctoral Research Fellow in the China Research Centre at the University of Technology, Sydney. He researches Chinese media and communication with a particular focus on the sociology and politics of digital media. He is the author of *Media Events in Web 2.0 China: Interventions of Online Activism* (Sussex Academic Press, 2016).

Haiqing Yu is Associate Professor of Chinese media and culture in the School of Humanities and Languages, University of New South Wales, Australia. Her research focuses on the "effect" and "affect" of digitally mediated social economy, social movements, and cultural transformation. It explores Chinese digital and informal economy, associations, and social activism; rural e-commerce and its impact on gender and ethnicity; social enterprise, digital economy, and disability; social media and Chinese diaspora. Her published works have also explored the implications of the Internet and mobile communication on Chinese journalism, youth culture/sexuality, HIV related health communication, and everyday life politics. Her publications include: *Media and Cultural Transformation in China* (Routledge 2009) and *Sex in China* (co-author with Elaine Jeffreys, Polity 2015).

He Zhang is a PhD candidate at the School of Media, Culture and Creative Arts in the Faculty of Humanities, Curtin University. She holds a MA in translation studies from Shanghai International Studies University. Her research interests include digital literacy, co-creative media practices, cultural citizenship and migration activities of Chinese young people.

Danjing Zhang (Joy) works with Professor Michael Keane at the Digital China Lab at Curtin University. After working in the knowledge based industries like ESPN Sports Channel, IDP (Australian Education Placement) and Shanghai Tongji University, Joy completed her Masters by Research degree in 2012 at Queensland University of Technology (QUT) exploring the topic *Impressions of China: Zhang Yimou's outdoor theme productions* in the field of cultural and creative industries. In 2015 she accomplished her PhD at QUT with a focus on Chinese urban youth and their networks and social media platforms. Her research interests are cultural consumption, urban youth's digital engagement and community activities such as crowdfunding in China.

Tianyang Zhou is a PhD student from the University of Sussex, UK. His PhD research focuses on LGBTQ culture in contemporary China.

Index

For Product Safety Concerns and Information please contact our EU
representative GPSR@taylorandfrancis.com
Taylor & Francis Verlag GmbH, Kaufingerstraße 24, 80331 München, Germany